Table of Contents: Gamut of Speedy Rockets

"Hello, let me guide you through the rocket book."

Book 1:

1.	Rocket Types and Future Ideas	4
2.	Thrust and Acceleration When You Push Something Away	14
3.	Why Have Rockets?	32
4.	Popular Culture Weighs In	49
5.	Different Rockets, Thrust, and Videos of Super Cool Launches and Accelerations	61
6.	Launch Pads: From $10 Bucks to $100 Million	69
7.	What Force and Acceleration Does to Us	74
8.	Fun Toy Solid Fuel Chemical Rocket	82
9.	Summary of Thrust and Rockets	87

Low flow water

Toy water rockets

High flow water

Toy chemical rockets

High flow hot gas

Human endurance testing

Rockets to space

This book is one of two versions. This version is lighter and talks about general ideas, without going into any engineering analysis. This lighter version is more fun and appropriate for someone who is not interested in engineering equations. If you want the engineering analysis, then read the heavier version 'Gamut of Speedy Rockets, for Parents and Kids', which is for parents, kids, and engineers. The two versions are mostly the same except the heavier version has some added slides and has appendices with the analysis.

Copywrite © 2021 by Court Rossman
All rights reserved. No part of this book may be reproduced or transmitted in any form or by any means, electronic or mechanical, including photocopying, recording, or by any information storage and retrieval system, without permission in writing from the copyright owner.
Publish date: 7/02/21, Revision date: 11/7/2024

Table of Contents: Gamut of Speedy Rockets

"Hello, let me guide you through the rocket book."

Book 2:

1. $Millions To $Billions - Modern Space Rockets — 7
2. Rocket Engines: Liquid Fuel, Solid Fuel, Hybrid Liquid/Solid, and Electric — 24
3. Flight Path to Orbit Earth or Go to Other Planets — 35
4. Uses, Competition, and History of Rockets — 43
5. Multiple Rocket Stages are Your Friends — 57
6. The Dream of Faster-Than-Sound Commercial Flights with Cascaded Engines and Piggyback Rockets — 61
7. Improbable Ways to Launch Astronauts Into Space like Rail Guns, Elevators, and Nuclear Power — 72
8. Where Does Nuclear Power Fit In? — 91
9. Thrust and Rocket Speed, the Quick Estimates — 107
10. Hardware to Visit Other Planets and Moons — 116
11. Summary of Existing and Improbable Ways to Get to Space — 124

Mach 3 inter-continental travel with piggyback launch

Rockets to space

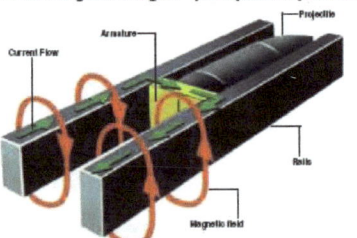

Improbable Rail Gun to space

Probably impossible balloon to space

Ground laser heat of exhaust

Space elevator

Lunar base for Planned Artemis Moon missions, 2020s

This book is one of two versions. This version is lighter and talks about general ideas, without going into any engineering analysis. This lighter version is more fun and appropriate for someone who is not interested in engineering equations. If you want the engineering analysis, then read the heavier version 'Gamut of Speedy Rockets, for Parents and Kids', which is for parents, kids, and engineers. The two versions are mostly the same except the heavier version has some added slides and has appendices with the analysis.

Copywrite © 2021 by Court Rossman
All rights reserved. No part of this book may be reproduced or transmitted in any form or by any means, electronic or mechanical, including photocopying, recording, or by any information storage and retrieval system, without permission in writing from the copyright owner.
Publish date: 7/02/21, Revision date: 11/14/2024

Rockets Launch Satellites ... Imagine This Without Satellites

No rockets means no satellites. Imagine this... A world without internet, or at least much less coverage. Less access to 'Zoom', 'Skype' or 'Hangouts' or other video calls. Much less accurate weather forecasting. No fireworks. No satellite TV or radio, no missiles or close pictures of Mars or anything farther. No humans on the Moon, and a lot of common knowledge about space and planets we would not know. No GPS. This is a world without rockets. Rockets are all about thrust from an exhaust, and about control of the flight path.

"I like GPS giving me driving directions ...when it is night and I'm on roads in a strange town, GPS is a god-send."

Sensors and Communications

Storms and crops

Monitor the Earth: Using cameras and radar, meteorological satellites see more than clouds and cloud systems. City lights, fires, effects of pollution, auroras, sand and dust storms, snow cover, ice mapping, boundaries of ocean currents, ocean temperatures, etc.

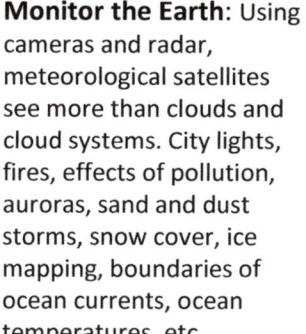

Direct TV, from satellites

Competition between communication satellites and ground cables:
Satellites have always competed with ground cables. We still have internet using land cables and antennas, just not to remote locations far from cities:
- First inter-continental cable across the Atlantic ocean laid in 1851 for the telegraph.
- Cables on land and satellites in space still compete (Cable versus Satellite TV) but also help each other.

Global Positioning System (GPS)

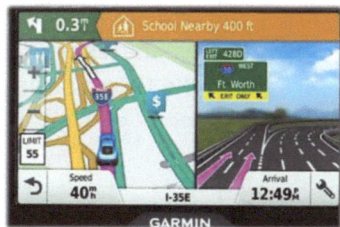

GPS navigation for cars

GPS navigation for boats

Of course, GPS does not know about blocked roads from winter snow, construction, or traffic jams.

Have a paper map handy just in case, if you are led down a dirt road or through a congested downtown.

Space Clutter

Satellites are so successful that there is space junk (satellite and rocket stages debris).
Space junk, unfortunately, needs to be tracked with radar to protect other rockets and satellites.

Among the more than 8700 objects larger than 10 cm in Earth orbits, only about 6% are operational satellites and the remainder are space debris.

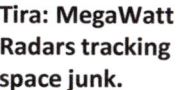

Tira: MegaWatt Radars tracking space junk.

Haystack Xband radar

Satellites have been a huge success story: we use them every second for communications and weather forecasting, whether we know it or not.

Introduction: Who Should Read This General Rocket Book?

Here's who will get the most out of this book. Anyone, from middle school kids to adults!

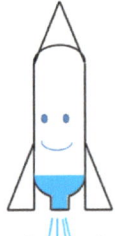

"Everyone can get something out of this book."

Elementary School student:

'Hey, these are great pictures of bottle rockets and Estes toy rockets and how to build these rockets. And I like building stuff."
To avoid the math, you could also read the shorter version **'Gamut of Speedy Rockets, for Kids'**.

Water bottle rocket:
1. Mom or Dad, please buy a water bottle kit! I'll cut cardboard and build the bottle rocket.

Toy chemical rocket:
1. Please buy an Estes or Quest chemical toy rocket! I'll use Elmer's glue and assemble the rocket.

Middle School student who is thinking about Engineering:
'Hey, I like these explanations, and want to learn more about them.'

Water bottle rocket:
1. Mom or Dad, please make a bottle launch tube, or buy a water bottle kit!
2. Cut cardboard and build the bottle rocket.
3. Apply techniques, like top weight, to make the bottle rocket more stable and go higher.

Toy chemical rocket:
1. Let's go get an Estes toy rocket!

Knowledge:
Hey, there are physical concepts that are working here, like the rocket equation and Newton's laws for thrust and drag.

High School student who is thinking about Engineering:
'Hey, I really should know about thrust and gravity, and back of the envelope estimates of thrust. I want to measure the thrust using a video camera.'

Water bottle rocket:
1. I can make a launch tube myself, or buy a water bottle kit.
2. Cut cardboard and build the bottle rocket.
3. Apply techniques, like top weight, to make the bottle rocket more stable and go higher.

Toy chemical rocket:
1. Let's go get an Estes toy rocket!

Knowledge:
1. Hey, there are physical concepts that are working here, like the rocket equation and Newton's laws for thrust and drag.
2. Hey, I can use formulas for thrust to estimate the thrust, just using a bucket and a timer.
3. I want to compare a bottle rocket to an Estes toy chemical rocket to a Space Rocket.
4. I can learn about possible other ways to get into space, like cascaded-engine rockets or elevators or rail guns.

Person with engineering and physics background:
'Hey, this is some fun. A bottle rocket or toy chemical rocket do demonstrate a lot of ideas that relate to Space Rockets, like thrust, gravity, air drag, energy and momentum.'

Water bottle rocket:
1. I can demonstrate this bottle rocket launch to other people, like cub scouts.
2. We can have bottle rocket challenges even in college.
3. Apply techniques, like top weight, to make the bottle rocket more stable and go higher.

Toy chemical rocket:
1. Let's show chemical launches to other people!

Knowledge and mentoring:
1. I want to help others understand these thrust and altitude ideas, and relate them to Space Rockets.
2. I can learn about possible other ways to get into space, like cascaded-engine rockets or space elevators or rail guns.
3. Those appendices show me how to relate thrust equations to real backyard measurements.

Come on, give bottle rockets and toy chemical rockets a try.

Book 1 reprise: Summary of Thrust and Rockets

First liquid fuel rocket, with top nozzle

Landing on the Moon using rockets

"Rockets are just the vehicles that enable satellites and exploration of the solar system. Let's make them less expensive and more reliable."

In Book 1, we've introduced toy bottles and chemical rockets, and the ways rockets work using fuels and thrust.

We're now just starting the age of space tourism. Would you be brave enough to get in a capsule and say 'Light this candle', like the early astronauts? It has taken a lot of trial and error to develop the rocket technology, for stable fuels, cryogenic liquid fuels, efficient nozzles and reliable fuel pumps, high temperature materials, non-flammable materials, well insulated electronics, nuclear fuel cells, solar cells, space suits, and air and water filters for the astronauts.

You can launch toy rockets in a local park or field by building water bottle rockets, or buying a toy chemical rocket starter kit.

If you *get* Newton's laws, then you are doing great. Newton's 2nd law is that force = mass*acceleration, so the exhaust thrust or force will accelerate the rocket. Newton's 3rd law is that for every force (Action) there is an equal and opposite force (Reaction), so thrown out exhaust will push the rocket the other direction.

As an accepted part of current lifestyles, the satellite payloads in rockets have helped the digital age. We have launched satellites for communication, GPS, earth monitoring, weather forecasting, and for science. Rockets also have kept alive the dream that humans may live on other planets.

Unfortunately, rockets are still far far too expensive, a 1000 times more expensive than an airplane ride per pound of payload. The cost and efficiency are poor. If we could instead design and treat a rocket like a run-of-the-mill bus or airplane ride to space, that would be great. Improvements are on-going. People are succeeding at more mass manufacturing, 3D printing of rocket engines, and re-usable rocket stages that land and are re-filled with fuel.

And what about hovering? Beautiful pictures of quiet spacecraft hovering over land in the movies can not be hovering peacefully because of rockets. We need Newton's 3rd law of Action and Reaction. But we all want hovering spacecraft. If we take hints from the movies, then we'd already have imaginary anti-gravity devices, and anti-matter engines with matter/anti-matter reactions powering the flight such as 'Star Trek'. But we don't, yet.

Going beyond rockets to more far-out concepts, let's get out there and break the limitations of the rocket equation and try other things, like cascaded air-breathing engines before rockets, or piggyback launches from supersonic airplanes, or rail guns.

Thrust and acceleration are directly related, using Newton's 2nd law:

$$Force = Thrust = Mass * Acceleration$$

The thrust for a rocket can be expressed as, using Newton's 3rd law:

$$F_{rocket} = (v_{exhaust})(mass\ flow\ rate)$$

Rockets are in a Wild West new era of development, with both NASA and commercial companies doing the innovating.

Book 1 reprise: Main Concepts of Rockets

Many technical hurdles had to be jumped over to get successful space flights. The rocket industry has been around for more than 60 years. People keep achieving better communication, better science, and better defense, so steady effort has been done.

"A lot of good history has been done to make rockets reliable."

It takes force to throw exhaust out the bottom of a rocket, which gives an opposite thrust.

From Newton's law, for a each force there is an equal opposite force.

Nozzle are fed with turbo pumps and nozzles use converging / diverging shape to get exhaust to all go straight.

Ironman actually obeys Newton's law with exhaust:
Extreme heating of air with nuclear fusion power source (real in concept, although not in practice).

thrust

exhaust

Space rockets use semi-explosive chemical reactions to get fast exhaust flow and high thrust.

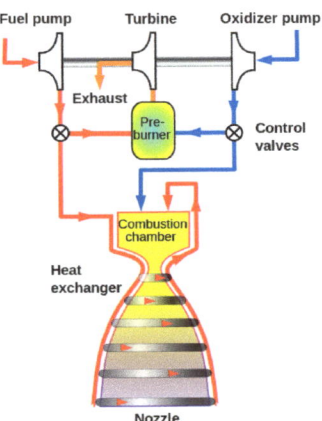

Turbo pumps feeding the thrust chamber

Bottle rockets, toy solid fuel rockets, and space rockets all share the same rocket thrust idea.

Rocket in space without air will steer and rotate by aiming the nozzles.

1-stage water bottle rocket:

1-stage toy Estes rocket:

Multi-stage powerful launch of space rocket with boosters

Space Shuttle engines: gimballing engines, with independent movement, allow tilting and rotation about the axis.
Directed thrust allows full maneuvering in the vacuum of space.
Direction is known using gyroscopes.

Basic rules are used for rockets. One, there is action and reaction, so we need to have an exhaust in order to have thrust. Two, in space without an atmosphere, we need to aim the nozzle and exhaust in order to change directions and roll.
Fuels, nozzles, materials, space stations and electronics... all have been developed.

Chapter 1: $Millions to $Billions - Modern Space Rockets

Space rockets come in a crazy amount of designs and fuels, with billions of dollars of investment and launch costs. Design differences are fuels, materials, construction techniques, number of stages, re-use, and landing.

There are many rocket companies and they each seem to go their own way, with different fuels, stages, and re-use. The larger companies are building medium rockets, and also building bigger rockets to escape Earth and visit other planets, such as the Moon and Mars.
- Designers need to choose between two stages or three stages, boosters or just strap on fuel tanks (both done with Space Shuttle).
- Designers need to choose between liquid, solid, or hybrid-fuel rockets. Different liquid fuels are kerosene, hydrogen, methane, or natural gas.

Let's look at the rocket manufacturers for manned and unmanned rockets. Some manufacturers focus on unmanned rockets, and some have options for both manned and unmanned. Some manufacturers focus on very large rockets to get to the Moon or Mars, and some manufacturers focus on medium size rockets just to get a small payload into Earth's orbit.

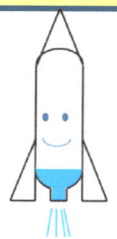

"I'm a bottle rocket, using a bicycle pump. Can you believe that I'm related to space rockets?

Space rockets have a lot more power and electronics, but bottle rockets and space rockets all have the rocket principal using exhaust for thrust."

Rocket design: Payload weight, number of stages, fuels, and materials.
Rockets are optimized for certain types of missions, like Low Earth Orbit or Escape velocity. The number of stages is a function of how high the rocket needs to go and how heavy the payload is. Typically 2 stages are used for Low Earth Orbit, and 3 stages are used for higher orbits for geostationary satellites, or visit other planets.

Manufacturers need to choose the right fuel, which is a trade of the fuel properties: most convenient, highest performing, and easiest to handle. Liquid hydrogen it has the highest performance. But todays manufacturers are backing away from the coldest liquid hydrogen because it is difficult to store and handle. Liquid methane is easier to handle and potentially methane can be made on other planets. With all these fuels – hydrogen, methane, or kerosene – they still need the cryogenic liquid oxygen for the chemical reaction.

All the materials for the rocket structure need to be light weight, strong, and handle high and cold temperatures.

Manufacturers: the old players and the new players.
The main manufacturers of space rockets, at least in the USA, are defense and aerospace companies like Boeing, Lockheed, and Northrup-Grumman, and the more commercial companies like SpaceX and Blue Origin. Each of these rocket manufacturer's designs are discussed in this chapter.

The new SpaceX and Blue Origin rockets are the result of NASA opening the bidding process to startup companies, after the Space Shuttle was retired. NASA wanted to get out of the space rocket business and focus more on the science of the satellites and manned exploration. NASA is also not known for low cost efficient rockets, or even the most reliable rockets, so the option was given for new companies to participate.

Part of NASA's purpose is to educate the USA population in technology and science, especially during the Space Race of the 1960s. Another purpose of NASA is to provide a backstop for research funding for all companies around the country that participate in science. There is always long term science progress that is needed. NASA's purpose is not to be the most efficient, but rather to be a leader in pure aerospace advancement, science, and exploration.

The NASA contracts are from the government. NASA deliberately spreads the fabrication of the rocket parts across the country, so the economic investment and money is shared across the country. More private companies can produce more of the parts locally to reduce cost.

Rockets can use different fuels, stages, and re-use. Many companies manufacture rockets of different designs.

Manned and Un-manned – Modern Space Rockets

Space rockets come in a crazy amount of designs and fuel, with billions of dollars of investment and launch costs. Design differences are fuels, materials, number of stages, re-use, and landing.

There are many rocket companies and they each seem to go their own way. The larger companies are building medium rockets, and also building bigger rockets to escape Earth and visit other planets, such as the Moon and Mars.
- Designers need to choose between two stages or three stages, boosters or just strap on fuel tanks (both done with Space Shuttle).
- Designers need to choose between liquid, solid, or hybrid-fuel rockets. Different liquid fuels are kerosene, hydrogen, methane, or natural gas.

The big traditional companies are betting on cheaper disposable rockets with more lifting power, with Boeing/Lockheed Martin 'Atlas' rockets and Boeing 'SLS' rockets. The new billionaire companies, instead, are betting on re-usable rockets, with booster landings back on ground. These billionaire companies, and some big traditional companies, got into the commercial rocket development business partly because rocket design takes a big initial investment, and partly because it is a beautiful dream to start bringing more people to space and to explore and inhabit other planets, to help humanity.

Traditional big rocket companies, like Boeing, Lockheed Martin, Northrop Grumman, are the backbone of space launches such as the Atlas and the Antares rockets and for the upcoming Space Launch System SLS.

New companies like SpaceX and Blue Origin, started by rich entrepreneurs of Tesla car and Amazon delivery fame, are building rockets to launch satellites, supply the Space Station, and compete for missions to the planned Moon base for the Artemis program.

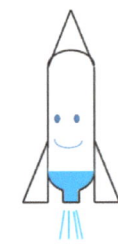

"I'm a bottle rocket, using a bicycle pump. Can you believe that I'm related to these space rockets?

These are US rockets. Russia, China, Europe, Japan, and India have their own too."

Un-Manned Rockets

Atlas and Delta design
- Many mission successes.
- Not re-usable.

Antares design

Built and launched many times

Manned Rockets

SpaceX design
- Many mission successes.
- Re-usable side boosters using liquid fuel, and an ejection and parachute for the entire capsule at launch, for safety of astronauts

Liquid re-usable boosters

Built and launched many times

Blue Origin design:
- Instead of using side boosters, the first stage core is re-usable and liquid fuel.

No boosters, re-usable 1st and 2nd stage

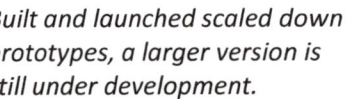

Built and launched scaled down prototypes, a larger version is still under development.

NASA's Space Launch System design
- Solid fuel boosters, 1st stage, disposable.

Solid fuel boosters, nothing reusable.

Built and launched in 2022

SLS should have 3 times the lift capability as the Falcon Heavy. SLS uses disposable Space Shuttle boosters and engines, and can escape Earth.

Here are the main contenders for missions to supply the Space Station, launch satellites and astronauts, and go to other planets.

Wild West of Modern Space Rocket Design, the Actors

Welcome to the Wild West of rocket design. After the Space Shuttle was retired in 2011, the US government decided to open up rocket contracts to anyone who could demonstrate a good rocket, and people (rich entrepreneurs) and companies responded that have deep pockets to fund the development themselves.

"Can you believe that I'm related to these space rockets?"

Consider a car. There are lots of different technologies that go into making a car. Practically all new technology goes into making a car. There are different fuels, like gasoline, diesel, hydrogen, and electric. There are long lasting engines with many moving parts and low wear with lubricant. There is electronic injection of fuel, with sensors to control the fuel ratio. There are different car shapes to allow the most safety during a crash, like an according compression. There are sensors to avoid collision, like radar and cameras.

Consider a space rocket. There are different fuels, like kerosene, hydrogen, and methane. There are rocket engines with spinning fuel pumps, with a controlled flow rate. There are navigation sensors, more than in a car. There is no driver in a rocket, so the sensors need to do most of the work.

What companies make rockets: traditional and new aerospace companies?
Traditional big rocket companies are the backbone of space launches, such as the Atlas and the Antares rockets. The big traditional companies are Boeing, Lockheed Martin, and Northrop Grumman, especially for NASA's Space Launch System.
New companies, like SpaceX, Blue Origin and more, started by a few billionaires and with NASA's help, are building rockets to launch satellites, supply the Space Station, and help humanity get to Mars.
All companies get contracts from NASA and commercial companies to launch rockets, usually after a demonstrated launch of a rocket design.

Commercial and Military rockets: orbital and non-orbital rockets:
Both the commercial world and the military world design and build rockets.
The commercial world typically needs to get into orbit, to launch communication or earth sensor satellites.
The military world also launches communication, location (gps), and camera and radar satellites, at orbital speeds. Besides orbital launches, the military world, with missiles, only needs to briefly get to space and then arc back down, at sub orbital speeds. If military rockets stay in the atmosphere, the rockets have the option of using oxygen from the air with turbofan engines as a cruise missile, to travel farther, instead of storing their own oxygen as a rocket.

Companies need to have a business plan to match the rocket design to the mission: number of stages, heat handling, and return capsule
The entire mission, like orbit and payload and manned or not manned, needs to be planned in advance to make the best design for the rocket.
- For hardware, how many stages are needed to lift the payload and get this payload to the destination? Nowadays, there are strap-on booster rockets, which make most rocket designs scalable. For example, if the rocket is launching a heavier payload, or going beyond Earth orbit, then strap on a few rocket boosters.
- For heat, how will the capsule handle the heat from air drag during re-entry, without burning up?
- For return, how will the capsule land back on Earth in a safe way, such as parachutes, gliding, or a retro-rocket?
- For launch, what day of year and time of day is the best to aim at the destination, like the ISS or Mars or the Moon?

Big established companies and smaller entrepreneurial companies are making rockets.

Blank Page Design for Lower Cost Rocket Competition

If you are designing a rocket, it makes sense to make friends with people who have done it before, such as in NASA. Besides fuels, there are so many things to think about, like strong, light and high temperature materials, and a capsule design with life support equipment like oxygen and shields from heat and solar radiation.

"There are quite a lot of different parts to build a successful rocket."

The mass-produced model, similar to mass production of cars:
- All companies support this. Use mass production of any design, like no-frills one-use rockets which the Russians or the Chinese use, or even new re-usable rockets in the US which land back down, or single use SLS. Mass production brings the cost down.

Carry astronauts and life support system?:
- Suddenly, with astronauts on board, the reliability needs to be much tighter, and the payload is partly taken up by life support gear and the capsule to return to Earth.

Emergency ejection system for astronauts:
- If the millions of pounds of fuel below the astronauts have a leak, then an astronaut might want to hit 'time out' and eject, let's try another day.

Re-usable versus one-shot rockets:
- SpaceX and Blue Origin are going for complex and re-usable rockets. Re-usable rocket stages could land vertically on land by re-lit rocket engines, or be caught by helicopter while parachuting down, be caught in a net, or be plucked out of the ocean after splashdown and floating.
- NASA's SLS is going for simple and one-shot rockets, not re-usable.

Larger rocket versus many smaller rockets:
- The large SLS will lift a 100,000 lb payload to the Moon, to allow large single payloads to be planted on the Moon as a single unit. The SLS needs 3 stages to get to Earth escape velocity.
- The light Electron rocket lifts a 200 lb payload to Low Earth Orbit (LEO), to allow custom single satellites to be launched to their exact orbit.

Multi-stage rocket design (1, 2, or 3 stage rocket):
- More stages allow a more efficient and powerful rocket, but more stages have more complexity.

Less parts:
- The best and most reliable part is no part.
- Use 3D printing to have all the shapes and functions built together in one part for less parts, especially for the engine.
- Less inventory, less management and hand labor.

	Strength	Weight	Hot Temp	Cold Temp	Cost
Stainless Steel			Good (1500F)	Good	$3/kg
Aluminum	Least strength	Add weight of thermal protection	Melts (1220F)		$3/kg
Carbon Fiber	Most strength		Melts (300F)	Brittle	$150/kg

Table of material properties for rocket structure

Blank page to start rocket design conversation, for low cost yet high reliability

Material choices: compromise of strength, weight, temperature handling ability, cost, availability:
- Stainless Steel can the handle high temperatures of 1500 degree F with less protective material, but is heavier than carbon fiber which handles 300 degree F. Stainless Steel can handle very low temperature and does not become brittle near cryogenic liquid oxygen.
- Aluminum and Carbon Fiber are lighter than Steel but need protective material from heat, which adds weight.
- Steel and Aluminum are lower cost ($3/kg), but Carbon Fiber (~$150/kg) is stronger and lighter if not exposed to heat.

Are modern rocket engines better than the old Saturn V rocket engines?
- Modern engines have more electronic sensors, and can turn off one of the many engines if fuel leaks occur or a valve breaks. More engines are better so that one engine can fail without aborting or at least allow a safer abort of the launch.
- Modern engines can use 3D printing, with fewer parts and less cost.
- Modern engines are optimized for ideal nozzle dimensions to get the most thrust per weight of the fuel, at each stage and altitude.

You need a mission plan before you design the rocket, because the rockets can be designed in many ways from carrying astronauts and going to different orbits.

Wild West of Modern Space Rocket Design, the Fuels

Liquid or Solid fuel is a number one decision for the start of a rocket design. Fuels are also discussed in more detail in the next chapter.

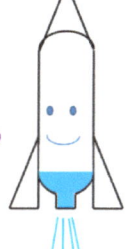

"Can you believe that I'm related to these space rockets?"

	Performance	Thrust	Cost	Complexity
Solid Fuel	Moderate exhaust velocity	Strong burn rate to generate huge thrust	Low cost because room temperature storage and less parts	Less parts.
Liquid Fuel	Highest exhaust velocity	Need large turbo pumps to get the larger burn rate.	Many parts, but can be re-usable.	Yes, cryogenic liquids and pumps.

Rocket Fuel: liquid and solid fuels
The fuel choice is always a good starting point for a design, based on performance, cost, and availability.

Liquid or Solid fuel:
- Solid fuels have more instantaneous thrust with huge burning surface area, can last for decades, but are less efficient and do not throttle. A typical use is 1st stage thrust.
- Liquid fuels are great for controlled burns, for re-starting, and for highest exhaust velocity. A typical use of liquid fuel is the upper stage thrust, because the highest exhaust velocity causes the highest rocket speed.

Liquid Fuel Choice: Cryogenic liquid fuel or room-temperature liquid fuel:
- For the fuel part choice of the fuel / oxidizer mix, the Liquid Hydrogen is cryogenic, Methane is moderately cryogenic and potentially can be made on other planets, and Kerosene is room temperature.
- Unfortunately, the common liquid oxygen oxidizer is still cryogenic.

<u>There are liquid fuel options.</u>
Liquid oxygen and liquid hydrogen are the best due to their high energy per weight, and were used for the Space Shuttle. But there are plenty of alternative liquid fuels, from other cryogenic liquids (methane), and room temperature liquids (kerosene).
- Cryogenic liquids need to be pumped into the rocket at the last few minutes on the launch pad, because the cold liquids are always boiling away.
- Liquid fuel rockets require pumps to squirt the liquid oxygen and the liquid fuel into the combustion chamber, in the right amounts. That thrust or burn rate is determined by the size of these fuel pumps.
- Methane is a heavier molecule and does not leak as much as hydrogen. Methane does not have as cold a boiling temperature and does not need as much thermal insulation.

<u>There are also solid fuel options.</u>
Solid fuels are great for large thrust, simplicity, and storage.
- Solid fuels are very stable, like clay, and can have a storage life of decades. Solid fuel rockets can have a very large thrust because the surface area of the burning surface, not a fuel pump, determines how much chemical is burning and how much exhaust provides thrust.

SLS rocket with 2 solid fuel boosters attached to the liquid fuel main engine.

Rocket Falcon Heavy with boosters, all liquid fuel.

Cascaded air-breathing rocket engines versus Pure Fuel/Oxidizer Rocket:
- Cascaded engines – subsonic to supersonic to hypersonic to rocket – are not yet demonstrated together as a system, due to high temperatures from air drag and added weight.

The Star-Raker cascaded-engine concept design by Rockwell.
See book 2 chapter 7.

Liquid and solid fuel both have their advantages and disadvantages.

Un-manned Workhorse Rockets in the US: Most Launches Don't Have People

There are thousands of satellites in orbit, and plenty of robotic missions to other planets.

Most missions are not manned, and the rockets just need to be a reliable way to get satellites and supplies into orbit. Of course most launches are not manned, because outer space is a dangerous place for people and people can't stay in outer space for decades.

Satellites with sensors and robots, powered by solar panels, are more practical. Unmanned satellites don't complain about the food, and they work for decades.

Generally un-manned launches only make the news if there is an exciting science mission, or they explode.

Atlas V rocket + Boosters

Launch of Mars Rover using 4 strap-on boosters to escape Earth, 2020

Atlas during launch

Atlas V rocket by United Launch Alliance (Lockheed Martin and Boeing)

- Liquid kerosene fuel / oxygen for first stage using Russian engine, and liquid hydrogen fuel / oxygen for second stage.
- Thrust can be augmented with up to five Aerojet strap-on solid rocket boosters
- Each launch costs about $150 million, and each strap-on Solid Fuel Booster adds another $6 million.
- About 5 launches each year, so extremely reliable.

https://en.wikipedia.org/wiki/Atlas_V

Some Missions, since 2002, about 5 launches per year.	Orbit
Solar telescope	escape
Jupiter Orbiter	escape
Mars Rover	escape
Van Allen Belts exploration	escape
ISS supplies	LEO
Military Comsat	LEO
Missile Warning satellite	LEO
Commercial Satcom	GTO
Navigation satellite	MEO
Earth Imaging satellite	LEO
Meteorology	LEO

*LEO: Low Earth Orbit
*MEO: Medium Earth Orbit
*GTO: Geostationary Transfer Orbit (to escape)
*Escape: leave Earth

Delta IV rocket + Boosters

Delta IV during launch

Delta IV rocket by United Launch Alliance (Lockheed Martin and Boeing)

- Liquid hydrogen fuel / oxygen for upper stages.
- Thrust can be augmented using strap-on solid rocket boosters
- Each launch costs about $150 million, and each add on Solid Fuel Booster adds another $6 million.
- About 5 launches each year, so extremely reliable.

Antares rocket

Antares during launch

Antares rocket, 2 stage, by Northrop Grumman

- Liquid kerosene fuel / oxygen for first stage using Russian engine, and solid fuel for second stage.
- Thrust can be augmented with strap-on solid rocket boosters
- Most launches send supplies to the ISS, up to 8000 kg (8 tons), for NASA, for small to medium missions.

Some Missions, since 2013, about 2 launches per year.	Orbit
Many ISS supplies	LEO

https://en.wikipedia.org/wiki/Antares_(rocket)

Heavier missions can strap some side boosters to a rocket, and the rocket becomes more powerful with more thrust and more stages.

Un-manned Workhorse Rockets in the US: Most Launches Don't Have People

Here is the launch of an un-manned space plane for the US air force.

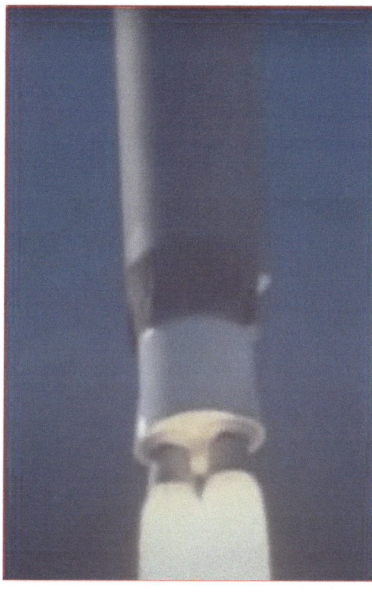

The space plane is fully re-usable and glides back down to a runway for a landing.

ULA's Atlas V rocket successfully launch a X37 space plane from Cape Canaveral FL, in 2020.
The huge faring on top protects the space plane from the heat of the air drag during launch.

ULA's Atlas V rocket two massive rocket engines for 1st stage.
These rockets are single-use only.

The payload is the X37 un-manned mini space shuttle.
The space plane is fully re-usable and glides back down to a runway for a landing.

The space plane gets a tow from a pickup truck.
The space plane is fully re-usable and glides back down to a runway for a landing.

Heavier missions can strap some side boosters to a rocket, and the rocket becomes more powerful with more thrust and more stages.

Un-manned Workhorse Rockets in the US: Liquid fuel Upper Stages and Solid Fuel Boosters

These solid fuel booster designs have been re-used on many rockets for the last 20 years. The core of the rocket uses liquid fuel, and the modular add-on boosters use solid fuel. More boosters are added on to carry more payload or to go faster.

Atlas V rocket + Boosters

Atlas V rocket by United Launch Alliance (Lockheed Martin and Boeing)

The Atlas V rocket has been launching satellites for two decades.
The first stage is powered by liquid kerosene and liquid oxygen, providing 0.9 million pounds of thrust. The thrust can be augmented by up to 5 solid fuel boosters, each with a thrust of 0.29 million pounds of thrust.
The Atlas V has launched many satellites, from science missions like Mars landers and the Webb telescope, to reconnaissance missions.

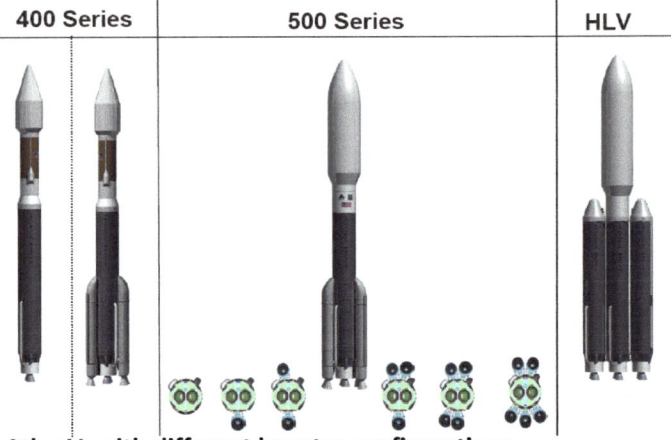

Atlas V, with different booster configurations

Delta IV rocket + Boosters

Delta IV rocket by United Launch Alliance (Lockheed Martin and Boeing)

The Delta IV rocket has been launching satellites for decades.
Now the fuel is liquid hydrogen.
Out of the many variations of the Delta IV rocket, the Delta IV Medium is getting retired because of the competition with SpaceX, Antares, and the European Ariane rocket. The Delta IV heavy will still be active.

Antares rocket

Antares rocket is a smaller rocket (Northrop Grumman).

The Antares rocket has been launching satellites since 2013.
Originally the 1st stage rocket engine came from Russia and Ukraine, and used kerosene and cryogenic LOX. The Russians have been launching rockets for 7 decades, and had developed a reliable engine. Currently, due to the Ukrainian war, the 1st stage rocket engine will be built by Firefly in Texas.
The 1st stage includes propellant tanks, pressurization tanks, valves, sensors, feed lines, tubing, wiring and other associated hardware.

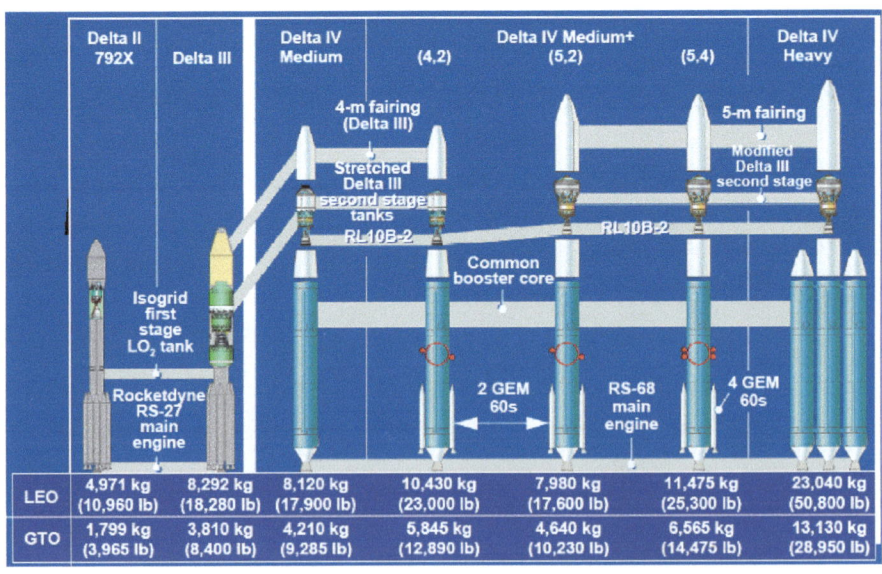

History of Delta rocket. Only the Delta IV Heavy will continue.
https://en.wikipedia.org/wiki/Delta_IV

Heavier missions can strap some side boosters to a rocket, and the rocket becomes more powerful with more thrust and more stages.

SpaceX: Land a Re-usable 1st Stage and Can Eject Astronaut Capsules

SpaceX designs, manned:

SpaceX has succeeded many times in landing their liquid rocket boosters on land, with re-started retro-rockets and not parachutes. On one design a booster even lands in a cradle, instead of landing on 4 legs.
- The booster engines only burn a few seconds to arrest their fall and touch down vertically, because at their return the booster rocket is much lighter.

SpaceX has a capsule ejection capability. Big rockets that carry people are now required to have an ejection and parachute for the entire capsule at launch, for safety of astronauts.
- Russians have had the ejection safety for a long time. The US Apollo mission to the Moon also had an escape assembly during launch. The Space Shuttle did not.

SpaceX has also been the first out the gate to launch its biggest rocket, which can travel to Mars.

"SpaceX was the first to re-land and re-use the 1st stage rocket."

SPACEX FALCON 9 LAUNCH PROFILE

- BOOSTBACK BURN — THE BOOSTBACK BURN PUSHES THE BOOSTER UP AND BACK TOWARDS THE LAUNCH SITE.
- BOOSTER FLIPS OVER — WITH NITROGEN THRUSTERS
- SECOND STAGE IGNITION
- STAGE SEPARATION
- MECO (MAIN ENGINE CUTOFF)
- REENTRY BURN — HYPERSONIC THREE ENGINE BURN
- GRID FINS DEPLOY — SPEED IS STILL ABOVE MACH 3
- FAIRING SEPARATION
- SECO (SECOND STAGE ENGINE CUTOFF)
- PAYLOAD SEPARATION
- LANDING BURN — SINGLE ENGINE TERMINAL BURN
- LANDING LEGS DEPLOY — USING COMPRESSED HELIUM
- SOFT TOUCHDOWN — MAX VERTICAL SPEED: 6 METERS PER SECOND
- LIFTOFF
- LAUNCH SITE
- DRONE SHIP

Flip First stage to land

First stage left atmosphere (about 60 miles)

Reverse direction of engines on falling boosters

Capsule can eject during launch if engines fail

Depiction of Falcon 9 landing trajectory for some of the floating-platform recovery tests

Release of 2nd stage

SpaceX tourism: Four new civilian astronauts

Returning boosters with retro thrust

Fuel: Room temperature kerosene in Falcon 9 and Heavy, and cryogenic methane in upcoming Starship. Liquid methane is not as cold as LH2 and can be made on Mars.

Some Missions, since 2009, about 3 launches per year.	Orbit
Commercial Sat, 2009	LEO
Jupiter Orbiter	escape
Supply ISS, 2012	LEO
First re-usable first stage, 2015	LEO
Heavy Falcon test, 2018	escape
Send astronauts to ISS, 2020	LEO
Launch many communication satellites, 2021	LEO

The landing burners do not need to be on for very long to stop and settle the nearly empty 1st stage boosters.
- 1 g deceleration (10 m/s^2) stops first stage in 500 meters, if falling at a terminal velocity of 100 m/s.

Rocket Falcon Heavy with boosters

Many nozzles: 9 engines and nozzles per booster, each with independent steering.

https://en.wikipedia.org/wiki/SpaceX_reusable_launch_system_development_program
https://www.bloomberg.com/graphics/2017-spacex-launches/

SpaceX rockets have supplied the ISS in low Earth orbit, and their largest rocket has placed a car in orbit around the Sun, with a payload of 37,000 pounds to Mars.

SpaceX: Launch and Re-use a Huge Starship Rocket

SpaceX designs, manned:

SpaceX has launched the massive 'Starship' 2 stage rocket to get to LEO, and then get re-fueled while in orbit to then re-fire and escape Earth's gravity and go to the Moon.
This Starship rocket will take supplies and astronauts to the lunar station in a few years.

"SpaceX has shown that bold re-usable rocket designs and willingness to go through a few launches until the rocket works did enable a re-usable rocket."

Most powerful launch in history of the Starship rocket
The launch shakes the ground around the launch tower.

Hot-fire 1st stage separation in near orbit
The hot-fire separation ensures that the 2nd stage rockets light up.

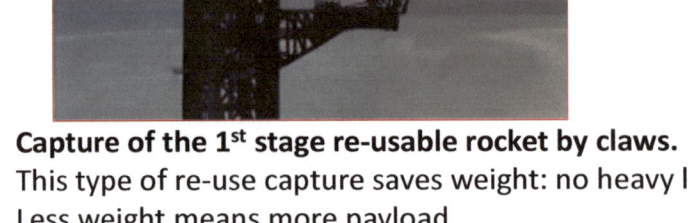

Capture of the 1st stage re-usable rocket by claws.
This type of re-use capture saves weight: no heavy legs. Less weight means more payload.

SpaceX Starship rocket has successfully landed the 1st stage using retro-rockets and a claw for capture.

SpaceX: Land a Re-usable 1st Stage and Can Eject Astronaut Capsules

SpaceX designs, manned:

SpaceX is a private company, founded in 2002, and is owned mostly by the tech titan Elon Musk. He largely funded the initial development of the company by the sale of his first business, PayPal, and sale of stock in his electric vehicle company Tesla.

SpaceX now has contracts to supply the ISS and to supply the upcoming Artemis lunar base program. In addition, SpaceX launches their own array of small satellites called Starlink to create a communications company.

During development, SpaceX pursued the same test-by-launch design method that the Apollo program did. There are so many parts on a rocket that it would take too long to test each part separately. Instead, just launch the prototype rockets with lots of sensors and see which part fails, during lift off or stage separation or engine ignition. After a few failed launches and vertical landings in the prototypes on the ground and on floating barges, the bugs got worked out.

"SpaceX has shown that bold re-usable rocket designs and willingness to go through a few launches until the rocket works did enable a re-usable rocket."

What was new with SpaceX, compared to the Space Shuttle or the Atlas rockets?

SpaceX was also taking on added risk-and-reward by designing a re-usable booster, and by experimenting with different fuels and rocket engines. There had never been a lower cost re-usable rocket, at least a lower cost and re-usable 1st stage, before SpaceX. Of course the Space Shuttle itself was re-usable, but that Shuttle could only get to LEO, and the cost was much higher. The Shuttle 1st stage solid fuel boosters and 2nd stage liquid fuel rocket were not re-usable.

Of course, this re-usable rocket business plan was the goal of the SpaceX business. At some point, rockets need to get away from building high quality parts only to fire them once and let them get destroyed or abandoned into the ocean during launch. For re-use, the engineers needed to optimize the control system to get the rockets on the 1st stage to re-fire and stabilize the rocket as it lands upright. In contrast, with one shot launches, lots of money has fallen to the bottom of the ocean or burnt up in the upper atmosphere.

SpaceX also wanted to build as much of the rocket in their local factory as possible. The design can be optimized at the place of the rocket where rapid modifications to parts can be made in the design, which speeds up the design cycle. The Space Shuttle design spread the design and money around the country.

With a single private company, parts could be built locally and there would be less need or restrictions requiring long distance transportation. For example, the Space Shuttle rocket boosters were built far from the assembly of the rocket. The boosters needed to be built in 4 sections to allow the transportation across the country to the Florida launch site. Each seam between sections is a risk.

Of course, local fabrication is not always the best approach to a cost effective product. Look at the automotive industry. Different parts, like engines, frames, and seats, are made in different countries around the world, and these parts are all sent to the final assembly plant where the final car is assembled.

Launch of SpaceX Starship, first attempt, 2023. This 2-stage rocket goes to LEO orbit.

An orbiting fuel station will be necessary to get this 2nd stage to re-burn and then escape Earth's orbit.

Fuels and Engine:

The Falcon Heavy has 5 million pounds of thrust, using liquid fuels. That takes a very fast flow and burn rate of the right fuels.

SpaceX needed to figure out fuels. The first decade of development had kerosene fuel, which is a liquid at room temperature. The next larger rocket uses methane, which has higher performance for the weight. Methane has a boiling point near liquid oxygen, and while cold it is compatible with the liquid oxygen temperature already on board the rocket.

SpaceX builds their own rocket engines, to enable different fuels, quicker design modifications, and reduced cost. Different rocket engines are needed for the different fuels, based on the cold temperature of the fuel.

Materials:

SpaceX needed to figure out the material of the rocket structure. The rockets are made from steel because steel can handle high temperatures and is very available. Carbon composite materials are lower density and higher strength but composite materials would have needed an extra outer heat protecting material (ceramic tiles or sacrificial material), are expensive, and do not handle temperature extremes, either too hot or too cold, as well as steel.

SpaceX rockets have been very aggressive for re-use, landing, and quick turn-around of design changes.

Blue Origin, Amazon's Project

Blue Origin designs, manned:

Blue Origin is building a huge rocket, where both the 1st and 2nd stages are re-usable to reduce costs, different than SpaceX. Like good engineering, the first step or prototype is the current non-orbital 1-stage demonstration rocket, for fuels, engines, and landing and re-use. This non-orbital small version still brings people up into space for 10 minutes. The larger multi-stage orbital version comes next.

- Blue Origin has been experimenting and launching a smaller non-orbital prototype rocket, to design the control system for landing back on the ground. The larger orbital rocket 'New Glenn' will launch in 2024 or later.
- Below is the non-orbital 1-stage prototype 'New Shepard' returning from launch into space. This prototype, which launches people too, is about 1/5th the height of the planned final bigger heavy lift rocket 'New Glenn'. Instead of using side boosters of solid fuel (like the Space Shuttle and the SLS), the first stage core is liquid fuel and re-usable.

"Blue Origin is making all stages re-usable, the first and second stage.

The first stage keeps some fuel after launch, so this stage's engine can turn back on just before hitting the ground, and land upright.
The first stage is much lighter, so not much fuel is needed to slow it down."

Fuel: Currently Blue Origin uses liquid hydrogen on the 'New Shepard', and in the future will use liquid natural gas (mostly methane). In the past Blue Origin has used kerosene and methane and peroxide.

'New Shepard' Non-orbital 1-stage Demonstration, for space tourism

Blue Origin tourism | Capsule with a center small rocket engine for emergency ejection

Launch of smaller demonstration 1-stage rocket, non-orbital.

Vertical landing of first stage for re-use, from demonstration rocket.

'New Glenn' Planned Orbital and Mars Multi-stage Rocket: Rocket Launch Profile:

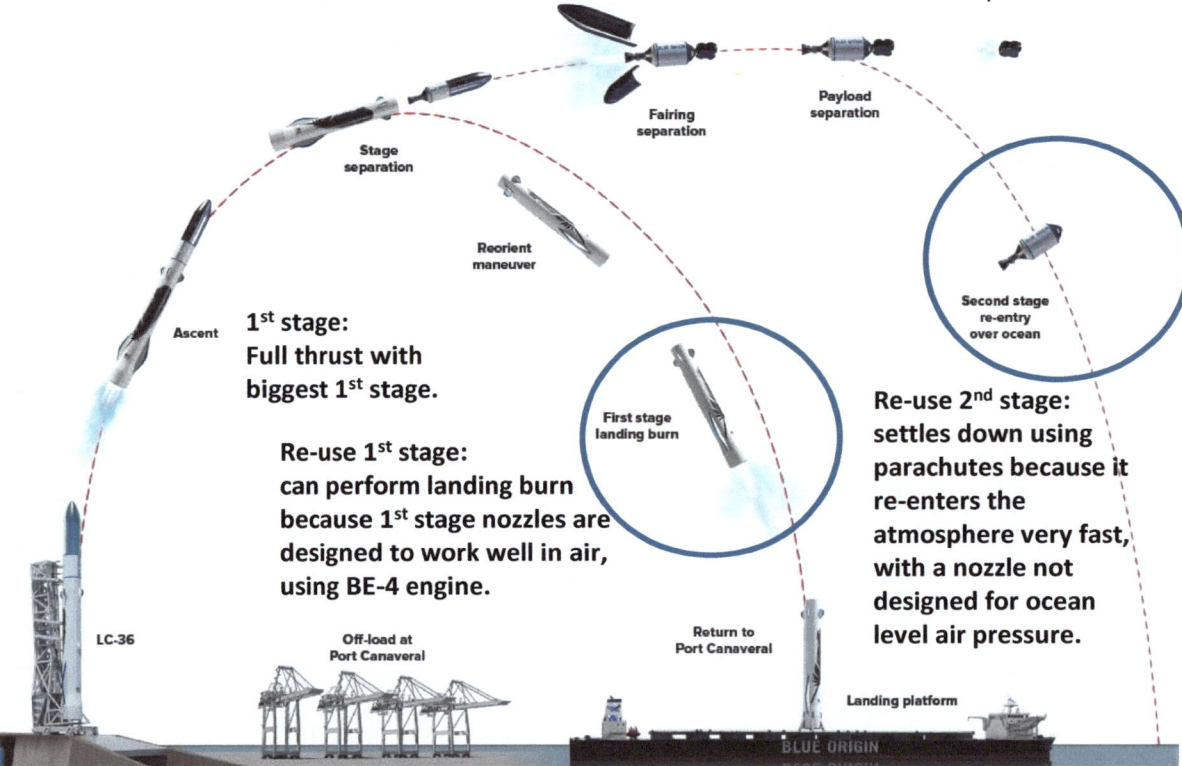

1st stage: Full thrust with biggest 1st stage.

Re-use 1st stage: can perform landing burn because 1st stage nozzles are designed to work well in air, using BE-4 engine.

Re-use 2nd stage: settles down using parachutes because it re-enters the atmosphere very fast, with a nozzle not designed for ocean level air pressure.

Concept for planned launch of larger orbital rocket: re-use of both 1st and 2nd stage

https://www.blueorigin.com/new-shepard/

For the upcoming larger orbital rocket, Blue Origin plans to save costs even more by re-use of the 2nd stage as well as 1st stage. Blue Origin also plans a rocket to Mars, the 'New Glenn' with 18,000 lbs payload to Mars.

Blue Origin, Amazon's Project

Blue Origin designs, manned:

The Blue Origin company is private, founded in 2000, and is owned entirely by the tech titan Jeff Bezos who started Amazon. Their development of a re-usable rocket stage is paid for from the sale of Amazon stock and its computer services.

Without the headlines, Blue Origin developed their re-usable rocket quietly without the news feeds. There were step-by-step tests of the re-useable 1st stage, which is the 'New Shepard' rocket. The second stage is also planned to be re-usable.

Blue Origin is the second provider for the lunar launch competition, to build and supply NASA's Artemis mission lunar base. Blue Origin's future orbital rocket will have a large payload. However, SpaceX is far ahead, already delivering supplies and astronauts to the ISS and already launching a heavier rocket to orbit the Sun.

"Blue Origin has taken a low visibility development, with many launches of the 1st stage, and many re-landings for re-use.
Blue Origin's final rocket will be orbital, huge and multi-stage to get to the Moon.
There is no re-fueling in orbit."

Fuel and Rocket engine

The current 'New Shepard' demonstration rockets are powered by the BE-3 engines, which burn liquid hydrogen.

Seven BE-4 engines will power New Glenn's reusable booster, for 3.7 million pounds of thrust. The BE-4 engine burns natural gas, which is mostly methane. This fuel can be made on other planets, and is not as cold as liquefied hydrogen.

Why the switch in fuels? The higher boiling point of methane means less fuel is wasted in boil-off and there are less leaks. Hydrogen, because it is so cold and so light, is difficult to contain.

Materials

Blue Origin is using aluminum and stainless steel for the rocket structure, which is more evidence that overall system costs matter, like lower cost materials, availability, and temperature properties.

Blue Origin BE-4 engines in production. The BE-4 is the engine for the larger orbital rockets.

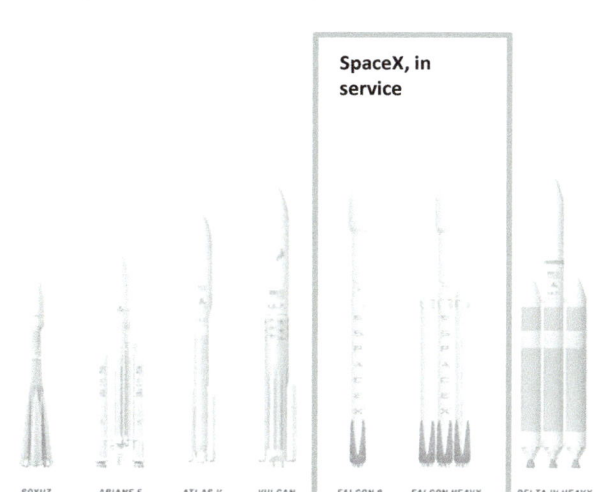

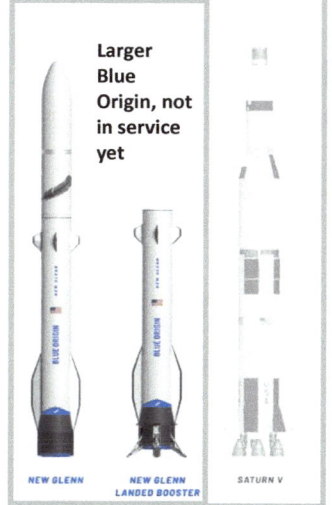

Comparison of Blue Origin's rocket size to other rockets

Engine	Propellant	Thrust
BE - 1	Peroxide	9 kN (2,000 lbf) at Sea Level
BE - 2	Kerosene + Peroxide	140 kN (31,000 lbf) at Sea Level
BE - 3PM	Liquid Hydrogen + Liquid Oxygen	490 kN (110,000 lbf) at Sea Level
BE - 3U	Liquid Hydrogen + Liquid Oxygen	710 kN (160,000 lbf) in Vacuum
BE - 4	Liquefied Natural Gas + Liquid Oxygen	2,400 kN (550,000 lbf) at Sea Level
BE - 7	Liquid Hydrogen + Liquid Oxygen	40 kN (10,000 lbf) in Vacuum

History of Blue Origin's rocket engines and fuels

Blue Origin's upcoming large rocket 'New Glenn' will compete for missions to Mars and the Moon.

https://www.blueorigin.com/engines/

NASA's Space Launch System, for Big Lifts to Other Planets

NASA's Space Launch System design, manned:

NASA wants huge lift capability, and the ability to get to the Moon or Mars. The NASA's Space Launch System (SLS) design, started in 2011 and built by Boeing and Lockheed Martin, fits the requirement.

SLS should have 3 times more lift capability than the SpaceX Falcon Heavy.
The SLS first stage is essentially a disposable Space Shuttle rocket, although very expensive. There are similar solid fuel boosters and hydrogen fuel rocket stages, like the Space Shuttle.
The SLS had a different cost strategy - make the parts cheap and disposable - compared to SpaceX or Blue Origin which have re-usable 1st stages. The cost should be much lower for a single-use solid rocket booster 1st stage than a liquid rocket booster, so the cost should still be competitive. NASA learned a lesson from the retired Space Shuttle: the Shuttle and the boosters were made re-usable, but that caused many of the cost problems over the lifetime of the program.

"For the NASA built SLS, the boosters are high thrust solid fuel, which re-uses the same idea as the Space Shuttle. The liquid fuel in second stage is still hydrogen."

SLS liquid fuel: extremely cold liquid hydrogen with liquid oxygen, also used in the Space Shuttle.
SLS solid fuel for boosters: aluminum fuel and ammonium perchlorate oxidizer

Launch of SLS, Sept 2022

On-going fabrication of SLS 2nd stage.

Liquid fuel rocket engine test run

Solid fuel booster test

Orion Crew Capsule, able to carry 4 astronauts and everything they need for 21 days

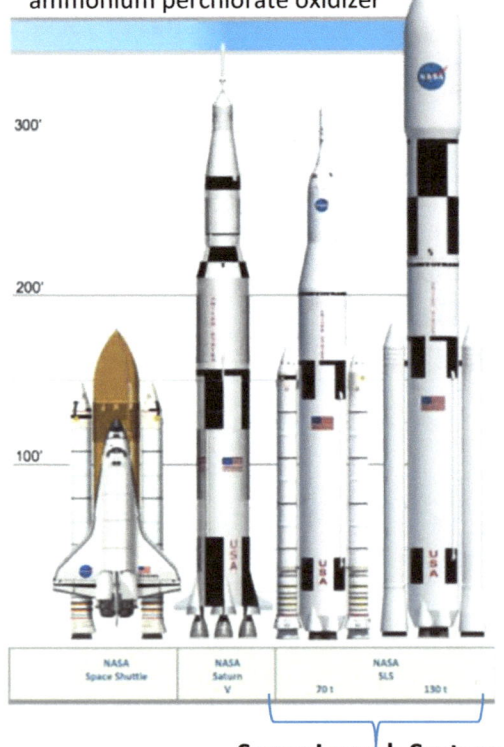
Space Launch System

Comparison of huge size of the SLS rocket to historic rockets Space Shuttle and Saturn V.

- SLS will be capable of bringing 66 kilo-lbs to the Moon in a single mission. Large payloads do not need to be broken up and re-assembled. There is a debate about whether large single payloads are necessary, or if 3 smaller payloads at lower cost would work.
- If the rocket costs $1 Billion, then the cost per pound of payload is $10,000/lb.

https://www.nasa.gov/exploration/systems/sls/

The follow-on rocket to the Space Shuttle is the Space Launch System, using many of the concepts that worked for the Shuttle, for 66,000 pounds payload to Mars. The same concepts are hydrogen fuel for 2nd stage, and solid fuel boosters for 1st stage.

NASA's Space Launch System, Why So Big?

NASA's Space Launch System design, manned:

NASA's mission statement is to explore the unknown in air and space, innovate for the benefit of humanity, and inspire the world through discovery. NASA should be developing next generation technology like robots for surgery in space, better video communications, search for life, and alternative rocket designs.

For the SLS rockets, NASA wants huge lift capability which does not exist yet, and the ability to get to the Moon or Mars. NASA tends to develop the rocket requirements. The heavy lift SLS is designed to fill this need, for super heavy and large payloads and to escape Earth.

This SLS design reuses the Space Shuttle launch approach with 1st stage boosters. The leveraged design was supposed to be an easy one-to-one replacement or an easy update : same boosters, same hydrogen fuel, same rocket engines. However, many of the parts needed to be re-designed anyway because the rocket is larger.

"NASA has designed their own very large rocket, in case other commercial companies have setbacks."

Large rockets for exploration:
Super large rockets don't make sense yet for profit, so this is where government missions or programs can step in. Commercial rockets to launch satellites around Earth orbit don't need the huge rocket. A super large rocket does not have a profitable business plan yet with commercial companies and the defense department, although a super large rocket can bring a large life-support habitat to Mars in one piece.

When a rocket will be developed by market forces by for-profit companies with existing commercial and defense customers, then NASA does not need to build a similar one.

Maybe in the future a very large payload rocket will make sense from satellite customers, but not now. Right now the purpose of a very large payload rocket is to start colonies on other moons and planets. There colonies out in the solar system are not a for-profit pursuit for the time being. Hence NASA can step in and a develop the technology. Hopefully in 20 years there will be a customer base for private rocket companies to build their own rockets, for mining, for colonies, and maybe space hotels.

One purpose of large rockets is to deliver a lunar or Mars base, with a sustainable habitat and happy astronauts. For a lunar base, NASA has gotten some heat for spending so much money for the SLS, as much as an aircraft carrier. But NASA is developing this larger payload rocket precisely because it is not profitable for other companies to do so. SLS should have 3 times more lift capability as the SpaceX Falcon Heavy. SLS is also a typical rocket that does not require any re-fueling in orbit, so it is a self-contained delivery unit.

NASA's SLS, direct to the Moon or Mars, without any refueling.

In parallel, SpaceX is building a 1st stage 'Super Heavy' rocket for the Starship rocket that should have much more lift capacity than the SLS. However, this SpaceX Starship is basically a 2 stage rocket, and requires refueling in low Earth orbit that has never been done. So, depending on how much extra fuel the upper stage wants to carry at the expense of cargo, there could be more than 4 rocket fuel refill launches just to allow the Starship rocket to escape LEO and to get to the Moon.

Typical size rockets and super-size rockets:
Bigger and more stages generally means more capability. There are three typical main purposes for rockets, to get a satellite into low Earth orbit, or into higher geostationary orbit, or to escape Earth to go to other planets. It takes more energy to launch a satellite into higher orbit. For the same rocket, a much heavier satellite can be launched into low Earth orbit than to geostationary orbit. Satellites in geostationary orbit are less than 20,000 pounds, which already can be handled by existing rockets (Atlas, Delta IV, Antares, Falcon). Double that weight can be launched into low Earth orbit with the same rockets.

A new fourth purpose of large rockets is to deliver a lunar or Mars base.

SpaceX Starship to LEO, requires an orbiting fuel station to escape Earth.

The Space Launch System can lift a large and heavy payload, such as Mars or Moon habits.

Small and Medium Lift Rockets, *We Do It Your Way*

A smaller satellite payload can use a smaller rocket with lower cost and quick response. Why use a huge rocket when only a small payload is launched to low Earth orbit? Here are some companies specializing in smaller rockets.

Existing launches: Rocket Lab from Australia

Upcoming, with existing contracts: ABL from USA, Relativity Space from CA, and Firefly Aerospace from Texas, and Richard Branson's Virgin Orbit from USA

Launch of 'Electron' rocket

Portable containers with rocket

Test fire

3D printing of rocket engine

Test fire

Stage 1 engines

Launch in Oct, 2022

Test fire

Rocket Lab
Already launched 100 rockets, since established in 2006, and has low cost launches.
Payload: 250 lb payload for $5 million ($20k per pound).

Fuel: room temperature kerosene and cryogenic liquid oxygen
Innovations:
- Electric fuel pumps, not powered by the fuel,
- Uses 3D printed engines
- Dedicated orbit trajectories, where payload does not need its own rocket after released in space.

Built and launched, 100s of rockets

ABL Space Systems
ABL testing 2nd stage rocket. ABL may produce 100's of modular rockets, for light payloads.
Payload: 2800 lb payload

Fuel: room temperature kerosene and oxidizer is cryogenic liquid oxygen.
Innovations:
- Rockets are in shipping containers ready to be shipped and launched from anywhere.

Under preliminary tests

Relativity Space
Test firing of 3D printed engine.

Payload: 2800 lb payload for $12 million ($4k per pound)

Fuel: room temperature liquid natural gas (methane) and cryogenic liquid oxygen
Innovations:
- 3D print rocket parts already assembled, to reduce the part count by a factor 100x for single use rockets.
- Uses a fuel that is the easiest to eventually make on Mars.

Under preliminary tests

Firefly Aerospace
Testing of thrust of engine.
Firefly will also be providing engines for the Antares rockets.
Payload: Less than 2200 lb payload into orbit for less than $20M, or less than 1100 lb to the Moon ($10k per pound).
Fuel: room temperature liquid kerosene and cryogenic liquid oxygen
Innovations:
- Carbon fiber composites for airframe

Under preliminary tests

This up-coming decade is a very active time in the industry for small rockets, with single payload and custom orbits.

New Small and Medium Lift Rockets, *We Do It Your Way*

A smaller satellite payload can use a smaller rocket with lower cost and quick response. Why use a huge rocket when only a small payload is launched to low Earth orbit? Here are some companies specializing in smaller rockets, shown on the previous page, with payloads of a 1000 lbs or less, and launch costs of $15 million or less. Included is a little description of the founders and what niche market or technology the rocket company has achieved.

Rocket Lab: established 'Electron' rocket
Peter Beck started Rocket Lab in 2006 in New Zealand. Beck built rockets and worked in machining all his life, and did not need to attend college. Rocket Lab started in Australia and has had a steady track record of success launches of its small payload rocket.
Rocket Lab is now providing an end-to-end business, from rocket launches to satellite designs.
The first rocket was launched in 2009 and used a monopropellant, which just needs a flame and it will self combust. However, monopropellants are dangerous.
Today, the fuel is room temperature kerosene with cryogenic liquid oxygen on the 'Electron' rocket. The performance is similar to other liquid fuel rockets, and there is no need for the fuel tank to handle the pressures and cold temperatures of cryogenic fuel.
Rocket lab is getting contracts to launch small satellites using its small orbital rocket 'Electron'.

ABL Space Systems: Rockets in containers to deliver anywhere
ABL Space Systems was founded in 2017 by Harry O'Hanley and Dan Piemont, former SpaceX (rockets) and Morgan Stanley (finance) employees.
ABL rockets are still in development, and there has been no successful launch into space at this time. ABL has been collaborating with the Air Force Research Laboratory, in 2020, for engine components.

Relativity Space: 3D printed engines
Relativity Space was founded in 2015 by Tim Ellis and Jordan Noone, both aerospace engineers.
Most every part of the rocket is designed to be reusable, from both stages to even the fairing which protects the payload. The rocket fabrication exploits 3D printing to the max, for the first stage and second stage. Relativity Space has the world's largest metal 3D printers, that create Terran 1, the world's first 3D printed rocket. The rocket engines are 3D printed, and even the structure of the rocket, including the walls, are 3D printed. The 3D printer of metals uses existing welding technology to melt metal wire, layer by layer, into precise and complex structures that have minimal joints and parts
Typically 3D printing is an advantage to replace many small parts and hand labor. Other companies just use rolled steel for the housing because that can be made cheaply using regular manufacturing.
Launches should start from Florida in 2024.

FireFly Aerospace: Carbon fiber airframe
FireFly was founded in 2014, also by ex SpaceX engineers, and from Blue Origin and NASA.
FireFly has teamed up with the larger company Northrop Grumman to provide engines for the Antares rockets, because the Russian engines are not available. Firefly has a two stage expendable rocket, with carbon fiber construction. FireFly is still debugging their rocket. Their first launch in 2021 got off the ground but failed due to a loose electrical connector a few miles up.

Here are 4 new rocket companies for small and medium rockets. Other companies are also building rockets.

Chapter 2: Rocket Engines: Liquid Fuel, Solid Fuel, Hybrid Liquid/Solid, and Electric

Space rockets are a complex design, and deciding whether to use liquid or solid fuel is one of the first decisions. There are fuel cost, performance, and peak thrust concerns.

The main purpose of the 1st stage is to get off the ground and lift the huge weight of all the other stages in addition to itself. Hence 'thrust is king' for the first stage. The efficiency of the fuel does not matter so much, as long as it can burn fast enough to create a huge exhaust flow and create the huge thrust. The 1st stage must fight the full weight of the loaded rocket against gravity, so the 1st stage needs the most thrust.

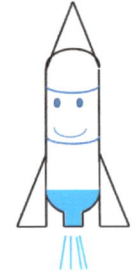

Solid and liquid fuels:
A solid fuel booster seems a natural for the **1st stage**, and indeed this is what the SLS is using. The SLS wanted a cheap and disposable 1st stage. However, solid fuel burns until it is gone, so solid fuel can not be turned off, can not be throttled, and can not be reused.

The **1st stage** can either use liquid fuel or solid fuel. Liquid fuel boosters can help off the ground, because they can be throttled, restarted, and landed for re-use. On the other hand, solid fuel boosters can be cheap and disposable, with larger thrust. A solid fuel rocket booster was used for the Space Shuttle. After the 1st stage, the rocket is already almost in low Earth orbit, flying sideways to gravity.

The **2nd and 3rd stages** are typically liquid fuel because efficiency (faster exhaust) and throttle are important, and because maximum thrust or burn rate is not required. The rocket is already in low Earth orbit, or close, and is flying sideways to gravity. Less thrust is necessary.

Liquid hydrogen and liquid oxygen are the gold standards for rocket fuel. The energy of reaction is high and the mass is low.

"Real space rockets are huge, and involve many companies.

The fuel is the basic question, and that leads to different rocket components."

Other fuel types, like hypergolic liquid, hybrid gas/solid, or electric ions:
There are other fuel types, besides a liquid fuel and liquid cryogenic oxygen, or a compressed powder of solid fuel.

Another type is hypergolic fuels, which ignite spontaneously when the fuel comes in contact with the oxidizer. This type of fuel is actually used for orbital corrections once in orbit, or for blasting off the Moon to return back to Earth. This hypergolic fuel is very reliable, but it is more dangerous and also the current chemicals cause cancer.

Another fuel approach is a hybrid approach. The oxidizer is still cryogenic oxygen, but it boils off and the O2 gas flows past something that will burn in oxygen, like wax. Unfortunately, the burn rate is low because the burning has a gas/solid interface that has limited mixing and burn rate.

Another fuel approach is electric acceleration of ions. A high voltage will accelerate an ionized gas out the back of the rocket. The electric power can be from a solar panel or from a nuclear generator. For chemical rocket power, typical chemical rocket power is Megawatts to Gigawatts. For electric power, no generator in space can generate anything more than Kilowatts, so this electric approach has low ion flow rate for the exhaust and low thrust.

Fuels can be different chemicals in liquid or solid form. The chemistry is chosen based on energy density, thrust, storage stability, and availability. The main purpose of the 1st stage is maximum thrust, which in practice means maximum burn rate and not so much the similar maximum exhaust velocities. Stage 2 and 3 care about exhaust velocity more, not maximum thrust, when not fighting the gravity of Earth.

Thrust Requirements

The first stage of a rocket is to fight the full weight of gravity and get the rocket off the ground. That means there needs to be a lot of fuel burning at once. The fuel efficiency does not matter as much.

First stage requirements and 2nd and 3rd stage requirements for fuel burn rate are different. The rocket is already nearly in orbit after the 1st stage, and is going sideways to gravity. The thrust or burn rate can be less.

Solid fuel is good for the 1st stage, with huge burn rates and thrust. Just make a large burning surface area, and the instantaneous thrust will be large. However, solid fuel boosters are disposable because they can not restart and re-land.

Liquid fuel is more efficient. That is, the energy per weight is better than solid fuels. But liquid fuel requires some major fuel pumps to get a fast flow rate and burn rate. These pumps, and the cryogenic fuel tanks, are more complicated than just having a large solid fuel surface area to create a large burning surface area and burn rate.

"Solid fuels with huge burn rate and thrust are a natural for the 1st stage, but not the 2nd stage.

Before the Space Shuttle, solid fuels were thought to be too dangerous because they can not be turned off.

All those previous designs like Mercury and Saturn rockets used liquid fuel only."

Solid fuel boosters

1st stage: Huge flow rate and thrust:
Solid fuel boosters can use a huge burning surface area.
Liquid fuel boosters must have huge fuel turbo pumps.

2nd stage: Maximum efficiency with highest exhaust speed, although less flow rate and thrust
Liquid fuels have more efficiency (specific impulse) and higher exhaust velocity than solid fuels.

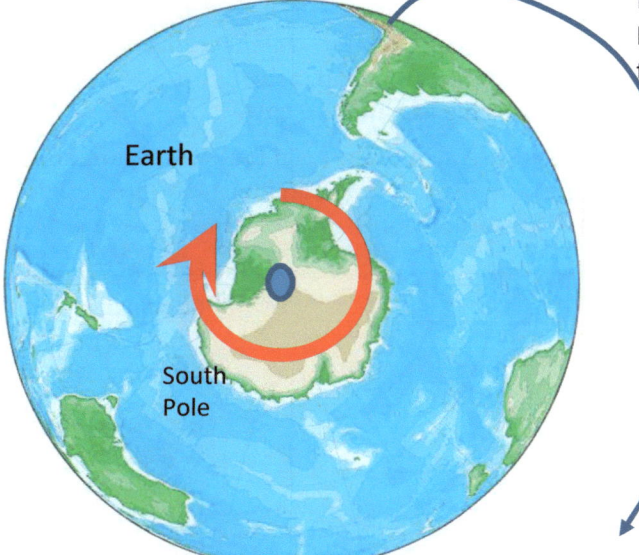

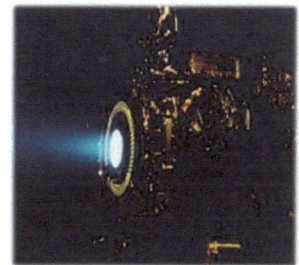

3rd or 4th stage: Very low thrust required
Ion engines have much more efficiency than any chemical reaction, but the limited electrical power available will limit the thrust. Ion rockets have larger exhaust velocity and do not need an oxidizer. The potential final rocket speed is much higher using ion rockets with fast exhaust velocity instead of chemical rockets.

The fuel choice for the 1st stage must still allow for a very fast burn rate to get the thrust and lift the entire weight of the fueled rocket. The fuel choice for the upper stages want a higher exhaust velocity, and do not depend so much on instant thrust and flow rate.

Liquid versus Solid Fuel, Cold Versus Room Temperature

Space rockets are a complex design, and deciding whether to use liquid or solid fuel is one of the first decisions. There are fuel cost, performance, and peak thrust concerns.

The **1st stage** can either use liquid fuel or solid fuel. Liquid fuel boosters can help off the ground, because they can be throttled, restarted, and landed for re-use. On the other hand, solid fuel boosters can be cheap and disposable, with larger thrust. A solid fuel rocket booster was used for the 1st stage of the Space Shuttle. After the 1st stage, the rocket is already almost in low Earth orbit, flying sideways to gravity.

The 1st stage must fight the full weight of the loaded rocket against gravity, so the 1st stage needs the most thrust or burn rate.

The **2nd and 3rd stages** are typically liquid fuel because efficiency (faster exhaust) and throttle are important, and because maximum thrust or burn rate is not required.

"Solid fuels can burn really quick, with exposed surface area. Liquid fuels need a pump."

Liquid fuel rocket with fuel and oxidizer tanks

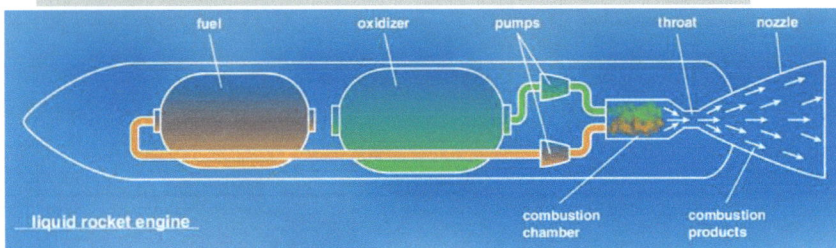

Liquid fuels are used for space rockets because:
- High thrust per unit weight (high specific impulse)
- Can be throttled to control acceleration, and start and stop the rocket.
- The liquids are evaporated into a gas before burning. Liquid fuel and oxidizer are typically cryogenic (cooled) to save space and tank mass.
- Liquid fuel rockets can be re-used if the rocket can land.

Here is a checklist to launch a rocket using liquid fuel into space: tanks of fuel and oxidizer inside thin metal walls, very cold liquid oxygen, and lots of sensors to know if the fuel is flowing properly and is not doing what it is supposed to be doing (low pressure in tank, clogging the pumps, leaking).

Liquid Fuel:
- Throttling,
- Faster exhaust

Liquid Fuel: Hydrogen, Methane

Liquid Oxygen

Liquid chemical reaction for throttled and controlled burn, 2nd stage

Solid fuel rocket with dry stable burning surface

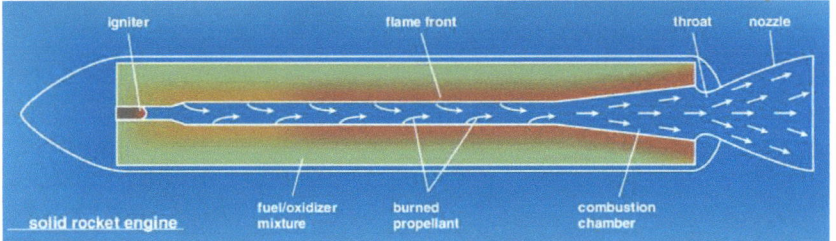

Solid fuels typically are used in the initial stage to help lift the core liquid fuel because:
- Solid fuels have higher absolute thrust, with faster burn rate when have a large burning surface area all at once.
- Solid fuel is less expensive and has convenient storage. The mold is made in advance and is room temperature and stable.
- Solid fuel rockets are single use and low cost.

The exposed interior surface area of the solid fuel determines how much fuel burns per second (burn rate) and the thrust. Solid fuel molds are designed to have more surface area exposed at start of launch, to lift all the rocket weight when the rocket is the heaviest.

Solid Fuel:
- Larger thrust

Solid or Liquid Chemical Rocket booster to quickly get initial speed, 1st stage

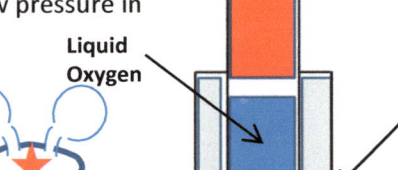

Fun Facts about oxygen

Combustion Engine: A car engine takes oxygen from the air and combines with gasoline in the car.

Rocket: A rocket carries both the oxygen and gasoline so the rocket can go into space, without an atmosphere, and fly faster than the exhaust speed.

Fuels can be different chemicals in liquid or solid form. The chemistry is chosen based on energy density, thrust, storage stability, and availability. The main purpose of the 1st stage is maximum thrust, which in practice means maximum burn rate and not so much the similar maximum exhaust velocities. Stage 2 and 3 care about exhaust velocity more, not maximum thrust, when not fighting the gravity of Earth.

Liquid Propellants Need Big Tanks and Pumps

Liquid fuel rockets have higher exhaust velocity than solid fuel rockets, but have a lot more parts, like turbo pumps, fuel lines, and cryogenic tanks. Liquid fuel rockets can re-start and be re-used if can land safely. The complication of liquid fuels is needing cryogenic liquid oxygen for higher performance, with special tanks and insulation, and needing fuel pumps to spray the fuel and liquid oxygen into the nozzle to burn.

"Quite a lot of separate parts to a successful rocket."

Liquid Fuels with air pressure: the 'Water Rocket'

Liquid Fuels with chemical reaction:

Liquid fuel choice:
Any liquid that burns will be considered. It should burn cleanly so that its byproducts do not clog the pumps that push the fuel into the combustion chamber.

Liquid fuels and liquid oxygen are typically super cold, to get these gasses into a liquid state. The liquid will only last a short time in the tanks because they boil away when surrounded by much warmer outside air.

Other room temperature fuels and oxidizers are also used in rockets, but they are acidic and do not have the same performance.

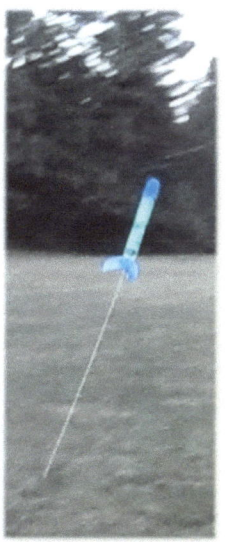

Cold water exhaust: water pushed out by air pressure

Water rocket has the same concept as liquid fuel, except space rockets have a chemical reaction and the hot gasses come out much faster, a 100 times faster (3000m/s exhaust speed for chemistry instead of 30m/s for air pressure).

Huge tank, with people below!

SpaceX fuel tank

Apollo Saturn V fuel tank

Turbo or Centrifugal Pumps:
- Turbo-pumps keep the right amount of fuel or oxidizer flowing to the combustion chamber, at a pressure above the nozzle combustion pressure.
- Turbo pumps can throttle down completely if a problem is detected (fire, low pressure) from a sensor, for safety

Below are the various combinations of liquid fuels :
- Liquid hydrogen (cryo) and liquid oxygen (cryo).
- Kerosene (room-temp) and liquid oxygen (cryo)
- Methane (cryo) and liquid oxygen (cryo)
- Gasoline (room-temp) and liquid oxygen (cryo)
- Alcohol (room-temp) and liquid oxygen (cryo)
- Monomethyl hydrazine (MMH) and Nitrogen tetroxide (NTO)

Hardware for liquid fuel engines:
Lots of engine parts...thousands of parts.
- Lots of parts keeps cost high, because each part needs to be maintained and quality checked.
- If can re-use the rocket, then cost can go down, like SpaceX and Blue Origin designs.

Liquid oxygen, very cold

Nozzle cooled with cryogenic fuel

Nozzle of the Space Launch System, with pre-heating of liquid fuel using cooling tubes wrapped around the hot nozzle.

Heat exchangers to vaporize cryogenic fuel:
Rocket engines can pre-heat the cryogenic fuel by wrapping gas flow tubes around the outside of the hot nozzle, for a heat exchanger.

Heat exchangers with cold fuel also stop the nozzle from melting, because the exhaust gas in the nozzle is hotter than the melting temperature of the metal. Liquid fuels are typically used to cool the nozzle before being mixed with the oxidizer as a gas

Fun fact about liquid to gas conversion:
Gasoline camping stoves also wrap feed tubes around the hot flame to pre-heat and vaporize the liquid into a gas (a heat exchanger).

Pre-heating of gas

There are a lot of fuel chemistry choices for liquid fuels. Liquid hydrogen has the best thrust per weight or highest energy density, but the other fuels don't need to be cooled to as low a temperature.

Cheap Solid Propellant for SLS booster, at Room Temperature!

These Solid Rocket Boosters for SLS are designed for high thrust, and to be single use and less complex (disposable) for more reliability. The solid fuel boosters were originally developed for the Space Shuttle in the 1970s. Thankfully, solid fuel is at room temperature, not cryogenic.

The booster solid propellant is molded in a unique shape with the most burning surface area to get the most thrust (star shaped perforation) right at the beginning of the launch, when the rocket weight is the largest.

The solid fuel has its own oxidizer mixed in. For high performance space rockets the oxidizer is ammonium perchlorate and the fuel is aluminum.

They still have nozzles, and gimbals to vector the thrust, to keep the rocket stable.

"Rockets are less expensive using solid fuel for first stage, with lower cost chemicals, more thrust, and without the complexity of mixing liquids.

However, before the 1970s, solid fuels were thought to be too dangerous for manned spacecraft because they can not be turned off."

Concept of Burning Surface Area

Solid fuel can have more thrust to start, based on shape and large starting surface area inside the mold. Cavity shape controls thrust profile versus time. Just ignite, and the thrust profile happens without throttling.

The 'negative' mold for combustion hole inside solid fuel:
11-point star-shaped perforation to increase surface area, flow rate and thrust at beginning.

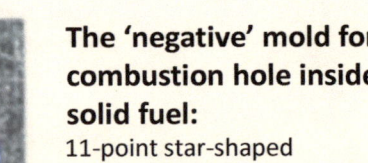

Toy Solid Fuel rocket: Same concept as large space rocket booster.

Initial Shape and Thrust: At first have huge surface area to burn, to get most flow rate and thrust at beginning, when lifting the most weight.

Trailing Shape and Thrust: Less surface area after inside 'star' burns away, so thrust deliberately drops off, when lifting less weight (half the fuel mass is already gone half way through the first stage thrust).

SLS Booster Testing

Mixing the propellant, for SLS booster

Pasting the propellant into the booster

SLS rocket with 2 solid fuel boosters attached to the liquid fuel main engine.

Static test of thrust: Ground testing is done to determine that the boosters have more thrust than their own weight, in addition to enough thrust to lift the rocket and not explode.
- 3.5 million pounds thrust, equivalent to a few GW of power (could power a city)
- Flame exits at Mach 8 (2680 m/s)
- If a rocket weighs 1 million lbs, that is a 2.5 g acceleration upward against gravity.

The SLS solid fuel rocket boosters, previously used for the Space Shuttle boosters, can be low cost and have high thrust due to a higher burn rate than liquid fuel. Solid fuel boosters are not re-usable.

Hypergolic Liquid Propellants at Room Temperature

Hypergolic fuels will ignite spontaneously when in contact with the oxidizer. Hypergolic fuels do not have the same energy density as cryogenic gases per kilogram, but these hypergolic fuels will not boil off during a long space flight. These fuels are liquid at room temperature, and not at a cryogenic temperature like liquid oxygen. Hypergolic fuel has been used on many rocket missions, partly because it is so reliable. The Apollo missions used this fuel to descend onto the Moon and blast off the Moon. The Space Shuttle used this fuel for attitude adjustments, and small tweaks to the orbit.

Hypergolic oxidizer is a carcinogen, and will explode in contact with the fuel, even without a spark. Precautions are necessary. For example, after landing, the Space Shuttle needed to have its hypergolic liquid bled off before the astronauts were safely able to exit the shuttle. Hypergolic fuel is highly toxic to wildlife and nature when used as a primary fuel for launches.

The Russian Proton missile uses hypergolic fuels as its main propellant. The USA Titan II ICBM used hypergolic fuel because of its room temperature storage, but was retired in the late 1980s due to aging.

"This room temperature liquid propellant fulfills a need. Rocket still need a fuel that won't boil away after a week in space, to lift off the Moon or do station keeping maneuvers."

Apollo Reactive Control Rocket System to Launch Off Moon

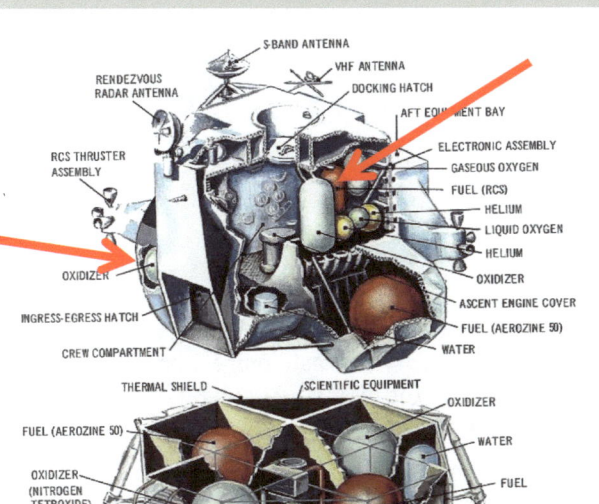

Two of four Reaction Control System thruster quads on the Apollo Lunar Module

NTO and Fuel for reactive engines on Lunar Lander.

Space Shuttle Reactive Control Rockets

Reactive hypergolic propellant tanks of the Orbital Maneuvering System of Space Shuttle Endeavour

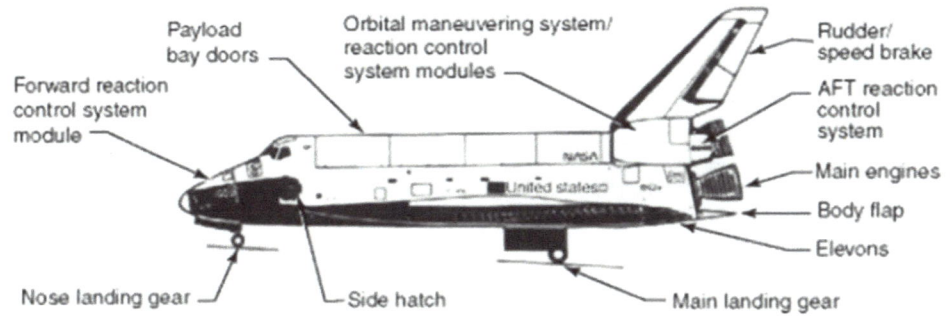

Below are the various reactive hypergolic liquid fuels :
- Monomethyl hydrazine (MMH) (room temp) and Nitrogen tetroxide (NTO) (room temp)
  - Used in the Cassini engines in 1997

Liquid gases are good to blast off Earth, but they boil away. Out in space for a week or more, a liquid fuel is used that is liquid at room temperature with no boil off, for landing on moons and planets, and for attitude (angle) control.

Hybrid-fuel Rockets for Throttling: Liquid O2 and Solid Fuel

There is also a hybrid-fuel rocket, used for rocket planes. Oxygen gas is blown past the solid fuel, like candle wax or rubber, which burns and shoots out the nozzle. The O2 gas is 'feeding the flames', like in the flu action of a fire.
For re-use, only the solid fuel needs to be replaced. The liquid oxygen tank just needs to be refilled.
Landing is done as a glider, without thrust.

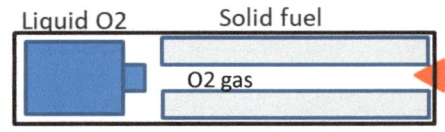

*"Put wings on me, and I push sideways into space.
That's the idea behind the 'Spaceliner'"*

This hybrid-fuel rocket can throttle, or be shut down and restarted during flight. Hybrid-fuel rockets are relatively safe because the solid fuel and liquid oxidizer are hard to mix, and are less likely to cause a huge explosion.
Hybrid-fuel rockets have been known for over 80 years, but to date have not produced the huge thrust of solid or liquid rockets. Low thrust is good for low force or slow acceleration applications, like faster commercial travel.

Hybrid Rockets have been a low-thrust alternative for years:

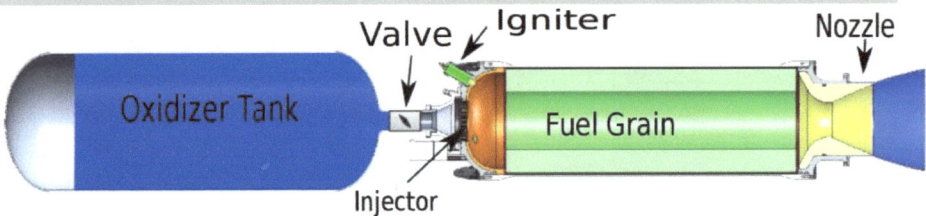

Hybrid fuel concept: Oxygen gas allowing solid fuel like wax to burn
Hybrid-fuel rockets have relatively low thrust due to slower evaporation off the surface of the solid fuel. Solid fuel and oxygen gas are hard to mix. A larger hybrid-fuel rocket will require a turbo pump to get enough gas in, and these pumps have not been developed yet.
Hybrid-fuel rockets have faster exhaust than solid fuel rockets. That is, hybrid-fuel rockets have more thrust per unit weight than solid fuel rockets, but less than liquid fuel rockets.

Test burn: A candle wax (paraffin)-fueled hybrid-fuel rocket motor undergoes testing in Butte, Montana. The oxidizer employed was liquid nitrous oxide (laughing gas), converted to a gas.

Virgin Galactic sub-orbital flights:

The goal here is space tourism, where passengers spend over an hour in space.
A longer term goal could also be faster travel between cities.

Virgin Galactic tourism

Spaceliner, version 2: Hybrid fuel sub-orbital plane returning after launch off mothership. The wings feather to create more drag at higher altitudes, which works because the air is very thin and the plane is not going as fast as returning orbital capsules.

Piggyback Booster plane using turbofan engine

Spaceship One, version 1
Space rocket using hybrid-fuel rocket.

There can also be a hybrid-fuel approach, where stored liquid oxygen is converted to gas and blown past a burning solid fuel surface like wax. Hybrid fuel means that the fuel is solid (wax or rubber) and the oxidizer is a gas (stored as a liquid and evaporated). Hybrid-fuel rockets can throttle. Unfortunately, the mixing and evaporation of solid fuel with O2 gas is slow on its fuel surface, so thrust is low. Hybrid-fuel rockets are a great rocket type for intercontinental supersonic flying, like the Virgin Galactic Spaceliner.

Ion Thruster: Weak Flow and Thrust But High Exhaust Velocity

Hey, here's something completely different, like electrical power to accelerate the exhaust. Don't use chemical reactions for heat and exhaust velocity, but instead use accelerated ions that get their power from solar panels and electric fields on the already orbiting rocket.

The exhaust velocity is huge, 10 times faster than chemical exhaust, but the thrust is very weak from a low flow rate. Recall that thrust equals exhaust velocity times the mass flow rate.

Ion thrusters have been used for decades as altitude and attitude (angle or orientation) adjustors on satellites, even with low thrust.

Ion thrusters have been used for 'station-keeping', keeping the satellite at the right orbit location. Ion thrusters are now used to keep over 100 geosynchronous Earth orbit satellites (used for communication) in their desired locations, and the ion thrusters are powered by solar panels. Satellites in LEO have their orbits decay due to residual atmospheric drag even at 200 miles up. The weak thrust from the ion rockets boosts the satellites back up to the original orbit radius.

Ion rockets also power the Dawn spacecraft, and allow the craft to orbit multiple Moons. The Dawn spacecraft was launched in 2007.

However, an ion drive at a few kWatts would require two days to accelerate a car to only highway speed in a vacuum. The low thrust due to low fuel rate and limited electrical power makes ion thrusters unsuited for launching spacecraft into orbit from the ground against gravity, even though weak thrust can be effective for in-space propulsion. The thrust of current ion rocket engines is only a few pounds.

Solar panels can generate the power at few kiloWatts to keep the high kV voltage for acceleration.

"Ion rockets are like old cathode ray tubes for TVs and oscilloscopes, but where the accelerated stuff is a heavy ion and not a light electron, and the ion can pass through the high voltage grid."

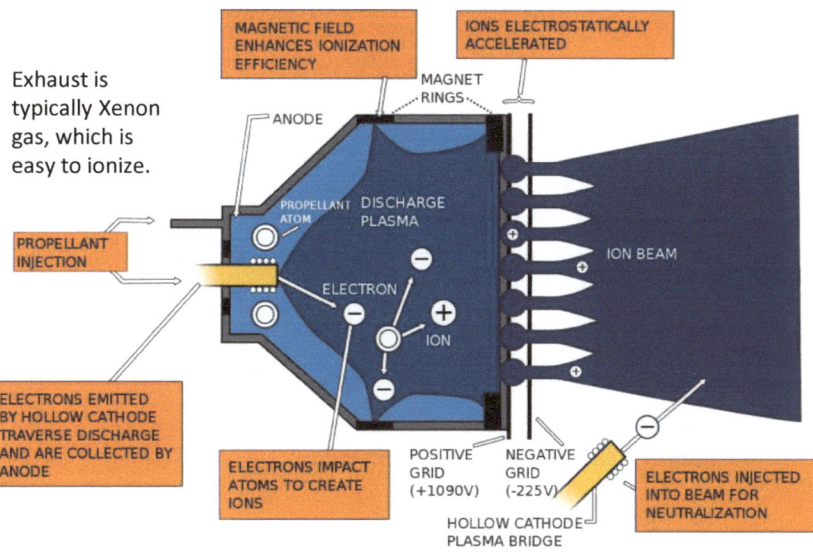

Ion rocket: electric voltage will accelerate an ion out the back.

Ion Rockets: Station keepers and interplanetary travel, after reach orbit

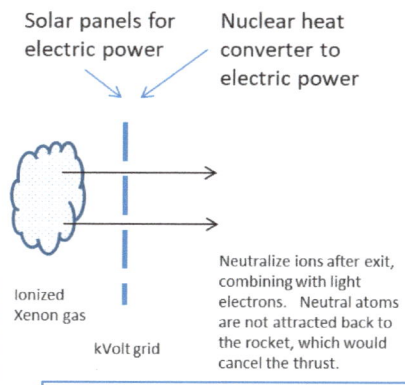

One future variation of an ion thruster is a plasma.
In a contained plasma, hot ions are circulated around an invisible magnetic pipe, so the heat does not touch the walls and materials are happy. The ions can then be ejected at a controlled rate.

Ion engine: There is a difference between exhaust speed and thrust, depending on the mass flow rate.
- If use an ion rocket, thrust is very low. To get a reasonable thrust at a fixed power, the exhaust velocity is actually reduced in favor of a larger mass rate. Ion rockets only apply a few kilovolts (dc) to accelerate the ions, and the exhaust speed is about 30 km/s, or 10 times larger than chemical rockets.
- Ion rockets can have theoretically an exhaust speed approaching the speed of light, but not enough power. A low power means a low mass rate so very low thrust. The flow rate would be very small to keep the same power level. With solar panels, the ion rocket power is only a few kWatts and must be near the sun. In contrast, typical chemical rockets use GigaWatts of power over 6 minutes, but an ion rocket to date only uses Kilowatts over years due to limited electric power sources.
- Higher electric power can be generated with nuclear generators, and then the ion rocket could fly away from the sun without depending on solar panels.
- For the same amount of fuel for a chemical or ion rocket, there is more energy or impulse in the ion rocket, but that energy is given over a very long time.

Currently ion thrusters only have Kilo Watt power, not the Giga Watt power of chemical rockets. So the magnitude of the thrust is only enough to lift a few pounds. That thrust can be a few pounds acting for many months.

Ion Rocket and Power Limits for Faster Travel

> Low thrust and low electric power are the issues with ion rockets. With very low ejected mass rate, the ion rocket does not have enough mass flow rate to get thrust anywhere near approaching the weight of the rocket on Earth. Ion rockets may have super high exhaust velocities, but this higher specific impulse from an ion rocket does not mean larger instantaneous thrust when this high exhaust velocity is combined with a dribble of a mass rate.
> At the same power for ion rockets, the energy is going into exhaust velocity and not mass rate.

For the same given power, say a power of 10 kW typical of solar panels, the more efficient ion rocket would have much, much less thrust compared to a chemical rocket.

Some things are just obvious. If the ion rocket can only get a kiloWatt of power, it will not have much thrust. In fact, the thrust is only about 1 pound-force, which is less than a toy water bottle or chemical rocket.

Still, an ion rocket is what you want to travel between stars, or even go to the outer planets. The faster exhaust velocity means, over time, the final rocket velocity can get much faster than a chemical rocket. The faster exhaust velocity also means that much more energy goes into the rocket over time, compared to the quick burn of a chemical rocket.

A square kilometer of solar panels could provide nearly 100 MW of power, so there is potential here when the rocket is close enough to the Sun. In fact, people dream of solar power stations in orbit, with the energy beamed down to Earth. More practically, there are already efficient solar panel power stations installed on Earth, so maybe orbiting solar panel stations have been overcome by improvements in solar panels.

Meager Kilo Watts of power for electric ion rockets, for a long time:
Thrust: Pounds of thrust
Power Source: Power sources are solar panels if near a star and nuclear power if away from a star.

Huge many Giga Watts of power for chemical rockets, for a short time:
Thrust: Millions of pounds of thrust
Power Source: Power sources are chemical reactions, approaching a controlled explosion. This is more than a million times more instant power than the ion rocket.

Ion Rockets: Station keepers and interplanetary travel, after reach orbit
Ion rockets with Kilo Watts of power have extremely weak (few pound) thrust but long duration to keep speeding up the rocket.

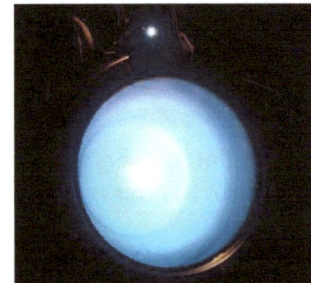

NASA Evolutionary Xenon Thruster (NEXT) ion thruster in operation
Deep space can use a gradual thrust from ion rockets. Ion rockets give steady low thrust, but gradually get the satellite to faster speeds than chemical rockets.

SLS: Rockets to Mars, by NASA and Boeing
Uses semi-explosive LH2 fuel, with Giga Watts of power for huge thrust

Ion rockets have great exhaust velocity but not much thrust, because the power source and mass rate are limited.

What Fuel Would You Like? High Energy and Light Weight? Liquid or Solid?

Liquid fuels have a higher exhaust velocity than solid fuels, to attain a faster final rocket speed. Solid fuels have the largest burning surface area, huge flow rate, and the largest thrust, good for the 1st stage.

Chemical rockets can generate an explosive million pounds of thrust at a few Giga Watt of power for 100 seconds. This Giga Watts of chemical semi-explosive huge power is more than large power plants.

Liquid/Solid Fuel 1: What are the major characteristics of solid fuel? -It is a solid mixture of chemicals at room temperature, both fuel and oxidizer, with a large surface area for burning.
- Solid fuel can't throttle, can't turn the burning off.
- Solid fuel storage life is long. There are also fewer parts than a liquid fuel rocket with pumps.
- Solid fuel has more instantaneous thrust (large surface area burning) than liquid fuel rocket engines, so solid fuel is good for boosters.

Liquid/Solid Fuel 2: What are the major characteristics of liquid fuel? -The fuel is vaporized and pumped into the combustion chamber of a rocket engine.
- Rocket engines using liquid fuels can throttle, and turn on and off.
- The best liquid fuels are usually very cold. Cryogenic liquids (oxygen, hydrogen) are not just for science labs, but for huge rocket tanks. These fuels are usually a gas at room temperature, because they are so light, but the gas state is not dense enough to fit in a reasonable sized tank, so the fuel needs to be cooled to get into a dense liquid state. If the fuel stayed in the gas state this gas would require a ridiculously large tank and rocket.
- There are room temperature liquid fuels and oxidizers, called hypergolic fuels, used for attitude control and landing and launching from the Moon. They self combust immediately upon mixing and are hence very reliable, but they are cancerous and have a lower exhaust velocity than liquefied gas (H2 O2).

Liquid/Solid Fuel 3: Are re-usable boosters, using liquid fuel, a good idea? -Yes, if the boosters can be made cheaply enough and re-used enough times to make the whole complicated design worth it.
- Liquid-fuel SpaceX boosters are already proving themselves in launches to re-supply the Space Station, since 2015, with re-use of boosters over 5 times on launches. SpaceX keeps launching commercial and military payloads, so their re-use approach must be cost competitive.

Liquid/Solid Fuel 4: Can a solid fuel rocket burn more quickly and get more thrust than a liquid fuel rocket? -Yes, because all we need is a large burning surface area, not a very fast spinning pump.
- Yes, with solid fuel there are no fuel pumps to limit the flow rate of fuel, which need to spin really fast. Instead, solid fuel thrust is all about the surface area of the burning fuel. So if you start out with a huge amount of surface area, then the thrust will also be huge, without much mechanical complexity.

Liquid/Solid Fuel 5: Why do SpaceX and Blue Origin use *liquid* fuel rocket boosters, and the Space Launch System SLS uses *solid* fuel rocket boosters? -Liquid fuel designs are typically re-usable and can re-ignite to land, while solid fuel designs are just one shot.
- Use liquid fuel rocket boosters when want to re-use the booster, by a re-ignition and throttling to land vertically back on the ground.
- Use solid fuel rocket boosters when the booster is disposable and the rocket can take advantage of the larger initial thrust due to a huge burning surface area of the fuel.

Rocket Booster: Solid fuel for SLS.

Cryogenic liquid oxygen: A cold liquefied gas in a glass boils away quickly

What Fuel Would You Like? High Energy and Light Weight? Hybrid or Electric?

Hybrid fuel rockets are used for the Virgin Galactic non-orbital airplane, but the burn rate and thrust is only moderate because flowing oxygen gas has a slower reaction rate with the solid wax fuel surfaces. A hybrid fuel rocket can not to date provide more thrust that the weight of the rocket, so vertical launches are not possible using this approach.

Ion rockets have very fast exhaust from electric fields, the fastest, for long burn times but ion rockets have low flow rate and low thrust, and are good after achieve orbit and good to achieve the fastest rocket speeds.
Again, ion rockets currently generate a measly few pounds of thrust at a few kilo Watt power from solar panels, versus chemical rockets that generate an explosive million pounds of thrust at a few Giga Watt of power for 100 seconds.

Hybrid Fuel 1: Can hybrid-fuel rockets, which is just oxygen gas flowing over wax or rubber solid fuel surface, launch straight up? -No, the chemical reaction at the gas/solid interface is just too slow to create much instantaneous burning.

- No, there is not a fast enough chemical reaction (not enough burn rate) and therefore not enough thrust. The gas oxygen and solid fuel surface just don't mix quickly enough on the surface to get the high burn rate, even though the exhaust velocity is the same as other chemical rockets.

Electric Fuel 2: Why are ion rockets not bigger news? The upper limit for the rocket final velocity using an ion rocket is much larger than chemical rockets, due to faster exhaust velocity, so why not always use them? - Because ion rockets are run on electricity, and we can only make kWatts of electric power, not the Giga Watts of power used during a launch.

- Ion rockets have very little thrust, even though the exhaust velocity is much faster than chemical rockets. That low thrust is because the amount of matter getting ejected, or mass flow, is just small. It is difficult to ionize a lot of gas without a chemical reaction. Currently ion rockets have 1 or 2 lbs of thrust using a few kW power from solar panels.
- Ion rockets are good after the rocket is in space, for gradual and efficient acceleration or for highly controllable navigation changes or station keeping.
- Ion rockets are used commonly in space, for attitude (orientation) readjustment and for the Voyager spacecraft, launched in the 1970s. The low thrust means that the exact bearing change can be accurately and slowly approached.
- Ion rockets still require a cylinder of high pressure atoms to eject. Once the gas in the cylinder is empty, then the ion rocket is done.

Faster Rockets: Ion rocket provide high exhaust velocity for travel to outer planets or between stars (interstellar)

Storage Fuel 3: Why are cylinders used as high pressure storage tanks, as opposed to rectangular volumes with corners? -Cylindrical shapes have the most volume for the liquid with the least wall material.

- The circular shape keeps a constant stress on the wall, while corners would have a huge amount of stress focused on the corners, which would then break.
- Circular shapes also store the most amount of volume for the least amount of wall material to make the storage tank (least surface area for greatest volume). Space rockets use cylindrical tanks.
- Rockets are mostly cylindrical for the same reason. Circular shapes have the most volume for the least amount of wall material.

Chapter 3: Flight Path to Orbit Earth or Go to Other Planets

Flight Plan using limited energy:

Rocket flight trajectories need to be planned before a launch, before a rocket is designed and put together from modular parts. The rocket needs the right amount of energy and thrust to accomplish the mission.

The rocket needs to coast in a path or orbit that will get to the target planet or moon at a future time. The rocket needs to use its limited chemical energy in the most efficient way possible.

There is only a limited amount of rocket fuel on board, so rockets need to exploit so many passive things – Earth's spin, Earth's orbit speed, planet alignment, and other flyby planet slingshots – to get to the destination moon or planet the quickest and with least fuel. This is not 'Star Trek' technology where the captain says 'Let's go that way' off the cuff, backed by an engine room with matter/anti-matter reactions 1,000,000 times more energetic than existing chemical reactions, and with short cuts through space using 'worm hole' black holes.

Every rocket first needs to launch with the Earth's spin direction to get to Earth orbit. Before the rocket can go anywhere, it needs to already have achieved Earth orbit.

Moon and Outer Planets:
To go to the Moon, after in Earth's orbit, then the rocket fires the last stage rocket to aim for the Moon, at a time of day when the Moon is visible. If the coasting velocity to the Moon is the same as the orbital speed to be captured by the gravity of the Moon, then very little fuel is needed at the Moon to match speeds and get into orbit.

To go to Mars, again the rocket should launch with the Earth's spin, when Mars is closest to Earth. Then the last stage rocket fires for the 9 month journey to Mars. Mars has a weak atmosphere, 1% of the Earth atmosphere, but the air drag from the atmosphere is still enough to slow the capsule down for a landing on Mars.

To go to Jupiter or any outer gas giant planet, the rocket also exploits the slingshot effect off convenient other planets. The journey would be much longer than 2 years without using the slingshot effect from Venus or Earth or Mars to get catapulted at a faster speed to these outer planets.

Inner Planets:
To go to the inner planets, Venus or Mercury, and fall into orbit around these planets, then the rocket actually needs to slow down as it falls toward the Sun. It can take more energy to slow down than to speed up. A satellite falling toward the Sun will pick up speed, and that speed is too much to get captured by the gravity of Mercury or Venus.

When leaving Earth's orbit, the rocket will fire its rocket engine in a direction opposite to the Earth's orbit, to be slower relative to the Sun. The rocket can also do the opposite of the slingshot effect, and use other planets to slow the rocket down, such as repeated passes of Mercury and Venus. Also, to have the time to do multiple passes of other planets to slow down, it takes 6 years just to get to the inner planets with a controlled speed that can get gravitationally captured.

The entire flight of the mission needs to be methodically determined well before the launch and flight or even the design and construction of the rocket.

Launch direction East with Earth's spin

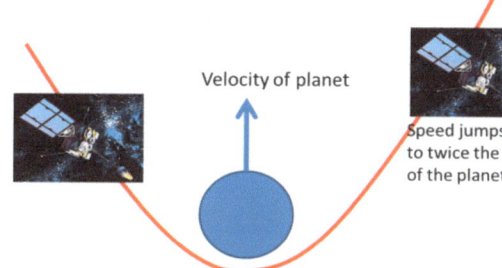

Gravity Assist to speed up, or Slingshot effect.

Apollo capsule during re-entry, using air drag to slow down.

35

Flight Path to Land On Moon and Return to Earth

Rocket flight trajectories need to be planned before a launch. The rocket needs to coast in a path or orbit that will get to the target planet or moon at a future time. The rocket needs to use its limited chemical energy in the most efficient way possible.

Engineers need to know the rocket weight and thrust, and orbital forces. In the 1950s beginning rocket era, design tools were limited. Engineers used slide rulers, and then used computer punch cards and main frames. Now engineers use keyboards and laptops.

1: Use Earth's spin and orbital velocity to launch

Rocket gets a free head start by using the spin of the Earth to get an automatic 1000 mph boost, to save energy and reduce rocket mass.

Orbiting in the same spin direction also means the rocket is traveling with the space junk, instead of getting hit with opposing traffic. (At relative speed of Mach 50, or 50 times faster than a bullet.)

"I need the boost of confidence from knowing my entire flight profile, from start to end."

5: Use drag from Earth's atmosphere to brake and land.

The returning capsule uses drag from atmosphere to slow down for landing, but the capsule outer surface must handle the heat.

4: The 'burn' to leave Moon's orbit

An even lower thrust will allow capsule to leave Moon's orbit, because gravity is lower than Earth's.

Return

Escape Earth orbit

Launch into orbit

Orbit the Moon, with option to land

Go in same direction as Earth's spin toward the east, to get a little extra help.

Earth's surface speed is about 1000 mph (460 m/s), and LEO orbital speed is 17,400 mph.

Similarly, Earth's orbital speed is about 67,000 mph (30 km/s), which is helpful to get to other planets when going into solar orbit. All planets generally move in the same direction about the Sun.

2: The 'burn' to leave Earth's orbit

The last stage of the rocket is already in orbit, and has already dropped most of the weight of the fuel and 1st stage hardware. Now a smaller thrust can get a capsule to leave orbit.

3: The 'retro burn' to be captured by Moon's gravity and orbit without the benefit of air drag to slow down

A slingshot

Capsules need to slow down using reverse thrust to let the gravity of the Moon capture the capsule.

Without an atmosphere for drag, the capsule needs just as much fuel to decelerate (slow down) as to accelerate (speed up).

The entire flight of the mission needs to be methodically determined well before the flight or even the design and construction of the rocket.

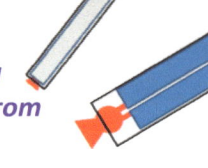

Launch East to Let Earth's Spin Help get Rocket to Orbit

Rockets get a free head start by using the spin of the Earth to get an automatic 1000 mph boost at the equator, to save energy and rocket mass. Rockets still need to get to the much faster 17,400 mph for orbit.

Use Earth's rotation

Launch direction

Earth's surface speed is about 1000 mph. This surface speed helps, even though a rocket still needs to get to 17,400 mph for orbit.

Launch and orbit in same direction as Earth's spin, to get a little extra help.

Rockets need less energy and fuel when launch with spin (rotation) of Earth to get to orbit:
- Due to rotation, when launch in the direction of Earth's rotation toward the east, then rockets gets about 1000 mph boost (460 m/s) at the equator without even trying. That's more than any existing piggyback launch at Mach 1.
- If launched in the direction opposite to the Earth's rotation, then rockets would actually lose 1000 mph speed, so what is the point of that?
- The closer to the equator you can launch where the surface speed from spin is fastest, the faster the boost from the Earth's rotation, and also the orbit can be more parallel to the equator.

Orbit tilt from equator:
- When the satellite has a tilted orbit to cross the equator, the Earth rotates under the satellite, and the satellite will pass over more of the Earth or different parts of the Earth over many orbits.
- For ISS, when tilt the orbit a little away from the plane of the equator, then all countries will get a time when the ISS passes overhead, and they can launch a rocket then. For example, the ISS passes over Russia and Canada, and both are a big collaborator at the station.

Florida and Texas launches, over water, East with Earth's rotation

Launch direction: Long exposure of launch

Florida, launch east over the Atlantic ocean

Texas Southern coastline, launch east over the Gulf of Mexico
- Launch close to equator for most speed boost, using Earth's spin.
- Launch above lots of open ocean, so booster and 1st stage can fall in the ocean, and if rocket has a malfunction the rocket will not fall on a populated area.

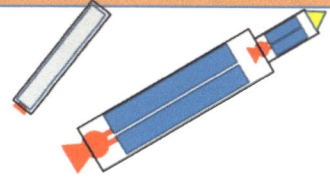

"I need a safe place in the ocean water to drop my boosters, and I need the helpful extra spin of the Earth to give me a boost."

David and Goliath, with sling.

A slingshot uses spin to get the rocket to high speeds before release.

The Earth's spin is already providing the slingshot to help get to orbit, before the remaining upper stage fires the last stage engine to get to the Moon.

The Earth's orbit speed around the Sun also provides energy to get to other planets.

It is kind of a no-brainer that rockets should be launched in the direction of the Earth's spin, to reduce fuel.

Rocket Trajectory Planning: Controlled Burns

To control the flight path, or trajectory, mission planners need to get thrust at the right time and for the right amount.
There are a million wrong ways to fly off to empty space instead of aiming for the destination planet.

"Key the suspenseful music in any good Hollywood movie during launch and re-entry...
- (excitement and dread...) Will the rocket explode during launch?
- (ready for action...) Will the astronauts need to eject, or abort the mission during launch?
- (silent tension...) Will the astronauts slow down enough during re-entry without burning up?"

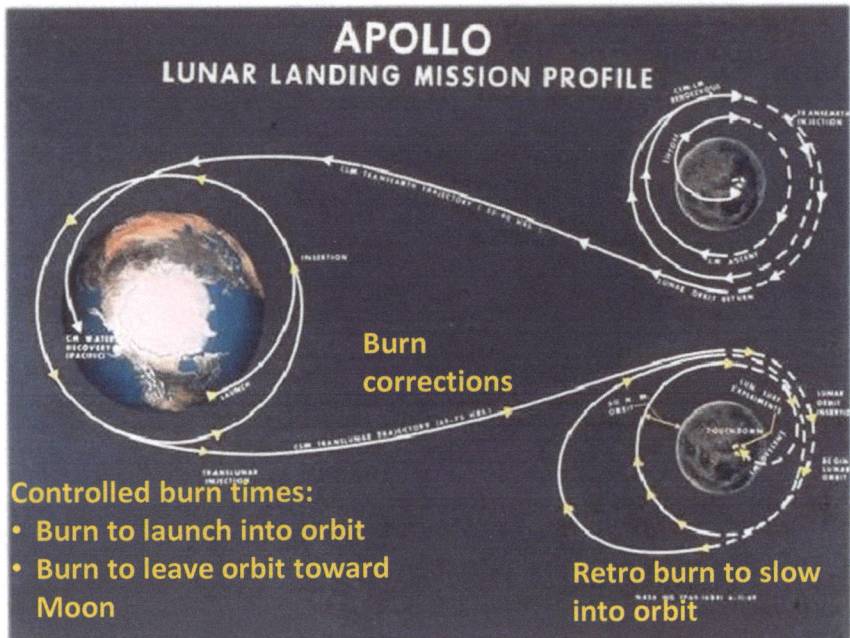

Burn corrections

Controlled burn times:
- Burn to launch into orbit
- Burn to leave orbit toward Moon
- Retro burn to slow into orbit

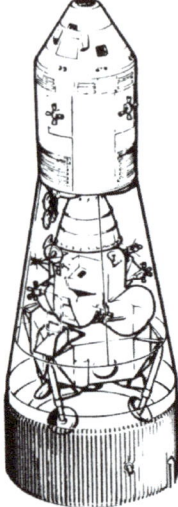

Payload of Apollo rocket with Command Service Module and Lunar Lander

Command Service Module: 1-stage rocket with crew capsule to escape Moon and return to Earth

Lunar Lander: Land on Moon, and then launch back to CSM and discard, using hypergolic fuel.

Controlled burns to coast to and brake at the Moon:

After the main stages have completed their thrust and released, the course of the capsule spacecraft is not changed in large ways, just adjusted or corrected. When a course correction is done, the spacecraft will fire small attitude (orientation) rockets to change the direction the spacecraft is pointing. After that, the remaining engine on the capsule can give the rocket a push in the new direction. In order to do this, the location and heading of the spacecraft must be known perfectly.

The spacecraft can take readings of heading and radio them down to people back at Earth, where computer calculations indicate how to change course, where to aim the capsule, and how long to burn the main engines. Or there may be an auto-navigation system on the capsule, with its own computer calculations, for course changes and burns.

A space rocket spends most of its time coasting in an orbit, after the thrust is over, around a planet or the sun. A space rocket can take advantage of the spherical Earth for Earth orbit (always falling but always missing the ground by going sideways), or escaping Earth to orbit around the Sun. In contrast, a toy Estes rocket in a parking lot or grassy field will go up and then back down to the ground, never making orbit.

Hypergolic fuel is used for orbit corrections or maneuvers around the Moon. The fuel is liquid hypergolic MMT and NTO which self combusts when mixed together, no spark required. This fuel is at room temperature, so it does not boil off on the trip there. The same fuel is used for attitude (angle or orientation) control on the Space Shuttle. Unfortunately, the fuel is a carcinogen so it is not used for launches from ground.

Lunar landers and their abandoned fate:

The lunar lander brought the astronauts to and from the Moon's surface back to the Command Module.

After the mission, the lunar lander is left in orbit around the Moon, to crash back down on the Moon at an unknown location. The lander met its end on the Moon, just like the rocket stages during Earth launch met their end falling into the ocean or burning up reentering the Earth's atmosphere.

The lander was not designed for the heat of re-entry into Earth's atmosphere. If the command capsule kept the lander for the return trip to Earth, the lander would be dead weight and slow the return from the Moon back to Earth.

The rocket burns need to be tightly controlled to get into the right flight path, with right time, thrust, and duration.

Flight Paths to Other Planets, Minimize Time with Limited Energy

There is only a limited amount of rocket fuel on board, or limited energy, so rockets need to exploit so many passive things – Earth's spin, Earth's orbit speed, planet alignment, and other flyby planet slingshots – to get to the destination moon or planet the quickest and with the least fuel. Generally the least fuel takes the upper priority.

Let's discuss choosing the right time in the orbits to launch the satellite, when the two planets are closest together or somehow the satellite would intersect the destination after some complicated flight path.

Also, there are different flight paths to just do a quick fly-by over a few minutes to get some pictures versus matching the planet's speed so the rocket can be captured by the planet's gravity for orbit and landing.

Launch rocket from Earth when the planets align, to save fuel and travel time.

Trajectory and launch date, typically to Mars and outer planets:

Let's not be foolish. The launch date needs to agree with the shortest path to the other planet, and needs to take advantage of the Earth's rotation surface speed and the Earth's orbital velocity to give the rocket the most energy. Even with these practical decisions, the travel time takes over a 9 month journey to get to Mars.

When starting the rocket stage to leave Earth's orbit, the rocket needs to be aiming at the destination planet, and the rocket needs to be in the part of its orbit around the Earth that is flying along the direction of the Earth's orbit around the Sun. We catch up to the other planet like a car slowly passing another car on the highway, with both cars moving very fast, but in the same direction. Then the velocity difference is small enough to let gravity capture the satellite.

To gain energy, we use the Earth's rotation speed at surface (Mach 1.4, or 15 times highway speeds of a car) to help get into orbit, and we use the Earth's orbit speed (Mach 100, or 1000 times highway speeds of a car) to help catapult the rocket to the destination away from Earth for orbit around the Sun.

To gain more energy to get to the outer planets, the spacecraft can bounce off another planet, or get deflected by its gravity, to increase the spacecraft's speed relative to the Sun. The spacecraft approaches the planet head on, like a tennis racket hitting a ball.

Mars and Earth on same side of sun every two years.

Mars and Earth on opposite side of sun every two years.

Go for launch
Get to same orbit and close in

No-Go for launch
Get to same orbit but far away

Flight profile, example to land the Mars Perseverance Rover

Energy of each orbit, and losing energy to go to inner planets:

It's all about energy. We want to conserve all the energy we can to go to outer planets, but we need to lose some energy to go to inner planets.

When we fall toward the Sun, we typically build up a lot of speed falling toward the Sun, which is bad if we want to orbit an inner planet. To get to Mercury, the innermost planet, the rocket needs to lose energy and slow down, to fall toward Mercury without getting accelerated by the Sun too fast to get captured in Mercury's orbit. If you've every looked at an extremely elliptical orbit, where the object is whipping past the destination at close distance but incredible speeds, we don't want that. Here are two ways to lose energy. One, the rocket might fly against the Earth's orbit to lose energy to get to Mercury. Two, the satellite can also be deflected by other planets by approaching from the back in a slingshot effect, like trapping a soccer ball with your foot moving your foot backwards.

Let's do smart: launch rocket when the desired planet is closest. We can also 'bounce' off other planets to pick up or slow down speed.

Flight Paths to Other Planets, Sling Shot Effect

There is only a limited amount of rocket fuel on board, so rockets need to exploit so many passive things – Earth's spin, Earth's orbit speed, planet alignment, and other flyby planet slingshots – to get to the destination moon or planet the quickest and with least fuel. Let's discuss bouncing off other planets to increase or decrease speed. This is a cosmic game of mini golf, without any physical touching with the planets so there are no collisions where the spaceship goes splat.

To understand the slingshot effect, imagine being on the planet. The satellite 'bounces' off you without losing energy. Relative to you, the satellite's velocity is reversed and has not lost any energy. The bounce is perfect and there is no loss of energy due to a collision. The satellite can gain or loss energy, but not through a crash.

If your planet is traveling in the opposite direction as the satellite originally, the satellite gained twice your velocity relative to the sun. It had to for you to see it fly away at the same speed relative to you. If your planet is traveling in the same direction as the satellite originally, then the satellite lost twice your velocity relative to the Sun.

No friction energy is lost in this bounce. There is no crash. There is just the force of gravity and no physical contact.

Use other planets to boost the rocket's speed mid flight to get to the outer planets.

Gravity Assist to speed up, or Slingshot effect.

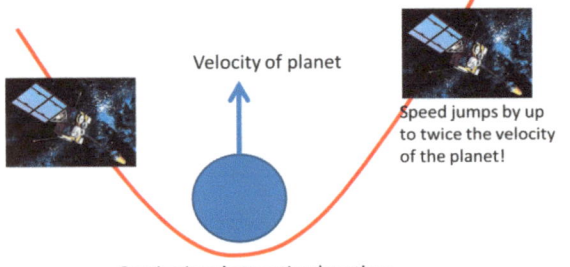

Speed jumps by up to twice the velocity of the planet!

Gravitational attraction by other planet (Venus, Jupiter)

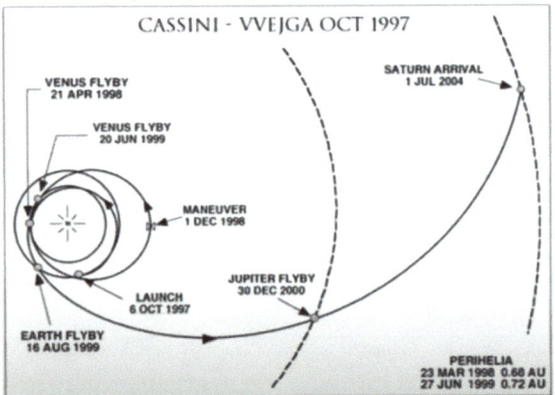

Cassini mission slingshot trajectory to Saturn:
The probe weighed 6000 pounds, and needed gravitation slingshots to get faster speed after leaving Earth.
The satellite used 4 slingshot effects to gain additional speed to get to Saturn.
Cassini got a boost or flyby twice by Venus, and once by Earth, and once by Jupiter.
The path was also risky because it takes 90 minutes to communicate to a probe from Earth.
The velocity of the rocket can be increased by up to twice the speed of the planet.

Use other planets to slow the rocket's speed mid flight to get to the inner planets.

Gravity Assist to slow down, or Slingshot effect.

Velocity of planet

Speed slows down by up to twice the velocity of the planet!

Gravitational attraction by other planet (Venus, Mercury)

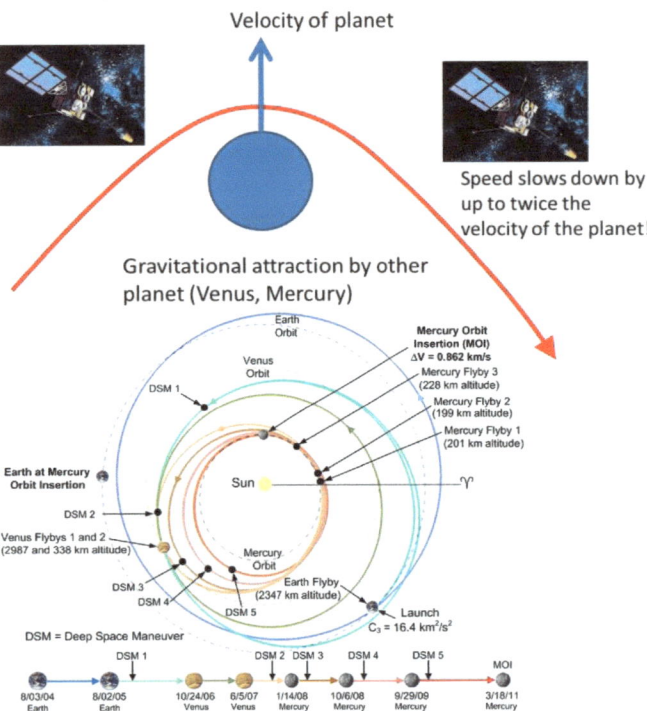

Mission slingshot trajectory to orbit Venus or Mercury:
The satellite used 4 slingshot effects over 6 years to lose speed to get to the inner planet Venus and be slow enough to be capture by its gravity for orbit., instead of quickly passing by.
The velocity of the rocket can be decreased by up to twice the speed of the planet.
Missions to orbit Venus have been Magellan, Venera (Russian), Pioneer.

Slingshots happen in other regular situations here on the ground.

Tennis: Swings are comparable to speeding up the satellite. Ball gets the addition of twice the racquet speed.

Soccer: Comparable to slowing satellite down. Trap the ball by moving foot back from the ball.

Here are closer-to-home examples of the slingshot effect:
- Speeding up: When throwing a tennis ball at a truck coming toward you, the rebound velocity of the ball gets a velocity boost equal to twice the velocity of the truck.
- Speeding up: A tennis ball will also get twice the racquet speed in regular tennis.
- Slowing down: When a soccer player traps a soccer ball by moving their foot backwards, they are using a reverse slingshot effect.

Let's do smart: launch rocket when the desired planet is closest. We can also 'bounce' off other planets to pick up or reduce speed.

Use Air Drag to Slow Re-entry

Air drag is a good thing for returning back to Earth, during re-entry. There is no need to carry an extra rocket engine to slow down to land, if there is an atmosphere to cause drag and deceleration.
Air drag creates heat, but air drag is a free way to slow down and stops the need to carry fuel to reverse thrust and slow down.

"Key the suspenseful music in any good Hollywood movie during launch and re-entry...
- (human's biting nails...) Will the capsule survive as the shield burns away?
- (human's straining to hear radio chatter...) Will radio communication be re-established after the glowing plasma is gone?"

Re-entry using air drag

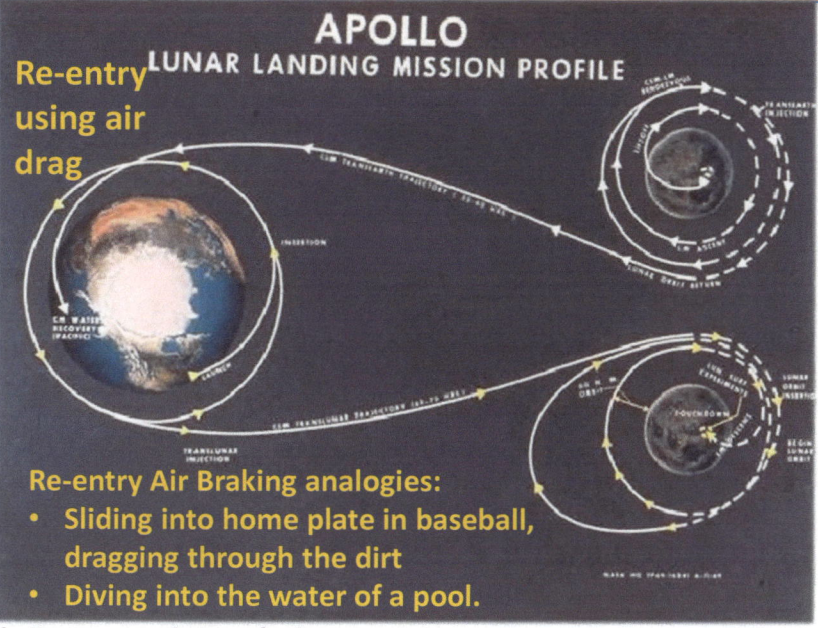

Re-entry Air Braking analogies:
- Sliding into home plate in baseball, dragging through the dirt
- Diving into the water of a pool.

Heat on bottom of blunt Capsule

Unwanted thrill of re-entry:
- 10 g's deceleration in low pressure upper atmosphere.
- Deceleration and heating are still half as terrible 5 miles up, at half the atmospheric pressure.

Heat profile on bottom of Space Shuttle

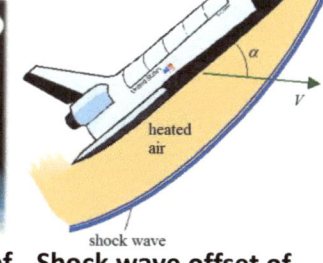

Shock wave offset of heat profile

Goal of the ceramic tile:
- Withstand the heat of the air.
- Keep the heat on the tile surface, and not transfer any of the heat through the tile to the rest of the capsule.

Air Drag experience during re-entry:

Why does NASA slow the returning space capsule using air drag, instead of a retro-rocket?
- Because air drag works, even in less than 1/100 atmosphere pressure at high altitudes.
- Don't need to carry fuel to reverse thrust, just let the air drag do its thing. The amount of fuel required for reverse thrust would almost be equal to the launch fuel.

Why a blunt surface on returning capsule, instead of a sharp aerodynamic point?
- Strangely, the hot air stays in front, offset, from the blunt front surface. The shock wave can not slide past the capsule, and stays out in front of the capsule. Most of the hot air is at the shock wave, offset from the surface and away from the capsule.

Why does NASA burn up the ISS trash in the atmosphere, instead of landing it?
- Building capsules not to burn up but to withstand the heat of re-entry is expensive. For example, air drag likes to burn up meteors because re-entry is hot. So just let the trash burn during re-entry.

Why do most meteors melt or explode before hitting the ground?
- Because air drag causes heat, and metals or frozen liquids melt and vaporize.

Why did Space Shuttle Columbia blow up during re-entry?
- A heat shield tile got knocked off the Shuttle leading edge of the wing during launch due to falling insulating foam from the external tank. During re-entry and braking, hot air got past these broken and missing ceramic tiles, and melted the soft aluminum structure underneath.

Air drag for braking is very convenient. Without free air drag, rockets would take the same fuel for reverse braking as launching.

Fun facts about air drag

Geminid meteor shower: Meteor velocity relative to Earth is about 30 km/sec

Natural: Meteor explodes over Russia due to heating from air drag

Ballistic: A long heavy rod would probably make it through Earth's atmosphere...look at supersonic titanium kinetic projectiles for tanks.

Heat Protection for Capsules and Astronauts Re-entering Atmosphere

Pick how the spacecraft will handle the heat on re-entry due to air drag: sacrificial surface material or insulating tiles like the bricks inside a kiln?

- If the returning capsule is going very fast, like the Apollo capsule, then there can just be a sacrificial layer that burns away. Instead of building some very expensive ceramic tiles, just let some material burn away.
- For slower re-entry speeds, the ceramic tiles should work, developed for the Space Shuttle. The heat stays on the outside of the tile, because the ceramic does not let heat flow through it to the metal parts underneath, similar to the brick walls in pottery kilns and inside furnaces.
- Because of the cost of heat protection, most expired satellites (expired due to broken gyroscopes, or no more propellant for station keeping) and ISS space garbage are allowed to burn up in the atmosphere after the mission if they are not carrying astronauts.

"Heat, Heat, rockets have to withstand extreme heat."

1st development: Faster re-entry:
Materials that burn away for extremely 'hot' re-entry (greater than 2000 C)

Apollo capsule during re-entry

The blunt bottom surface is coated in sacrificial 'ablative' material that burns away, providing a few minutes of protection from the heat.

Small capsules:
- The capsule has low mass during re-entry, so air drag can slow the capsule quickly and reduce heating.
- The capsule's blunt surface actually does not get as hot as a sharp edge, because the compressed air insulates the surface from the shock wave.

Blunt burnt bottom surface of capsule.

'Arc' test of material.

Layered ablative material.

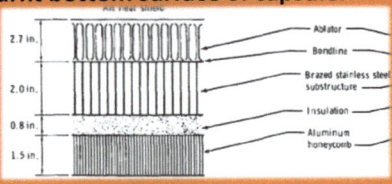

2nd development: Slower re-entry:
Insulating ceramic materials that are light weight and stop heat flowing through for just 'hot' (less than 2000 C)

Shuttle enters atmosphere at Mach 23, because in low Earth orbit.
Shuttle travels at below escape velocity (Mach 35, or 11.2 km/s, or 25,300 mi/hour).

Space Shuttle during re-entry

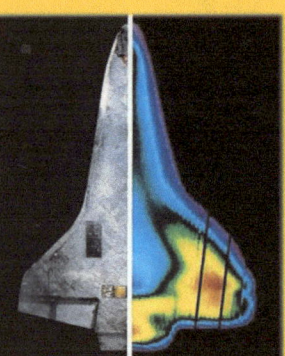 

Silica tile from Atlantis Shuttle

Tiles: Shuttle is coated in insulated ceramic tiles, so heat stays on the outer tile surface. The tiles are super light

Infrared image during re-entry: The orbiter was 56 kilometers (184,000 ft) high and travelling at Mach 15.6.

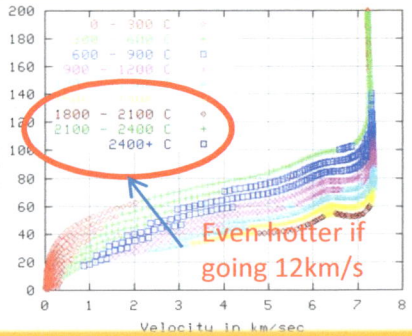

Even hotter if going 12km/s

Heat map: Shuttle surface temperature versus speed and altitude.

Metal melts…
Air drag and heating: Air drag is why a bullet, given all the velocity at ground level, will not get through the dense lower atmosphere.

Where do you protect yourself from heat?:
- When baking, use oven mitts
- If doing pottery, there are insulating bricks in a ceramic kiln.

Returning spacecraft get hot when braking from air drag even at low pressure in the upper atmosphere and lower speeds.
This drag reveals the problem with ground based cannons. Imagine the even more drag and heat from going the same >11km/sec at the high density air near ground level.

Chapter 4: Uses, Competition, and History of Rockets

A huge amount of time and development, in the last 7 decades, have gone into making rockets the workhorse to get satellites and people into space. We need fuel, oxidizer, rocket engines, high temperature materials, navigation, sensors and communications, and life support equipment in the case of manned missions.

In the last 2 decades, we also need a competitive cost. There now are more commercial rocket launches and more launch companies.

"Rockets have so many uses – launching communication satellites and science satellites and for the military - it is not surprising that there has been a steady funding for development over the last 70 years."

First there were the military reasons for rockets, to replace bombers with something faster, more lethal, and cheaper. Rockets also don't need to just go to space. There are air-to-air missiles to replace bullets and dogfights, at farther ranges. Believe it or not, rockets are just cheaper, faster, and more accurate with their own guidance or homing.

In parallel with the military development of rockets, there was the commercial Space Race, to get people and satellites into orbit. Basically the USA and Russia get to improve their technology with the help of the commercial world, and all that civilian technology will then help the military technology. It is a win-win case for rocket improvement.

Rockets replaced bombers

To get rockets to work, there was investment in all the different kinds of fuels, from solid fuels to cryogenic fuels to acid hypergolic fuels. There was also investment in the rocket engines, from the fuel turbo pumps to the heat withstanding materials to the navigation control using gyroscopes and gimbals. Rockets needed steady thrust to avoid tipping over, so fuel pumps need to be large and reliable. Ejection mechanisms were necessary for the safety of any astronauts.

There are also major technology developments that have come from the challenges of building space stations and exploring the solar system. Solar panels were developed to power the satellites, which otherwise would not last long on a few batteries. There is no town power grid to plug their satellite into. Solar panels are now commonly seen on house roofs for power and potentially a huge power supply for our homes. Materials for heat shields and designs for supersonic drogue parachutes were developed to survive reentry. RF communications and satellites were developed, which we depend on everyday for cell phone calls, instantaneous news reports, and weather updates and predictions using pictures from above the storms. Sensors for satellites were developed, such as radar and IR cameras.

Mercury rocket engine

Connecting two spacecraft in orbit

Returning capsule with blunt end to handle heat and create an offset shock wave.

There have been a few space stations in the last 40 years. At first these stations were just small capsules with extended solar panels. Now the International Space Station is many capsules all linked together, and the power relies on 10's of kiloWatts of solar panels. Space stations need to be resupplied or maintained every few months, for a few reasons. One, fresh oxygen and food is needed. Two, any low Earth orbit satellite needs to get periodic boosters to keep its orbit, due to the small residual air and air drag at 200 miles up. Three, astronauts and experiments need to come home at some point.

Two major people had large contributions during the beginning of the Space Race in the 1950s and 60s. For the US, Wernher von Braun brought his knowledge from Germany and basically led the concept for the Saturn rocket, with multiple stages, that brought astronauts to the Moon in 1969. For the Russians, Sergei Korolev led the development that launched the first orbital satellite Sputnik. He was a master organizer, recruiting talented engineers and keeping the funding flowing from the government. The Russians, as well as the USA, used German rocket engineers to speed up the development.

Wernher von Braun, 1940-70

Sergei Korolev, 1940-60

Rockets were a huge development effort in the 1950s, 60s, and 70s, in 'Space Race' competition between the USA and USSR. The Space Station is the core of an international astronaut program, where astronauts conduct human and earth sensor experiments.

Uses, Competition, and History of Rockets

A huge amount of time and development, in the last 7 decades, have gone into making rockets the workhorse to get satellites and people into space. We need lots of fuel, oxidizer, rocket engines, high temperature materials, navigation, sensors and communications, and life support equipment. In the last 2 decades, we also need a competitive cost. There now are more commercial launches and more launch companies. Costs must now be reasonable against future profits.

"The current International Space Station is orbiting the Earth every 90 minutes, with about 6 astronauts doing maintenance and experiments."

Space Race: Rocket development and competition between USA and Russia: 'firsts' to get to space, launch satellites, get to Moon (1950 – 1970)

USA Apollo Saturn V rocket, to the Moon in the 60s and 70s.

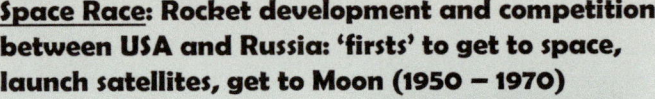

Russian Soyuz rocket, with first space station, and launches for decades

Rocket improvements and fails: One-stage Mercury rocket in the 1950s

Rocket plane in the 1950s (X-15), to test rocket engines and their narrow design and to test heat insulating materials

Military uses: Replace bombers and guns, and launch surveillance satellites

PATRIOT ground-to-air missile, single stage, against larger missiles or airplanes.

Inter-Continental Ballistic Missile: replaced B52 bombers. These Titan rockets also launched commercial payloads.

Air-to-Air missile
Launch beyond visual range to hit targets in a fire-and-forget engagement (replacing bullets and dog fights)

Launch Space Stations: Conduct space experiments

International Space Station Current (1990 -)

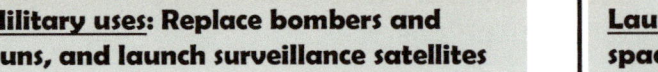

Chinese Space Station (2021 -)

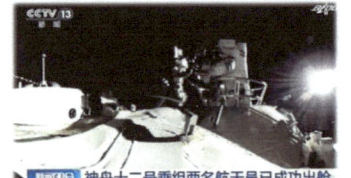

USA Skylab (occupied for 24 weeks in 1970s)

Russian Mir 'Peace' (occupied between 1981 and 2001)

Rockets were a huge development effort in the 1950s, 60s, and 70s, in 'Space Race' competition between the USA and USSR. The Space Station is the core of an international astronaut program, conducting human and earth sensor experiments.

Rockets Frequently Supply the International Space Station

In addition to carrying satellites, the Shuttle had a large payload and supplied life support, experiments, and astronauts. In fact, the Shuttle was designed to be a low cost frequent 'bus' to the ISS. What is the International Space Station (ISS) up to? The ISS is conducting experiments on human endurance (muscle and bone loss), human exposure to radiation, crystal growth in micro-gravity, growing food in space, and monitoring the Earth's oceans, crops, and atmosphere. This orbiting station is also a political effort of unity between nations, with shared supply ships, experiments, and additional modules. Visit a real Space Shuttle on display at the Smithsonian Museum, Washington DC.

Nope, get to ISS inside the rockets, not outside!

"How do astronauts eat their ice cream? In floats...

What do Astronauts eat on? Flying Saucers!

The current International Space Station is orbiting every 90 minutes, with about 6 astronauts doing maintenance and experiments."

Piecemeal Delivery and Assembly:
This International Space Station required many, many rocket launches, to bring up all the parts. Notice that all the ISS sections look like cylindrical rocket sections.

<u>Question of Cost</u>: How much of the cost of the ISS is the delivery price in the rocket?
- <u>Fact</u>: The cost of the ISS was $100 Billion dollars, as of 2017
- <u>Answer</u>: If assume $1000 dollars per pound to launch, and the ISS weighs 50,000 lb, then most of the cost is in the rocket delivery. The actual parts are not the price driver, except for their weight.

Future Space Hotels? More rockets will be necessary to supply the guests.

Space Tourism:
In the future, will there be spinning space hotels, like the '2001 Space Odyssey' movie?
The donut shaped hotel spins and creates an artificial gravity by constantly pushing the tourist person in a circle, as a centrifuge.
No, people will not get dizzy. The force is just to the floor while spinning. However, if you threw a ball, the ball would appear to aim to the floor as the floor rises up to hit it while spinning, because the ball goes straight.

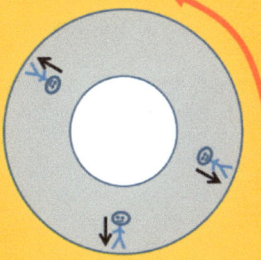

Spinning space hotel

Weightlessness:
Without spinning the spacecraft, astronauts in low Earth orbit do not 'feel' gravity because they are constantly falling as they travel in a circle. Astronauts can do backflips and float in orbit in free fall. Gravity g is still there and gravity is about the same as on ground, only about 5% less in low Earth orbit. People falling don't feel gravity (until they hit the ground).

ISS with solar panel power, docking ports, science and sleeping stations

A tribute wall at Cape Canaveral, FL

Shuttle visit to ISS, before Shuttle retired. Now the US and Russian capsules supply the ISS.

The Space Station was designed and postponed many times in the 1980s, but now this station has been up there for over 20 years and is the core of an international astronaut program, conducting human and earth sensor experiments.

Historic Space Rockets on Display at Kennedy Space Center

Rockets have progressed from just 1 or 2 nozzles or engines per rocket stage, to many nozzles with improved fuel pumps and efficiency and reliability. The modern SpaceX rockets have 9 nozzles per stage.

The tolerance for failure for rocket engines is near zero, especially on flights with astronauts. But being an astronaut is still dangerous. Just look in history at the fatal Apollo 1 fire in the 1960s due to flammable material in the capsule, and the two Space Shuttle disasters in 1986 due to rubber o-rings and 2003 due to broken heat ceramic tiles.

"What did the astronaut say when he crashed into the Moon? 'I Apollo-gize.'

USA and Russia paved the way into space in the 1960's, in a competitive space race.

...Hey, I'm mostly filled with liquid fuel, not solid fuel. Designers in the 60's didn't think that solid fuel was safe enough without a turn-off."

Gemini rocket, 2-stage: launched into Earth orbit, 1961-66

Apollo rocket, 3-stage: rockets to the Moon take a lot of fuel, 1969.

Saturn V huge rocket nozzles, 5 nozzles in the first stage. Compare size or nozzles to visiting tourists below.

Capsule for astronauts and Command module.

Apollo Command Module for astronauts:
- The astronauts sit in the small capsule on top of the explosive rocket.
- There was an assembly for emergency ejection during launch in rockets before the Space Shuttle which has been re-introduced for safety.

Cape Canaveral Museum, FL

Gemini Rocket: two independent nozzles per stage.

Nozzles dynamically change direction with fast updates to re-aim and balance the rocket, using gyroscopes for guidance.

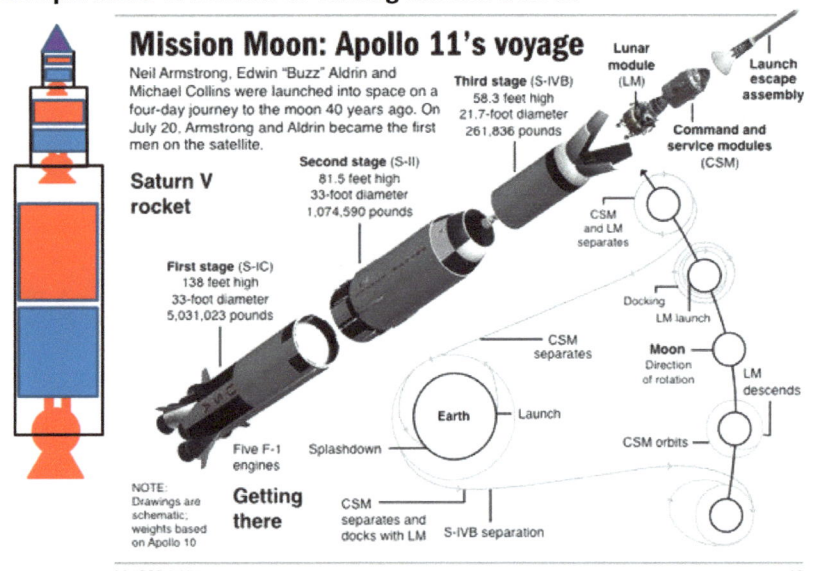

Saturn V multi-stage sections, using kerosene and oxygen for 1st stage and hydrogen and oxygen for upper stages.

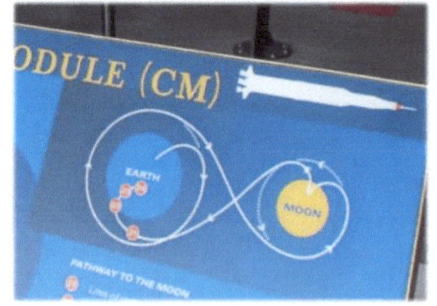

Flight path of rocket payload: Command module and moon lander

The 1960s was a decade of huge rocket programs, to orbit the Earth, to get to the Moon (USA), to launch a space station (Russia).

Historic Rockets in USA, from Greek Gods to More Functional Names

The Apollo rocket Saturn V, to the Moon, had been the biggest rocket from when it was retired in 1973 until quite recently, 2010. Now there are new heavy lift rockets, such as SpaceX Heavy, and upcoming NASA Artemis SLS rockets and Blue Origin New Glenn.
The new rockets need to be much less expensive and more reliable than the technology of the 1960s. Rockets are a mature industry for communications and exploration, as well as a military capability and a political status symbol.

"Multi-stage rockets get farther into outer space."

Space programs in past decades

Upcoming NASA Space Launch System

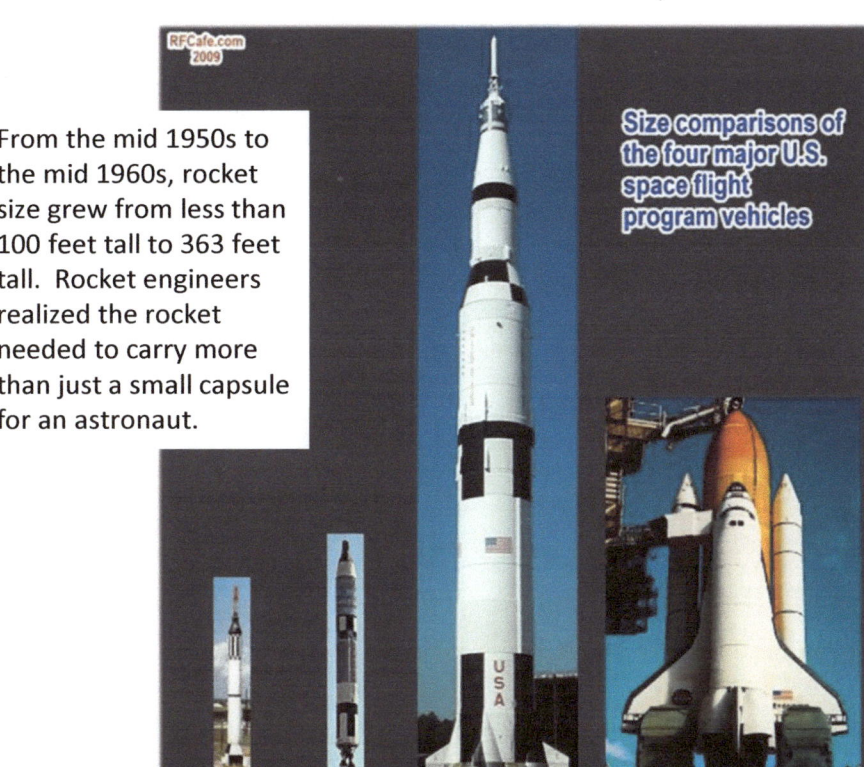

From the mid 1950s to the mid 1960s, rocket size grew from less than 100 feet tall to 363 feet tall. Rocket engineers realized the rocket needed to carry more than just a small capsule for an astronaut.

Mercury 1.5-stage rocket (2nd stage fired at liftoff): into Earth orbit at 120 miles up, 1958-60

Gemini 2-stage rocket: into Earth orbit, 1961-66

Apollo Saturn V: 3-stage, to Moon 1967-73.

Space Shuttle: 2-stage, low Earth orbit, 1981-2011

SLS rockets, huge and upcoming in 2023?

See the rocket history at Kennedy Rocket Garden at the Space Center: Here you can experience the very same Redstone, Atlas and Titan rockets that first put NASA astronauts in space, or climb aboard Mercury, Gemini and Apollo capsules – and get an idea of the cramped quarters America's astronaut pioneers endured.

Apollo, 3 stage rocket, on its side, which escaped Earth and went to the Moon

Comparison of the huge sizes of the SLS rockets to historic rockets.

1950　1960　1970　1980　2020

Bigger rockets are necessary to get heavier payloads into space, but cost per pound and safety are the main goals of rocket design.

47

What USA Learned in the 1950s and 60s

"Multi-stage rockets get farther into outer space."

The USA needed to master the multistage rocket, even to get to Low Earth Orbit. We needed space suites. We needed to be able to rendezvous two capsules in orbit around Earth.
There was a plan to get to the Moon, using a lunar lander and a command module. But none of this had been built yet. The USA had not even placed a man in orbit around Earth, let alone escaped Earth to get to the Moon.

Here are some successful developments in the 50 and 60s:

Rocket engines that fit into the rocket cylindrical shape, in the late 1950s:
The rocket plane X-15 tested smaller rocket engines and heat protecting materials. This X-15 is the test rocket plane over on the box to the right.

First use of liquid fuel rocket to space:
The X-15 plane used liquid oxygen and a liquid acid for fuel.

2 and 3 stage rocket development to get into orbit:
The separation of stages for rockets was developed, on the Mercury, Gemini, and Saturn rockets.

First rendezvous in orbit:
Two space capsules united in orbit. Due to the behavior of orbital mechanics, sometimes the pilot needs to push down in order to go up.

First space walk, in 1965:
Astronaut Ed White became the first USA NASA person to exit the capsule in orbit.

First radar to guide landing on the Moon:
There were various radars. There was a landing radar, or altimeter. That altimeter is necessary to know when to ignite the thrusters to land.

Calculations for trajectory:
Orbital flight predictions are not easy, almost anti-intuitive. There were new mainframe computers, with punch card input files. There were estimates of air drag to slow the re-turning capsule down to land back on Earth.

Training for walks on the Moon:
The astronauts trained in Iceland. The rocket landscape is about the same as the Moon.

Heat shields and parachutes to return to Earth:
The capsule can slow down without burning fuel.

Mercury rocket engine

Connecting two spacecraft in orbit

First space walk by USA in 1965, with astronaut Ed White

We had a lot to learn to get rockets to space, like multi stage rockets, high temperature materials, orbital dynamics, re-entry into the atmosphere.

The rocket plane: X-15 test plane in the 1950s for supersonic rocket

X-15 test plane

X-15 test plane dropped from a B-52 Stratofortress
This piloted rocket plane was dropped from the wing of another plane, piggyback (similar to the test pilot opening scenes and fiery crash in the TV show '$6 Million Dollar Man'). This rocket plane was a test bed for technology, like rocket engines and heat shields, that went into the liquid fuel Mercury and Apollo mission rockets, and into the Space Shuttle.
The X-15 only had enough fuel to burn for 80 seconds, but that is similar to typical stages of a space rocket.
Here are some achievements of the X-15 testing:
- Achieved Mach 8, which is what is typically achieved in the first stage of the rocket.
- Tested temperature handling of materials, and tested ablative paint.
- Developed a new powerful rocket engine to fit in narrow body of plane or rocket.
- Developed throttling of thrust (variable thrust output) by varying the rate of the turbo pump, to bring fuel to the combustion chamber and nozzle.
- Used blunt edges to create a shock wave away from the surface, so the high temperatures would mostly heat the shock wave in the air and not the surface.

Contribution from Von Braun to USA Space Program

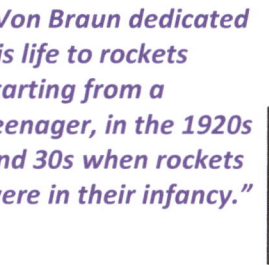

"Von Braun dedicated his life to rockets starting from a teenager, in the 1920s and 30s when rockets were in their infancy."

Von Braun led the development of the multi stage Mercury and Saturn V rockets, which brought the Americans to the Moon. He also tried to popularize commercial missions to space, for satellites, space stations, and visiting other planets like Mars. He also developed the single stage V-2 rocket for Germany during WW2.

German development, and the V-2 rocket:
Many of Von Braun's developments in Germany in the 1930s and 1940s were very similar to the patents of Dr. Goddard, such as fuel pumps, nozzles, and gyroscopes. Basically, the US government was not interested in funding rockets because they already had regular weapons (tanks, ships, guns), but the German government was interested because they had restrictions on those standard weapons and instead saw the potential for rockets.

As Germany was collapsing at the end of WW2, Von Braun deliberately surrendered, with most of his team, to the western side by driving to the western front. He also brought the blueprints for rocket parts with his team. Because of the recognized potential of the rocket technology, he and his team were brought to Huntsville Alabama to develop rockets for the US.

The USA got most of the German rocket engineers after WW2, and the Russians got most of the hardware for the V2 rocket.

Wernher von Braun, 1940-70
Developed the German V2 rocket and the USA Saturn V

US development, and the Redstone and Saturn V rockets:
Von Braun and his team worked for the US Army for 15 years and led the development of multi-stage Inter-Continental Ballistic Missile (ICBM)s. The single stage V2 rocket and its limits were known, and it was known that multi stage rockets were needed to get to orbit.

At Huntsville, he was permitted to work on multi stage rockets for the Moon missions, as a backup 'plan B' team to another rocket development team led by American engineers. One concern was his war past. Another concern was that the USA did not want to raise the heat on the Russians by using a rocket that can also be used as an Inter-Continental Ballistic Missile (ICBM), and the rocket designed by Von Braun can be used as an ICBM. Unfortunately, the American-only team kept having failures and falling behind the Russians in the Space Race, so Von Braun and his large multi-stage rockets were launched and proven successful.

Von Braun came to the US in 1945 and became a naturalized US citizen in 1955. Later, he worked with Disney to popularize space travel. He made videos about the design and fabrication of space stations orbiting the Earth, such as the circular ring concept that spins to create centrifugal forces instead of gravity.

Nazi and SS past:
Von Braun has a darker side. His initial rocket experiments in his 1920s were paid for by the German military, because rockets were not prohibited by the WW1 surrender agreements. He joined the Nazi party and the SS, and led the development of the V2 rocket which killed about 7000 citizens in London. There is debate about his involvement with the manufacturing of the rocket, which killed about 20000 slave labor people in Germany during production of the rocket.

Disney videos to show concepts and trips to Mars and Space Stations, in the 1960s

Von Braun led the US Space Rocket development during the Space Race, but also developed the V2 Rocket.

The Whole World Makes Rockets for Defense and Commerce

All big countries, with huge budgets, want to launch satellites and have rockets for defense and satellite communications.
Russia and USA started their rocket programs at the same time, in the 1950s and 60s. Russia was the first to launch a satellite (the Sputnik satellite in 1957, transmitting radio frequency pulses as a simple beacon) and have a man orbit the Earth. The USA put men on the Moon first in Apollo missions in 1969. The Russians put a space station 'Salyut 1' in orbit first in 1971.
The USA had the advantage of advanced electronics.

"Big countries around the world build rockets, for satellites (communications, TV, radio, earth sensors, astronomy), and for military."

Timeline:
- 1920 — Dr. Goddard prototype liquid fuel rockets.
- 1940 — V2 military rockets, 1-stage, in Germany
- 1950 — 2 stage rocket development, in USA and Russia
- 1960 — US and Russian Rockets orbit Earth
- 1970 — Man lands on Moon: Saturn V rocket
- 1980 — Space Shuttle
- 1990 — International Space Station; China
- 2000 — India
- 2010 — Japan

Intermittent unmanned launches from: Japan, North Korea, Iran, Ukraine, Israel, United Kingdom, France

Russian rockets

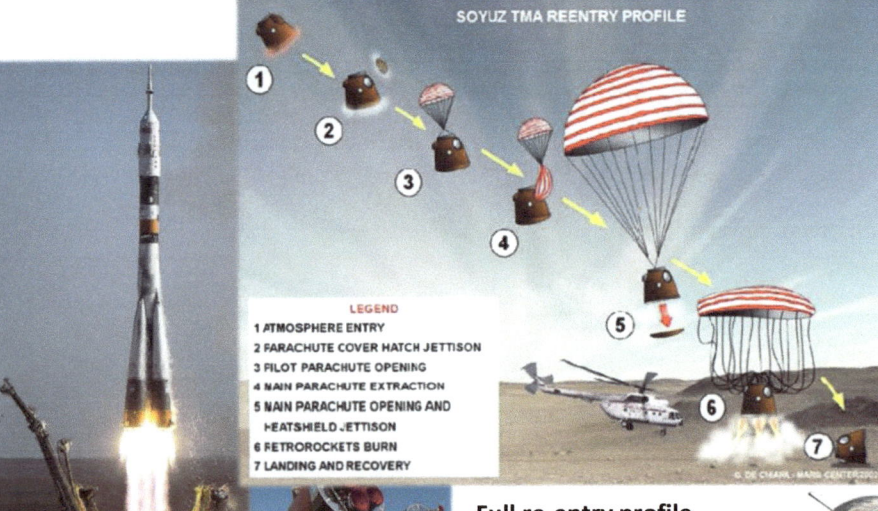

Full re-entry profile

Soyuz rocket 'Union'

Many nozzles per booster

Parachute landing of capsule on the Russian Steppes

Thump, roll, roll, roll

Instead of Russia picking up their returning capsules in the ocean, the capsules land on the long Russian Steppes with a good parachute and a few bumps and rolls. Russia does not have any tropical ocean nearby, or a consistently unfrozen ocean, so they needed to land on the large unpopulated ground of the steppes.

Chinese Long March-2F rocket, from Gobi Desert:

New Space Station, 2021

Old, de-orbited in 2017 (allowed to burn up in atmosphere)

Chinese Space Station: The Chinese have their own space stations. The Chinese are not part of the ISS simply because the US does not want to share its designs.

Indian rockets

The Indians have been active, starting in the 2000's. They are currently putting satellites in orbit and landing robots on the Moon.

Launch to Moon

Every big country wants their own rockets and satellites, to encourage science and technology and for defense.

Contribution from Sergei Korolev in USSR Space Program

Sergei Korolev was an aeronautics engineer who led the Soviet rocket program in the 1950s and 60s. He successfully led the launch for Sputnik, which was the first satellite in space, and the launch of the cosmonaut Yuri Gagarin, who was the first man to orbit the Earth.

"Korolev was a man of many hats, and was able to handle political, team building, and technical issues in the old USSR."

Korolev's contribution to Russian rocketry:

Korolev was originally an aeronautics engineer. In the 1920s he designed gliders and airplanes. In 1930 he became interested in the possibilities of liquid-fueled rocket engines to propel airplanes, while working as a lead engineer on the Tupolev TB-3 heavy bomber. Korolev earned his pilot's license in 1930 and explored the operational limits of the aircraft he piloted, wondering what was beyond his plane's altitude limit and how he could get there.

After WW2, the Soviets jumpstarted their rocket program by moving about 150 rocket engineers from Germany over to their Soviet startup program. After a few years, these German rocket engineers were no longer used and they were repatriated back to East Germany. Korolev himself went to Germany after WW2 to learn the techniques to build the V2 rocket.

Korolev was not publicly referred to by his last name, instead called 'Chief Designer', for fear that the West would try to assassinate him. Korolev's leadership included an ability to train younger engineers, an ability to secure funding for programs, and an ability to produce successful rockets. Many of his rocket missions, like the first satellite Sputnik, the first man in orbit, the first space walk or the first ICBM, were directly driven by deadlines based on beating the US.

Imprisonment:

Korolev was originally on the Soviets bad side because, during Stalin's purges in 1938. This was before Korolev's leadership of the rocket program. Korolev was falsely denounced by a colleague and sent to a forced labor prison camp, a 'gulag' with severe work and malnutrition. After 6 years, another colleague got the charges reduced and Korolev was sent to a prison camp for scientists and engineers to work on Soviet programs. Then he was cleared of all charges. In an amazing turn-around, he later headed the Soviet Space Program.

https://en.wikipedia.org/wiki/Sergei_Korolev

Korolev sitting in the cockpit of glider "Koktebel" in the 1920s

A U-2 spy plane photograph of R-7 launch pad in Tyuratam, taken on 5 August 1957

The launch center in Kazakstan is surrounded by open plains for clear radio communication, is closest to the equator in the old USSR, and is unpopulated.

Sergei Korolev, 1940-60

Korolev lead the development part of the Russian multi-stage rocket, which launched first satellite Sputnik and cosmonaut Gagarin, the first person to orbit the Earth. Korolev was brought out of a gulag as a political prisoner into the Red army, to work on rockets.
Ukrainian and Russian

Yuri Gagarin, 1961

Gagarin was the first man in space to orbit Earth. During re-entry, he ejected from his capsule as planned and landed by parachute. The capsule also landed by parachute.
Russian.

Korolev had many qualities that made him lead the Soviet Space Program, like the technical knowledge and the ability to train future rocket scientists and get funding for launch missions.

Military Rockets, for Long Range Air and Ground Targets

Missiles are relied on heavily in the military. Smaller missiles make possible long range defense against incoming airplanes or missiles, beyond visual range, and marked the end of WW2 dogfights. Larger missiles make delivery of nuclear warheads, as part of 'Mutually Assured Destruction', a political strategy for the last many decades. Larger missiles also marked the end of a huge fleet of bombers.

'Ballistic' missile means there is thrust at the beginning to get to speed and upper altitude, but then afterwards the missile has no thrust and is coasting like a fast bullet, gliding to the target.

During thrust, a missile in general can be propelled by either an air breathing jet engine or a rocket with fuel and oxidizer on board. A missile in air can use fins to steer. A missile in space needs two or more rocket engines to steer..

"More than half of rocket development was for military reasons."

Solid fuel rockets, 1 stage and 2 stage

Advantages of solid fuel:
- Easy to store for years
- Immediate time to launch
- Lower cost

Air to Air missile, AIM-54 Phoenix, single stage

Ground-to-air missile, PATRIOT, single stage.

These PATRIOT rockets are very similar in propulsion to solid-fuel toy chemical rockets, except for expensive stuff like the added guidance, a radar seeker in the nose, the control surfaces (a flap or gimbal), and a nasty payload.

Ballistic missile, Trident, launched from a submarine, 2 stage.

The Trident missile is ejected from its launch tube using high pressure steam produced by a solid-fueled boiler. The steam booster protects the submarine. The main rocket motor ignites automatically when the missile rises approximately 10 meters (33 ft) above the submarine.

Liquid fuel rockets

Advantages of liquid fuel:
- More range of the rocket because more thrust per weight

Intercontinental Ballistic Missile (LG-25C Titan II), in mid 1970s

<u>Older Liquid Fuels</u>: These larger liquid fuel rockets have nuclear warheads and used cryogenic liquid fuel (oxygen, RP-1). The liquid fuel took time to fill the rocket tanks. Hence underground silos were built to give the rocket some response time, 10s of minutes, to fuel the rocket and get ready before a launch.

<u>Newer Solid Fuels</u>: Newer ballistic missiles use solid fuel to avoid the 10 minute response time.

Previous military technology, before rockets:

WW2 fighter planes had dog fights using bullets, with limited and visual range. Now fighter jets launch air-to-air missiles using radar before the pilot even sees the target.

P47 Thunderbolt, a WW2 fighter

Bombers flew many hours to reach the target, with many personnel constantly on alert and in the air. Slow moving bombers needed to already be in the air. As an obvious improvement, ICBM silos have a 10 to 20 minute response time.

B-52 Bomber, a very large cargo delivery plane, which is still actively flying with new engine designs and periodic replacement of parts of the wings.

Instead of bombers, we have missiles (missiles are cheaper and faster). Instead of bullets for jet fighter dogfights, we have air to air missiles (shoot at longer range). Rockets are much more effective than bombers and bullets.

Military Missiles Using Turbofans for Longer Range, Not Rockets

Not all missiles need to be rockets, if they only travel in the atmosphere. Both rocket engines or airplane turbo jet engines work.
- Missiles and airplanes replaced battleships and big guns.

"If I'm flying in air, you don't need my rocket, you just need an airplane jet engine that burns oxygen from the air."

Cruise missiles in the atmosphere can use a turbofan engine instead of a rocket. The cruise missile can travel farther because the turbofan engine breathes air and does not need to carry the oxidizer, only the fuel. The oxygen is taken from the air instead. Most cruise missiles use a turbofan engine and travel sub sonic to reduce air drag and get more range.
As an option, a missile that needs to fly up to Mach 6 would use a ramjet engine.

Cruise missiles using Turbofan engines:

These turbofan missiles are just like airplanes, with liquid fuel combining with oxygen from the atmosphere. Because they are launched in motion in the air, there is no need for a quick start rocket thruster.

Cruise missile: Long Range Anti-Ship Missile (LRASM) Subsonic, using a turbofan.

Cruise missile with turbofans, like the Russian Kh-55-Kh-55SM.

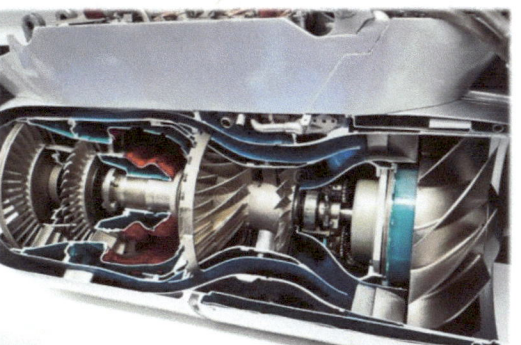

Turbofan engines, sucking in oxygen from air

Cascaded engines:

Combined initial solid fuel rocket booster to get up to speed, and turbojet for steady flight. The initial rocket allows these missiles to start from zero velocity, so they are ground to air missiles.

Rocket booster before turbojet with a thrust of 660 lb-force.

Ground to Air missile with booster rocket: Harpoon missile

Air intake (black triangle) for turbojet is visible.

Ground to Air missile: Exocet MM40

If the missile is not going into space, just use jet engines and not rocket engines. A turbofan engine needs less fuel, no stored oxidizer, and gets longer range. Some short range missiles still use solid fuel rockets, just for simplicity and storage.

Rocket Fails in Spectacular Fireworks, or How to Avoid Dying a Horrible Death

The development of rockets didn't come without setbacks along the way. Look at these failures in history (or teachable moments), and teachable failures for any new rocket program. The risk of explosion exists because rocket thrust is a controlled explosion of chemicals.
Recently there are many sensors and wireless telemetry to learn why a launch failed.

"Most rocket designs failed many times before they succeeded. Many parts need to work together."

When thrust is less than the weight, gravity wins.
Mercury rocket, late 1950s:
Possible reasons for failure are:
- Not enough thrust to lift weight?
- One engine did not turn on, or the turbo pump froze?
- Gyroscope failed to orient the nozzles?

Safe landing after ejection

Russian rocket fails, with safe recovery of crew from ejected capsule. Failures happen. The capability for safe ejection of the capsule is awesome.

Keep-out zone: Give your model rocket plenty of space.

SpaceX failed landing during test of re-usable rocket booster, at least for the initial few tests.

Engine turns off in middle of thrust
Private builder, Japan, 2018

Some launches are programmed to self destruct or explode if a failure occurs.

Early US rocket failure, buckling in flight
- Maybe the skin was too thin.

Trident II, 2013: Why the wild ride?
- Not enough thrust from steam?
- Not full thrust from chemical ignition?

Sea Launch: A sea launch, away from everyone, was probably a good idea by NASA given the explosion.

Inadequate thrust is usually the issue for failures. Sometimes a fuel pump does not turn on or gets clogged. One or more of the engines does not ignite. You always fail, even dramatically, before you succeed. Those who truly fail are those that stop trying.

The Expensive History of Rockets Didn't Come Cheap

Rockets started due to military advantages. Rockets are less expensive and less vulnerable compared to bombers, and smaller rockets are better than bullets to target airplanes, even beyond line of sight with seekers. Now, even from the 1970s, the commercial world gets some of the benefits with communication satellites, car navigation gps, and science and exploration.

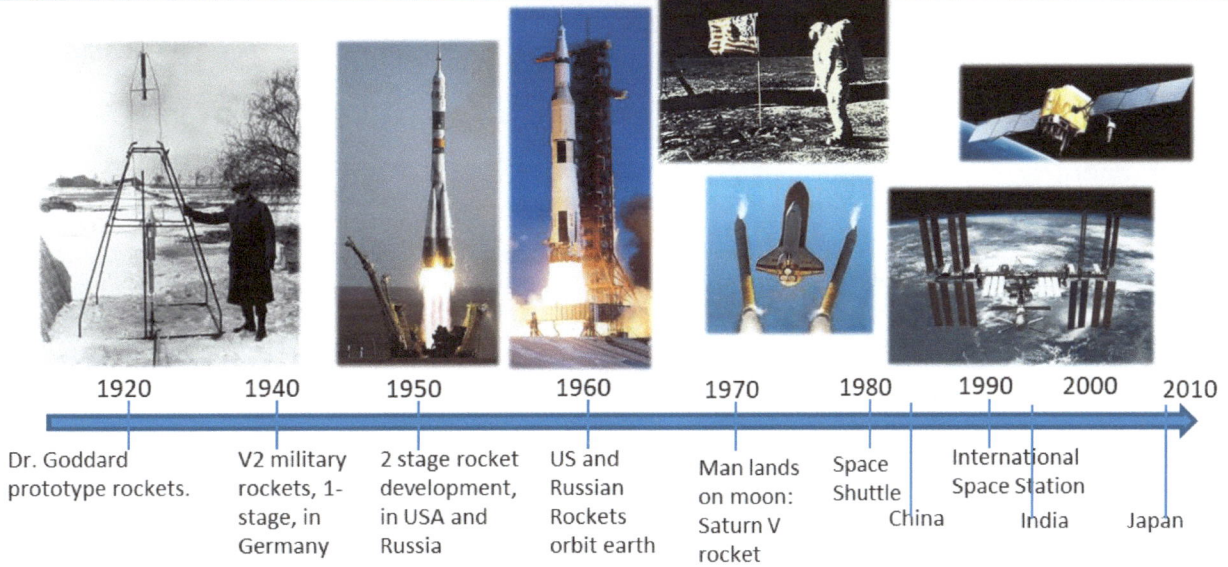

1920	1940	1950	1960	1970	1980	1990	2000	2010
Dr. Goddard prototype rockets.	V2 military rockets, 1-stage, in Germany	2 stage rocket development, in USA and Russia	US and Russian Rockets orbit earth	Man lands on moon: Saturn V rocket	Space Shuttle	International Space Station / China	India	Japan

Motivation 1: Why did the USA and Russia really get into the space race in the 1950s and 60s? -The generals paid for it, for less expensive and faster weapons delivery than bombers.
- Mostly the leaders wanted a fast, inexpensive vehicle to deliver weapons, to replace slow and vulnerable bombers. The ideas of communication satellites, earth monitoring for weather and crops, and manned missions to the Moon really did not 'do it' for the military generals with the big cash, even though rocket designers were aware of all the other commercial and peacetime benefits. Even GPS satellites, which are a great success for drivers to not get lost in a city, were started by the military in the 1970s for guiding airplanes and weapons for precision targeting.
- The same rockets that deliver weapons can also do all the other science and communication stuff, so the USA started a national mission to get men on the Moon. This mission allowed commercial companies to help develop the rockets and all the associated technologies like electronics, high temperature materials, space suits, and carbon dioxide filtering and breathable air.
- Both the USA and Russia exploited German rocket engineers after WW2 to kick start their rocket programs, such at Wernher von Braun and members of his team in the USA. The Russians relocated over 100 German rocket engineers to Russia after WW2.
- The USA used European scientists to help with the nuclear bombs and the Manhattan project. Russia used Manfred von Ardenne for nuclear isotope separation.

Motivation 2: How many countries are active in the space rocket game now? -Now space rockets are dominated by commercial uses, like launching communication satellites and GPS satellites.
- USA, Russia, China, India, Japan, Europe (European Space Agency)
- Other countries can pay to launch a satellite, or can buy a rocket from another country.

Motivation 3: What are typical missions for rockets? -There are both commercial and military missions.
- Re-supply Space Station (ISS)
- Launch communication satellites, earth monitoring satellites, GPS satellites, and science satellites.

Early rocket development came mostly to help the military, but now helps commercial projects.

Minor Luminaries in Rocket Development

Many people have contributed to all the great things that have happened in rockets, such as blunt capsule re-entry shapes to handle shock waves and heat, monopropellant fuels for reliable rocket ignition in space, and self igniting hypergolic fuels. This is in addition to the major players like Goddard and Von Braun.

Harvey Julian Allen in the 1950s first proposed the counter-intuitive blunt shape to reenter the Earth's atmosphere. He invented the blunt capsule shape for reentry.
Imagine saying let's use a blunt ball shape to enter the atmosphere at super fast speeds. Imagine saying we should go with the absolute most drag possible and get this heat and this slowing down over with as fast as possible. Do you think we would be met with skepticism?
Blunt surfaces are good because there is no one hot spot that is so hot that no material can handle it. Also, the broad shock wave actually insulates the surface below, and much of the heat stays in the compressed shock wave above the surface. Even warheads from ICBM were designed with blunt surfaces to handle reentry.
A pointy shape would have no shock wave in front of the point as insulation, and all the friction from air drag would touch that one point and melt it.

Returning capsule with blunt end to handle heat.

Yvonne Madelaine Brill in 1972 invented a hypergolic fuel rocket engine called Electrothermal Hydrazine Thruster (EHT/Resistojet). This thruster keeps today's satellites in orbit for station keeping.
She developed a single monopropellant because of the reliability and simplicity. The propellant is ignited by running an electrical current through it.

Hypergolic rocket engine on the Space Shuttle, for maneuvering in orbit.

Hellmuth Walter in 1935 discovered the hypergolic fuel hydrazine hydrate. When this is combined with high-test peroxide, they spontaneously ignite.
There are other hypergolic propellants as well.
This hypergolic fuel is a room temperature acid. Safety precautions are necessary when humans get near it. When the Space Shuttle landed after a mission, all the remaining hypergolic acid needed to be drained before the Shuttle could be approached.

Rocket development involves many different fields in science and engineering, and many different applications.

Chapter 5: Multiple Rocket Stages are Your Friends

Multiple rocket stages allow the remaining fuel to push on less weight to allow the final payload to go even faster. After most of the propellant is exhausted from each stage, then that lower stage rocket engine is turned off and the hardware released. Each stage brings the rocket payload to faster velocities and higher altitude, and each stage has its own fuel tanks and rocket engines.

"Space rockets need multiple stages to even make Earth orbit.

We don't want that last bit of fuel pushing on the huge used-up lower engine mass. We only want that last bit of fuel pushing on the relatively lightweight payload, not used-up hardware."

It takes a lot of hardware to store all the fuel to get off the ground. In the middle of the launch, after that major part of the total fuel is gone, then there is little reason to keep that extra hardware. The remaining fuel and thrust should be pushing on payload, and not pushing on the useless spent hardware. The goal is to get the payload to the highest speed, not to get the hardware for the stage one fuel to the highest speed.

A typical rocket to get to Low Earth Orbit has 2 stages. This number of stages is a good compromise of reasonable mass ratios per stage and the desire to keep a reasonably simple design. More stages means more disconnecting parts and more chance of failure.

A typical rocket to get to a higher orbit (geosynchronous or geostationary) or to escape Earth has 3 stages. Again, to have a reasonable mass ratio per stage, and to get the payload to the much higher speeds to escape Earth's gravity, 3 stages are required.

Modern rockets are modular to help production and lower costs, and to enable different size payloads and different orbits. There are booster side rockets that can be mounted to the main center rocket. Each booster rocket costs a few million dollars.

The original rockets during WW2 only had one stage during the 1940s. They were not designed to make Earth's orbit. During WW2 the rocket development had a complicated past. The man who developed the one stage V2 rocket during WW2, von Braun, was also the one who pushed for the development of 2 and 3 stage rockets during the 1950s and 60s.

Besides even considering the advantages of 2 and 3 stages, a lot of fuel is still necessary to get to orbit, without any other hardware weight. It takes a lot of fuel to even lift the fuel, so rockets have a hard job.

Toy rockets, like Estes or Quest, typically have much more rocket hardware than fuel, or low mass ratios. This small amount of fuel is one of the reasons these toys are in the toy category.

Multiple stages allow the empty hardware to be dropped after its part of the launch is over and its fuel is empty.

Cartoon of 3 stage rocket

3-stage rocket: Saturn V rocket went to the Moon.

3-stage rocket: Big Falcon Rocket escaped Earth, with modular boosters.

Multiple Rocket Stages are Your Friends

Multiple rocket stages allow the remaining fuel to push on less weight to allow the final payload to go even faster. Here is the velocity of a space rocket during a typical launch, for each stage.

After most of the propellant is exhausted from each stage, then that lower stage rocket engine is turned off and the hardware released. Each stage brings the rocket payload to faster velocities and higher altitude, and each stage has its own fuel tanks and rocket engines.

The force on the astronauts during launch is limited to three times their body weight, for safety reasons, by designing the thrust to keep the rocket acceleration below 3g's *.

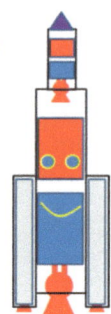

"Space rockets keep a lid on the acceleration to avoid hurting the astronauts and avoid air drag near ground in the dense air."

The 1st stage gets to 5 km/s velocity, and a 2nd stage will do the remaining work to get to low Earth orbit, all in under 8 minutes.
- Velocity of 8 km/s is just right for low Earth orbit, like the space station.
- Velocity of 12 km/s is good to escape Earth.

Falcon Heavy

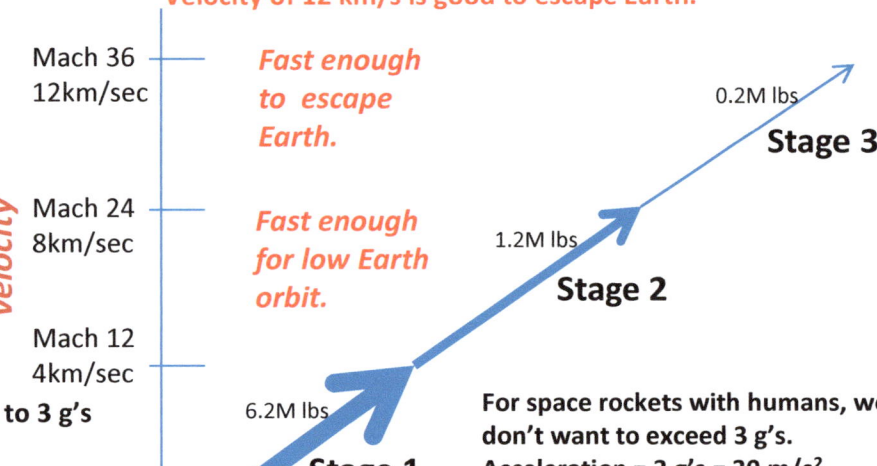

All 3 stages of the Apollo launch

Limit (throttling) acceleration to 3 g's for safety of astronauts:
- For astronauts, rockets are not allowed to have the huge accelerations.
- To control acceleration as the rocket gets lighter, throttle back thrust (burn rate) as fuel gets lighter, or turn off a few of the rocket engines.

For space rockets with humans, we don't want to exceed 3 g's.
Acceleration = 3 g's = 30 m/s²

Here are typical timelines and velocities during a launch.

The burn time for each stage rocket is about 140 seconds (over 2 minutes)

The velocity change per stage, using 3 g's acceleration, is about Mach 12:

$$speed = acc * time = \left(30 \, m/s^2\right)(140s) = 4200 \, m/s \sim Mach\ 12$$

Basic equations of motion:

$F = m\,a$ (Newton's 2nd law)

$v = at$

$d = \tfrac{1}{2}at^2$

* 3 g's in space and 2 g's above gravity, when fighting gravity during launch.

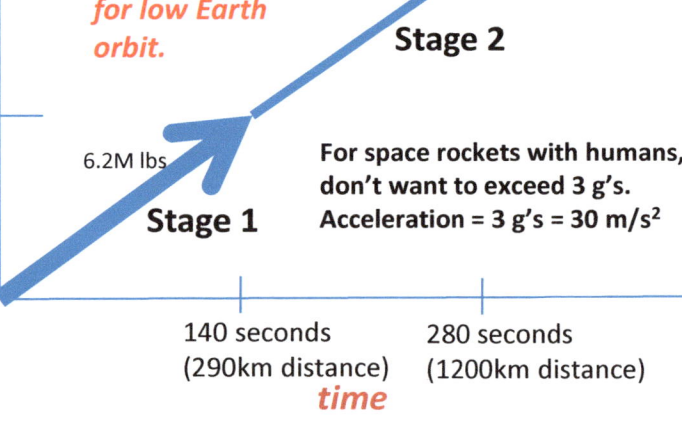

Falcon Heavy engines: Each rocket stage has many engines, for steering control, reliability, and modular lower cost engine.

Multiple stages allow the empty hardware to be dropped after its part of the mission is over and its fuel is empty.

Multiple Stage Rockets Drop Used Hardware and Weight

It makes complete sense to discard dead weight (empty metal fuel tanks, heavier lower stage rocket engines, hardware for rocket frame) as the fuel gets used up. The last bit of fuel, instead of pushing on all the dead weight, can be pushing only on the payload in the last stage.

"That 1st stage extra hardware weight, used only at the beginning of launch to hold fuel, does me no favors later on, when I have less fuel."

Drop lower stages, and push on less weight

Halfway through the launch, should the remaining fuel push this excess hardware weight (empty hardware), when it can push less weight by dropping the hardware? This gets back to acceleration idea of Newton's 2nd law.

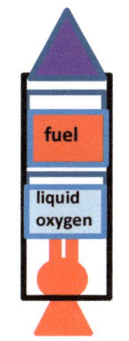

Bad choice after most fuel is used up — Why keep this extra hardware weight?

Remaining fuel

Good choice — Same fuel, and a lot less hardware to push in last half of launch.

For a single stage rocket, look at all this hardware left as most of the fuel is gone.

There is a limited mass ratio, if just use 1-stage rockets, because keep all the housing and engine weight, even after most of the fuel is gone.
- For example, a can of soda is 94% liquid and 6% can, so this soda can has a mass ratio of at most 20:1, without even a payload or engine.

What's better, pushing up a huge extra amount of hardware from the previous fuel tanks, or just pushing up only the hardware needed for the remaining fuel?

Why design 3 stage rockets?
Two answers:
1. Because multiple stages can get effective mass ratios of >50:1, as discard metal structure as fly along, which is necessary for heavy payloads to escape Earth's orbit.
2. Because it is easier to design lower mass ratios per stage (10:1), instead of a single very high mass ratio (80:1) in one stage, to get the payload to the same final velocity.

Purpose of each stage

Three stages are needed to escape Earth. But each stage can be customized.

3rd stage: This upper stage can allow a large capsule velocity change, because the mass is the least. Exhaust velocity is the most important, not exhaust mass rate.

2nd stage: This middle stage does not need as much thrust, because the lower stage mass is gone. The fuel flow can be low.

1st stage: This lower stage needs the most fuel and thrust, because the 1st stage needs to lift the most weight against gravity, including all the 2nd and 3rd stages. Thrust is king, not exhaust velocity or final rocket speed. Burn rate is most important.

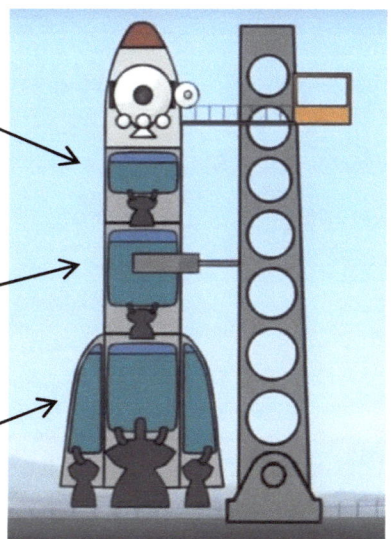

Cartoon of 3 stage rocket

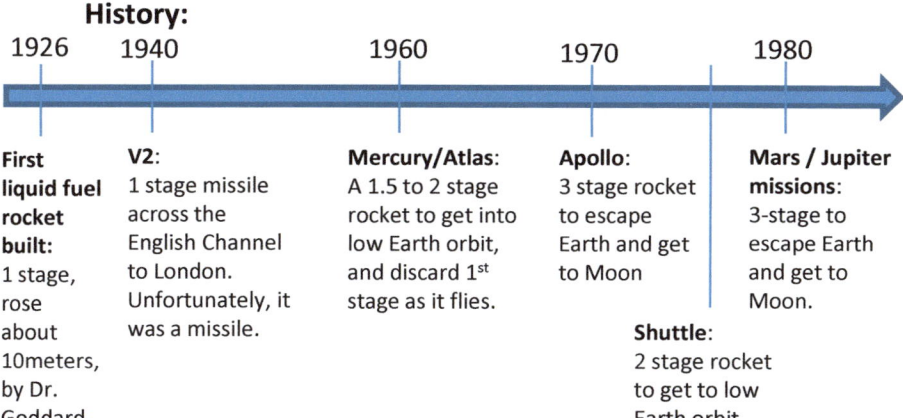

History:

1926	1940	1960	1970	1980
First liquid fuel rocket built: 1 stage, rose about 10meters, by Dr. Goddard.	**V2:** 1 stage missile across the English Channel to London. Unfortunately, it was a missile.	**Mercury/Atlas:** A 1.5 to 2 stage rocket to get into low Earth orbit, and discard 1st stage as it flies.	**Apollo:** 3 stage rocket to escape Earth and get to Moon	**Mars / Jupiter missions:** 3-stage to escape Earth and get to Moon.
			Shuttle: 2 stage rocket to get to low Earth orbit	

Why keep pushing up useless hardware, so just drop lower stages for re-use in the ocean, or to burn in the upper atmosphere. When fuel is mostly empty, we don't want to waste its thrust pushing on hardware that is not part of the mission anymore.

Multi-stage Custom Rocket Design, the Trade Space

A multi-stage rocket design on a blank sheet of paper would start by asking some basic questions: how heavy is the payload, what altitude is the orbit, is the rocket manned, what fuel is available?

Rocket design is a huge project that requires system engineering, with many companies providing separate parts and many people participating. After decisions are made, the consequences typically are etched in stone for 20 years. At least that was an old paradigm. Upstart companies like SpaceX and Blue Origin are building more parts in house for faster design cycles and improvements.

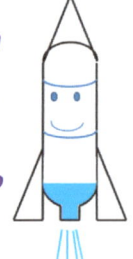

"I'm breaking up, in stages. Basically, you need to shed more hardware weight to go up higher."

System requirements of rocket design:

Design Goals	Different answers that impact the design
Final Orbit?	Stay in atmosphere (commercial flights, faster than sound), or launch to low Earth orbit, high Earth orbit, or escape velocity
Weight of payload?	Few 100 lbs (micro satellites), or few 10,000 lbs (trip to Moon)
Carry people?	Currently it is much cheaper not to carry people. With people, flight time is more limited before need to re-supply items like food and oxygen, and life support equipment occupies most of payload such as oxygen, air filters, seats, and added weight for fuel for return trip.
Lower cost?	No people, less payload, lower altitude, tolerate higher probability of failed launches.

Typical orbital solutions:

Mission	Number of rocket stages needed
Inter-continental travel	1 stage • Payload does not need to make orbit (sub-orbital)
Low Earth Orbit	2 stages • Payload orbits Earth in Earth's gravity, orbiting 200 miles above the Earth every 90 minutes.
High Earth orbit / escape Earth to or beyond	3 stages • Payload escapes Earth's gravity by dropping most extra hardware.

Multi-stage designs in history:

1 stage rockets:
- Sub-orbital flights in early 1960s

Mercury rocket

2 stage rockets:
- Got to low Earth orbit in the 1960s, on Mercury-Atlas missions.

Space Shuttle design for low-Earth-orbit satellites and ISS supply, 1970-90:
- Time per orbit = 90 min low Earth orbits
- Distance per orbit = 25000 miles circumference
- Speed = (60min/90min)*25000 miles/hour = 15 kmi/hour (Mach 25, below escape velocity)

2 Stage Rocket: Mercury Atlas 6, 1960s

2-stage rocket: Falcon X has been supplying the International Space Station (ISS), in low Earth orbit.

3 stage rockets:
- Escaped Earth's gravity and got to Moon, Mars, Jupiter, Saturn, and beyond the solar system (Voyager), 1960s.

3-stage rocket: Saturn V rocket went to the Moon.

3-stage rocket: Big Falcon Rocket escaped Earth.

There are some basic design questions that need decisions. Answers are based on payload, risk, cost, and re-use of proven designs.

Chapter 6: The Dream of Faster-Than-Sound Commercial Flights with Cascaded Engines and Piggyback Rockets

Movies that portray the future have concepts like world travel in space ships, underground pods in tubes, and molecular transporters. We all want to travel around the world faster and cheaper. Most people just expect technology to advance.

Even with jet airplanes, for a weekend outing, we can not conveniently cross a continent or an ocean. The airplane flight takes too long to be fun, except for a president with government planes or a rich person with their own luxurious private airplane.
- Want to get from New York in USA to Tokyo in Japan in less than 3 hours instead of 14 hours? Go Supersonic.
- Want to see kangaroos in Australia and live in New York, but only have a weekend and $100k for expensive tickets? Go Supersonic.

Will flying also make a major leap forward?

"Hey, super-sonic flight could all be great in 20 years! But super-sonic looks like a gas guzzler now. Also, the sonic boom is a real turn-off."

Supersonic Intercontinental Travel

Potential Concorde successor:
Boom Supersonic, using turbojet engines, with sonic boom directed upward.

Testing with Lockheed X59, to silence or dilute the sonic boon into many little booms.

Piggyback Commercial flights at Mach 3, with hybrid fuel rocket in middle ready to drop (Virgin Galactic sub-orbital flights)

Rocket plane (concept by Skylon): Cascaded engine single stage space-plane concept

Future Designs:
Maybe companies have created supersonic designs on paper, but few if any designs are built. The individual parts are there, but the business plan or cost is not. Here are some ways to go faster for passenger flights, for travel to the other side of the Earth.
1. Cascaded air-breathing engines before rocket ignition may make rockets more efficient and re-usable. Use air when in the atmosphere (different forms of jet engines) instead of the large 1st stage rocket, and then switch to a rocket at outer limits of the atmosphere.
2. Cascaded air-breathing engines, not rockets, that simply stay in the atmosphere.
3. Piggyback rockets, small and re-usable, can launch off the bottom of supersonic airplanes.

Maybe these cascaded-air-breathing engine airplanes or liquid/solid hybrid-fuel rockets are only a dream of the rich and famous or the powerful, but most things start out expensive anyway. Then, with improvements and mass production, these luxuries become standard for everyone. Look at indoor plumbing before 1900, expensive custom cars before 1920, short-flight airplanes before 1960, and large and expensive car radars before 2000.

In the history of travel using different modes of transportation, travel has been getting quicker for hundreds of years.
- On the oceans, first big canoes crossed the seas, then sailing ships crossed the oceans in months, then powered ships cross the ocean in weeks.
- On land, we had horses and covered wagons, then we had steam trains, then cars and highways.
- In the air, airplanes are new and have only been around in the last 100 years. We started flying across the Atlantic ocean at less than 300 mph in un-pressurized propeller airplanes, with many stops for fuel (Canada, Iceland) along the way. Now we travel over 600 mph non-stop, in pressurized cabins, in turbo-jet airplanes.

People are impatient, and have been trying to go faster since the beginning of time. Also, comfort improves, and economies improve.

Future 'Jetsons' Lifestyles, in the Next Solar System Age

Let's jump ahead to the future year 2200 and listen in on a telephone conversation about space travel (or holodeck conversation with virtual 3D holograms of people) or simply a conversation about faster ways to travel across the ocean:

Daughter on satellite phone: 'Hey, Mom. I'm going from New York to Japan today, and I don't want to be traveling for more than 4 hours. What the best way? Should I take the **Basic rocket**, or the **Hybrid engine rocket**, or the **Piggyback rocket**?'

Mom: 'Dear, I'd take the **Hybrid engine rocket**. It stays all in one piece, and is cheap. The **Basic rocket** is too expensive. The **Piggyback rocket** is too small. So I'd take the **Hybrid rocket**.'

Rockets don't need to only be for orbiting the planet. They can also just help us go between continents much faster, such as 2 hours to get to the other side of the planet. If the rocket stays in the upper atmosphere, we can have air breathing engines as well as rockets.

We could also piggyback a ramjet off another 1st stage rocket, and then use the ramjet to fly in the upper atmosphere at Mach 5. Air breathing ramjets need some speed to even work, so the rocket 1st stage can just get the ramjet to speed. The typical turbojet engine has a hard time getting to supersonic speeds for the ramjet to kick in.

That said, let's skip rockets altogether. Turbojets still can work hard to get to supersonic speeds. We could have cascaded air-breathing engines, and mostly use turbo-jet engines to start out at the airport runway and then transition over to ramjets as the plane exceeds Mach 2 in the upper atmosphere. The Blackbird Mach 3 airplane did this.

Piggyback a rocket on a supersonic airplane.

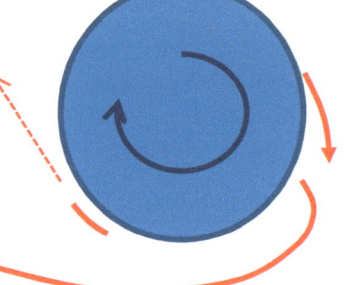

Chemical rocket, vertical launch

Hybrid engine air-breathing rocket, airplane launch

Hopefully we have more choices than airplanes in the future to fly between cities on different continents, like hybrid rockets, or piggyback rockets.

Supersonic Planes that Made It using Cascaded Engines

These supersonic airplanes were made in the 1960s. The commercial flight Concorde uses afterburners to get to Mach 2. Fuel is sprayed into the exhaust which still have remaining oxygen to get extra burning and extra thrust. The military Blackbird could go to Mach 3 and employs a cascaded turbojet and ramjet:

Concorde, a commercial airplane, launched in 1969:
The Concorde jet could fly steady at Mach 2, faster than fighter jets. The Concorde employed afterburners in turbofans.

Compared to a fighter jet, the Concorde could fly for many hours without refueling because it stores a lot more fuel in its wings because it is larger, and because it flies higher with less air drag. A fighter jet is smaller, flies at lower altitudes, and is more maneuverable, but needs re-fueling every half hour.
- The only commercial supersonic jet, the Concorde, did Mach 2, and flew for over 20 years, but this luxurious jet was retired in 2003 because it never made money, partly because of expensive tickets and partly because the 'shock wave' supersonic boom caused it to be banned from flying supersonic over land, which broke the business plan (broken windows, cracked walls, annoying bang on the ground).
- Many airlines in the beginning were lined up to buy the Concorde, but cancelled the orders when the Concorde got banned from flying over land in the continental USA and other inland countries due to the sonic boom, which is annoying like a gun shot, startling, and breaks windows.

Even if airplane engines are efficient above Mach 2, there is more heat and much more air drag. Supersonic airplanes need high temperature materials and extra airplane weight for strength to go to Mach 2.
- Look at the retired Concorde supersonic airplane. The engines on the non-profitable Concorde were actually very efficient, with after burners on turbojet engines, but the heating from air drag and weight to handle the stresses caused more fuel consumption. The force of air drag is 4 times as much going at Mach 2 compared to Mach 1, at the same altitude. So supersonic airplanes fly higher where there is less air. The lift is obtained by faster speeds and larger wings.

SR-71 Blackbird, a military airplane, launched in 1964:
The Blackbird could fly at Mach 3 and employed a cascaded engine, a turbo jet and then a ram jet.

The Blackbird did Mach 3 using turbojet engines with afterburners at lower speeds, converting to a ramjet at a speed of about Mach 2.2, retired in 1999.

Jets going this fast typically will fly more than 10 miles high to avoid air drag, and these jets are not designed for maneuverability. They are just designed to outrun opposing missiles, which is even harder to do these days.

In contrast, the current Joint Strike Fighter (F35) does Mach 1.2 using turbofan engines with afterburners. No ramjet is used. Current fighter planes don't try to outrun missiles. They instead use jamming, flares, and situational awareness.

Here are the two faster than sound airplanes that everything can be compared to.

Faster Commercial Flights and Cascaded Rocket Engines

Want to get from New York to Tokyo in less than 3 hours instead of 14 hours, and are you willing to spend $100k for a ticket?
We've had supersonic flights for decades, most notably the retired Concorde. But due to high cost of the fuel and heat resistant materials and the sonic boom there is no current supersonic airplane for commercial flights.
Aerospace companies have created new paper designs, but few if any are built.

*"Hey, faster flights could all be great in 20 years!
Supersonic flight has already happened, but it is not competitive with regular subsonic, was loud inside the cabin, and could not fly supersonic over land due to the shock wave."*

Ideas for Faster than Sound (Supersonic, Mach 1 – 4)

Mach 2 Concorde using turbojets, faster than fighter jets

Piggyback at Mach 1:
Release passenger rocket from booster mothership which uses turbojets.

Piggyback Spaceliner:
Prototype rocket-powered commercial Spaceliner, from Virgin Galactic.

Ideas for 'Way' Faster than Sound (Hypersonic, Mach > 3)

Piggyback release of Mach 10 Ramjet launched from a subsonic airplane:
This piggyback works well for a supersonic commercial flight skimming the atmosphere, when the rocket does not need to get to orbital speeds. A piggyback solution is not so obvious for space flight, because space flight still needs a much larger 2nd stage to even get to low Earth orbit.

Piggyback release of Glider or ramjet plane at Mach 20 from a rocket booster going Mach 5:
A hypersonic jet could have a rocket booster and a final ramjet passenger stage, which separate after being propelled into the mesosphere. The launch could be vertical, like the Space Shuttle. The concept above is for the SpaceLiner from Institute of Space Systems in Bremen, Germany.

Air density is less at altitudes higher up, so an airplane needs to fly faster to get the same lift.

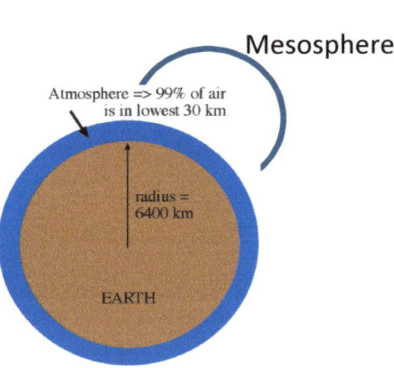

Where space begins: Can't fly an airplane fast enough without escaping Earth (somewhat arbitrary): altitude where air density is so low that an airplane needs to travel faster than escape speed (Mach 35) to get enough lift: this happens at an altitude 100 km (62 miles) where the pressure is at 1 millionth atmospheric pressure

Altitude for Hypersonic flights (>Mach 3) for lift

Altitude for Supersonic flights for lift

https://en.wikipedia.org/wiki/K%C3%A1rm%C3%A1n_line

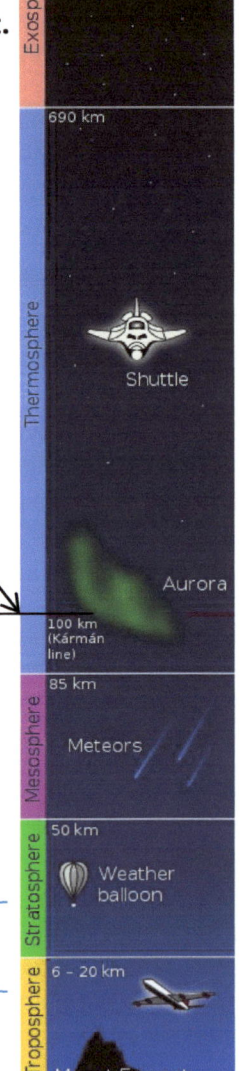

Using air-breathing jet engines, we could speed up to Mach 10 or so before we ignite the rocket engine, and save weight. Or we could do the reverse, and have a rocket booster to get to Mach 5 before we start the air-skimming scramjet engine.

Cascaded Engine Types to Breath Air, Getting to Space while Sipping Fuel

Here is the dream for future rockets: Fully re-usable rocket planes, that use oxygen in the air as they climb into outer space. Why not take advantage of the air in the atmosphere as the rocket goes up, using turbofans and ramjets, and not carry extra oxidizer? These dream cascaded-engine rockets are called Single Stage To Orbit, or STTO.

Order of cascaded engines, based on each engines sweet spot for speed:
- When in the air, use air-breathing engines before the rocket (cascaded engines), so the rocket plane does not need to lift the weight of the oxygen during the path through the atmosphere, and we can break the stranglehold of the rocket equation.
- Also, the cascaded-engine rocket is re-usable, so the promise is that the cost of launching the payload will drop dramatically. Of course, the Space Shuttle promised all this as well, and technical issues got in the way.

Below Mach 1, airplanes use turbo-jet engines, where fan blades are necessary to get enough back pressure so when the gas burns with fuel the gas will only exit out the back. Above Mach 2, airplanes use ramjets and scramjets, where the incoming air pressure, funneled through a narrow opening, is enough to force the burning gas to exit out the back: the pressure from the exploding gas provides thrust by mostly pushing on the flared metal of the nozzle, and not the incoming air.

Out in space, with no oxygen from air, we are back to a regular rocket, with its own carried oxidizer to burn the fuel.

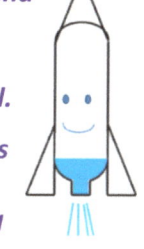

"Someday airplanes and rockets may look the same, if cascaded engines are successful.

Those future airplanes will have some huge temperature handling and material issues."

Multiple engine approach for STTO, air breathing to rocket: turbojet / ramjet / scramjet / rocket

SPACE — Rocket: does not need air.

Rocket: Final propellant: Liquid oxidizer rocket after reach outer space.

Cascaded single stage space-plane concept  | Engage Rockets

UPPER ATMOSPHERE — Jets: use air (not rockets)

Third air engine: Scramjets
from Mach 4 to 8 (supersonic-combustion ramjet)

X-43 Scramjet airplane

Scramjet: Compression from speed and narrow opening.
No moving parts:
Can not take off by itself

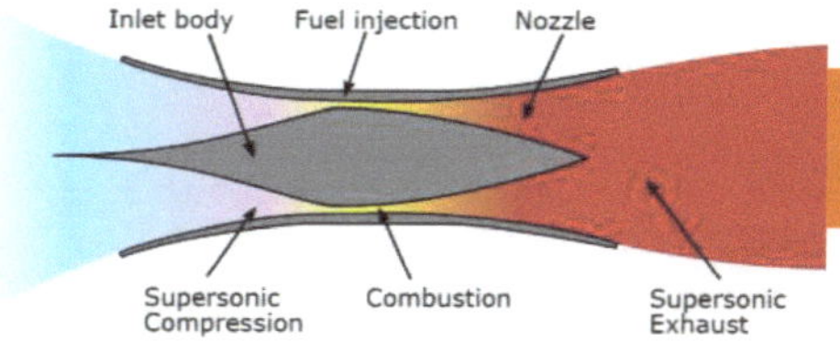

Second air engine: Ramjets
from Mach 2 to 4 (air rammed into engine)

Turbo RAM-jet Blackbird

Ramjet: Compression from speed

GROUND

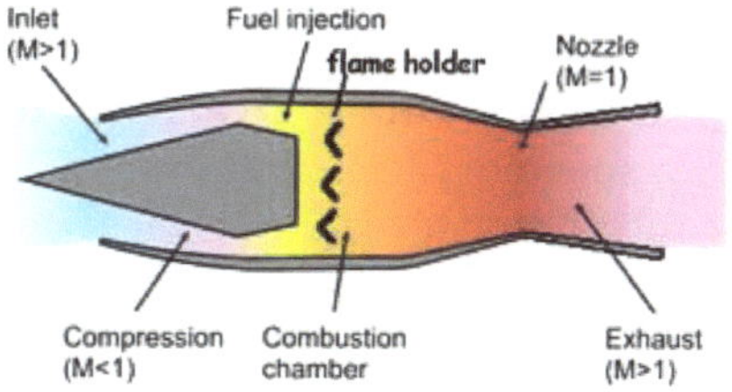

First air engine: Turbo-fan and Turbo-jets
like in commercial air planes, Usually less than Mach 1, but up to Mach 2

Turbo-fan

Turbojet, like turbo-charged cars: Compression from fans

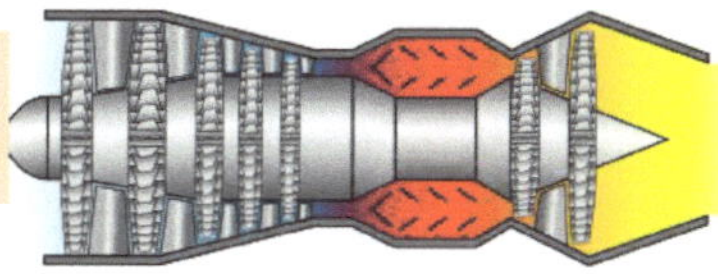

Many moving parts:
- Self pressurizing, so can work at zero velocity.
- Damage at high velocity

Afterburners can be applied in the exit nozzle by injecting fuel, if the exhaust still has oxygen, like a rocket.

Cascaded engines sounds great to exploit oxygen in the atmosphere, but there are huge heat and material issues to overcome.

Piggyback Rocket on an Airplane Booster that Breathes Air

One dream is the rocket piggybacks on an airplane to 5 miles altitude at Mach 1 or faster, and then the rocket drops and ignites. The mothership airplane needs to be going at some reasonable fraction of the final rocket speed to make this interesting, like Mach 5 to replace the 1st stage in orbital launches.

Design choices for a mothership airplane:
- **Space launches:** This piggyback airplane idea would work best if the mother airplane could get the rocket to 10 miles altitude with a starting piggyback speed greater than Mach 5 or so. If less, then the mother airplane does not provide enough starting speed to make the complexity worth it, when the payload needs to get to a much larger > Mach 25 final speed.
- **Inter-continental travel:** The 5 miles altitude and starting piggyback speed of Mach 1 works, when the final speed of the payload only needs to be Mach 6 or so.

"Piggyback might work for faster commercial travel. We could have a combination rocket / ramjet, or a combination turbofan / ramjet."

NASA and Air Force have been doing this piggyback booster idea a long time, for light payloads and to simplify tests of different engines and rocket designs.

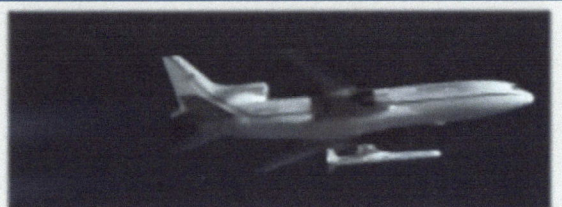

Low Earth orbit: Pegasus rocket launch from belly of large airplane, since 1990.
- Good for launching smaller satellites into low Earth orbit, because the orbits are customized and not because the piggyback provides much added velocity.

Piggyback Virgin Design, sub-orbital:

Design purpose: Mach 3 commercial travel, skimming the atmosphere.

Rocket-powered commercial space liner getting boost from mother ship. This current design carried civilians to space for faster travel.

Release from mother ship and ignition of rocket

'Spaceship One' in Washington DC. This was the first prototype.

Low Earth orbit: DARPA Boeing XS-1 Spaceplane concept in 2017, with payload on top of re-usable booster rocket that can land like a glider. (project cancelled in 2020)

Air-to-Air missiles: Solid fuel rocket engines or a turbo jet.

Air-to-Air missiles: Typical missile launch. Missiles are faster when launched at Mach 1.

An piggyback airplane booster might be economical to shuttle people from New York to Tokyo, between continents, where a speed of Mach 5 is a great achievement.
- In the Virgin design, the rocket propelled space plane is dropped from an air-breathing airplane, fires its hybrid fuel rocket to gain altitude, and then re-enters the atmosphere and glides to a landing.
- The rocket propelled space plane is above atmospheric drag.
- The Virgin design above allows the wings to pivot, to control the drag and heat of re-entry, and to allow the plane to fly down to an airport. Wings can have more pivot at the beginning of re-entry in the near vacuum of space.
- The Virgin rocket is made from composite material (fiberglass), for increased strength and lower weight.
- Ticket price goal if ever in full production: $250k (about $1000 per pound)

A piggyback ride to the upper atmosphere avoids the need for rocket launch pads, and allows more custom insertion into orbit. When the mothership is in the upper atmosphere, then fire those rockets and go into space. However, it would be better if the mother ship for the piggyback ride got to Mach 5 or so.

Future Space Designs: Piggyback/Air-Breathing Engine/Rail Gun Launches

Want to be more efficient than a vertical launch rocket, and use less fuel and be more reliable? Can the rocket launch sideways or breath the atmosphere as the oxidizer as it rises through the first 10 miles of atmosphere?

- **A piggyback design** can avoid some fuel on the rocket, if the rocket is just going to low Earth orbit. A mothership airplane can use the turbofan jet engine and ramjet.

- **A cascaded engine air-breathing design**, with a 1st turbofan jet engine, would not need a piggyback boost, and can accomplish a space launch all by itself.

- **A rail gun design** could boost the rocket to faster speeds than a piggyback design, but the rail is so long and complex. The Moon might be a better launch location. If we were building a city on the Moon with less gravity and less escape velocity, no air drag, with 1000's of launches each year, less access to chemical fuels, maybe a rail gun would make sense. On the Moon, not Earth, there is no air drag and we can install huge areas of solar panels to charge up the huge batteries for the rail gun (during the constant sun of 14 Earth days, or half the lunar cycle).

"Piggyback and cascaded air breathing engines have been investigated for decades.

Hopefully rockets will start using the oxygen in the atmosphere, when launching up, instead of carrying all the oxidizer for the fuel."

Alternative Future Designs

Piggyback launch

Piggy back sub orbital hybrid-fuel rocket

Pegasus rocket with light pay loads, launched from an airplane

Commercial supersonic Inter-continental travel:
- Piggyback launch from airplane
- Use rocket engines and then Glide back to earth

Cascaded engines

Piggy back inter-continental X-51 scramjet engine

X-43 Scramjet engine only, as prototype of cascaded engines

Rail gun launch

Scaled prototype rail gun to get to Mach 1

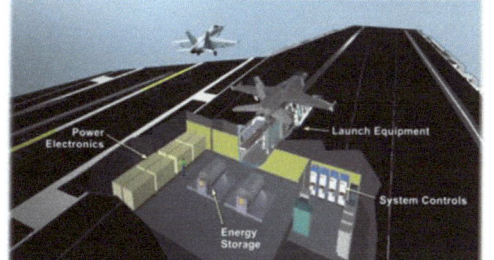

Rail gun on aircraft carrier, to aid take-off of subsonic jets with bombs and fuel

Alternate piggyback or cascaded designs may one day provide faster inter-continental flights, or maybe low Earth orbit.

Star-Raker Single Stage to Orbit, a Paper Design in 1980s

There have been giant space plane designs, using cascaded engines, to get huge payloads into Low Earth Orbit and to provide faster intercontinental travel. These designs were conceived, although never built, after the Space Shuttle was built. The concept designs still have technical issues to overcome like the huge surface temperatures when traveling over Mach 10 in air.

Why were big companies considering these designs? In the 1980s, the energy crisis was a big threat, with untapped crude oil and OPEC raising oil prices. Fortunately, the energy crisis also broke or was diminished when oil drilling technology improved using fracking and sideways drilling.

With this energy crisis as a backdrop, as a new way to power cities, people wanted to place huge solar panels in orbit, and then beam the energy back down as microwaves to be captured by rectennas which grab microwave beams and convert the microwave power to dc power.

  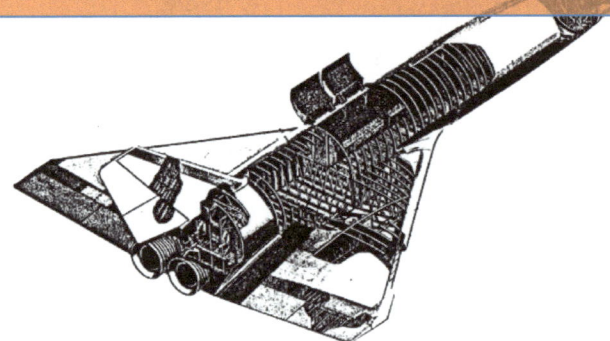

The Star-Raker design by Rockwell.

The Reusable Aerodynamic Space Vehicle design by Boeing

These huge space planes were designed to launch every day and bring materials up into orbit for these orbiting solar panel power stations.
The engineering challenge is the super hot temperatures on the surface, while going faster than Mach 5 in the atmosphere.

Solar panels in space, for power on Earth
Huge 2 x 5 mile solar panel array in orbit, to capture the power of the Sun's rays and beam the energy back down to Earth. The solar panels must be huge to generate huge power. The Star-Raker was designed to assemble and maintain the solar panels.

Nowadays, we really don't need the complexity of maintaining an orbiting solar panel power station. Instead we have solar panel farms here on the ground. Here are some reasons to keep the solar panels on the ground:
1. Solar panels on the ground are more accessible, upgradable, and less costly just to build on the ground, and accept the atmospheric losses of 50% reduction in solar power per square meter.
2. The designs of solar panels get more efficient rather rapidly, and it is hard to upgrade anything in space.
3. There would also be losses to convert from DC power to microwaves to beam the energy back down to Earth.
4. The materials required for the hot temperatures of a single stage of orbit vehicle are un-proven.

When there was a national need to find alternative energy during the 1970s and 80s energy crisis, people considered the huge investment in Space Planes and Solar Panel Power Stations in orbit.

Rockets Carry Oxidizer and Airplanes Burn Air

It is good to know the different capabilities of rockets and airplanes. Rockets don't need outside air for either lift or fuel. Rockets can go into space. In contrast, airplanes don't need to carry any oxidizer and don't carry as much fuel, because airplanes use the oxygen in the air as it flies, and airplanes are more efficient. However, airplanes can't leave the atmosphere.

"Rockets provide their own oxidizer, so rockets can have thrust in the vacuum of space. Rockets can also go faster than their exhaust."

Rockets:

1. Carry oxidizer and fuel, solid or liquid.
2. Can use on-board fuel oxidizer to escape air.
3. Rockets can travel faster than the exhaust velocity of the exhaust gas.
4. Rockets without wings must provide a thrust greater than the weight of the rocket.
5. Efficiency: Terrible at lower speed, but can go fast.
6. Typically burn through fuel quickly and then coast.

Cost to build the International Space Station:
~$100 Billion, mostly due to launch costs, such as one-time-use rockets and fuel.

Cost to build a 'gigantic' small moon (the Star Wars 'Death Star'):
cost of 'more money than exists'.

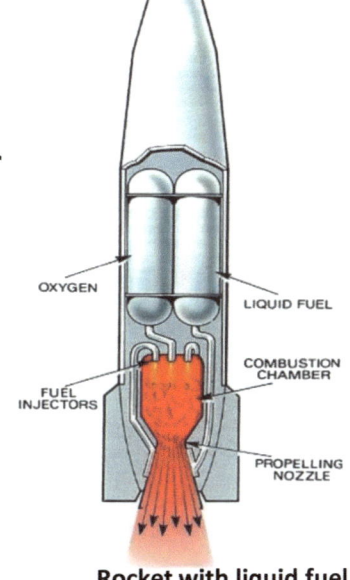

Rocket with liquid fuel

Toy rocket launch with solid fuel and oxidizer

Airplanes and Helicopters:

1. Do not carry an oxidizer. Use air instead.
2. Must stay in atmosphere.
3. Airplane can not travel faster than exhaust gas: Exhaust velocity must be greater than plane velocity.
4. Wings and air flow provide most the lift. Using wings, thrust only needs to be large enough to counter-act weight divided by glide ratio and air drag, not the full weight of the aircraft.
5. Efficiency: better at lower speeds.
6. Steady fuel use.

Turbofan jet airplane

Combustion engine airplane

Jet man turbofan

Turbofan back pack

Turbofan engine for helicopter

- The main difference is that rockets carry their own oxidizer and can go into space.
- The second difference is rockets can go much faster than their exhaust velocity. Airplanes can not, to get any thrust.

Pros and Cons of Supersonic Fast and Inefficient Air Travel

Yes, we already do a speed of Mach 2 or more with fighter jets, but oh so expensive and unreliable! Fuel runs out in 30 minutes doing over Mach 1, and the fighter jet needs re-fueling in the air. Also, the fighter jet engines need to be inspected after each flight, with an overhaul every 1000 hours.

Still, for an airplane or missile, it is better to use oxygen from the air using air-breathing engines when flying in the atmosphere, rather than a rocket engine which needs to carry its own oxidizer.

- The Blackbird did a speed of Mach 3 using turbojet engines with afterburners, and then converting to a ramjet at a speed of about Mach 2.2. This military plane was retired in 1999.
- The current Joint Strike Fighter (F35) does Mach 1.2 using turbofan engines with afterburners. This fighter is of course a military plane.
- The only commercial supersonic jet, the Concorde, did Mach 2, and flew for over 20 years, but this luxurious jet was retired in 2003 for many reasons: because it never made money, partly because of expensive tickets and partly because the 'shock wave' supersonic boom caused it to be banned from flying supersonic over land, which broke the business plan (broken ground windows, cracked walls, and annoying bang on the ground like a gun blast).

"If you care about cost and efficiency, then flying faster than the speed of sound is not an obviously 'sound' idea."

Pro: Military Flights Supersonic (faster than sound)
1. **Save time**: You get to the bad guys faster
2. **Outrun**: You escape from missiles.

Missiles for defense

Blackbird for surveillance

Pro: Commercial Flights Supersonic
1. **Save time**: You get to where you're going faster
2. **Bragging rights**: As a passenger, you get to be suave and sophisticated, and brag about how you have lots of money

Previous flights

Can't buy a ticket, since the Concord retired.

Potential Concorde successor 'Boom Supersonic', using turbojet engines, with sonic boom directed upward, or broken up into smaller booms.

New supersonic design

Con: Supersonic
1. **Fuel**: Guzzle down the fuel, worse than a Hummer SUV!
   - Poor aerodynamic lift, large air drag, and large heating, so heavier airplane.
2. **Heat**: Higher temperatures and more expensive materials
   - Air drag heats the metal
   - Compressing the air in the engine heats the metals
3. **Maintenance**: More maintenance of the airplane.
   - Fighter jet engines get overhauled every 1000 hours flight time, instead of 3000 hours for typical commercial jet engines.
4. **Expensive**: Much more expensive tickets (10x more)
5. **Loud sonic boom**: Only allowed to fly faster over the ocean.
   - A shock wave is constantly following the plane, like the wake of a boat, when going over Mach 1.
6. **Loud inside cabin**: Hard to have conversation.
7. **Risks of new technology**: Consider tragic events in history
   - Traveling on the Titanic (sank because could not avoid iceberg due to slow braking and turning, and due to poor metals),
   - Flying on the Hindenburg (burned up using hydrogen gas),
   - Flying on the Concorde (tickets did cost around $8000, never made a profit due to banned supersonic flights over land, and had one terrible accident)

Carry more fuel

More maintenance from heat

Expensive tickets

Loud sonic boom

Cost per pound,	$1/lb	$10/lb	$100/lb	$1000/lb
Airplanes and rockets	Standard sub-sonic jet	Concorde super-sonic jet, Mach 2		Space orbit

But still rooting for the supersonic underdog, even with more cost.

Faster than Mach 1 travel is going nowhere fast on commercial flights until supersonic flight is more reliable, fuel is less expensive, and until the shock wave doesn't create a loud boom over cities and noise in the cabin.

Examples of Cascaded Different Engines to Handle Different Speeds

The idea of using different engine types for different parts of the rocket journey (atmosphere, orbit, inter-planetary travel) is just a simple extension of other ways we use cascaded engines or different parachutes for different speeds.

Speeding up with cascaded engines: rockets, airplanes, and cars

Missile boosters, to get out of the water, or to start from zero speed and then use a turbo fan:

Poseidon ballistic missile with steam boost: first steam-exhaust thrust pushes rocket out of launch tube and water, and then chemical-exhaust thrust pushes rocket when in the air. Missiles from a submarine need to escape the water.

Turbojet breathing air for sustained cruise flight

Rocket booster, to start from zero speed

Harpoon missile with cascaded engines. Starting from a stand-still, a rocket booster is needed to get to speed where wings provide enough lift for the turbo jet engine.

Airplane thrust, with turbofan for lower speeds and after burners or ram jet to get added speed above Mach 1:
High performance turbofans use after burners to squeeze out more speed when you need it.

F35 fighter jet (Joint Strike Fighter): added boost for supersonic flight from after burners

Blackbird: added boost for supersonic flight from ramjet

Hybrid electric cars, with all electric at slow speeds or combined combustion/electric at faster speeds:

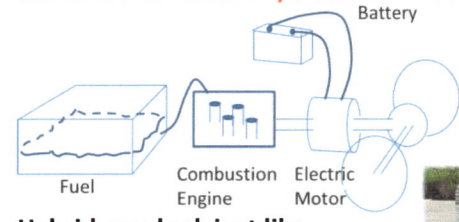 

Hybrid cars look just like regular cars with combustion engines from the outside ...no big deal.

Hybrid car: able to recharge batteries or recover energy while slowing down.

Cylinder deactivation on Durango:
Engines can de-activate half the cylinders (8 cylinder car engine with only 4 cylinders active) during low power, like cruising on the highway.

Engines that idle half the cylinders: less fuel when don't need the horsepower.

Slowing down with cascaded parachutes:

Different parachutes for different speeds:

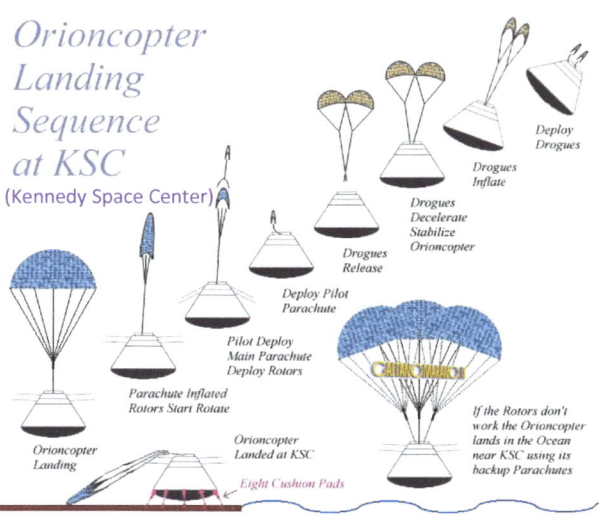

Orioncopter Landing Sequence at KSC (Kennedy Space Center)

SLS Orion capsule landing with main parachutes, after using drogue higher speed parachutes and the pilot parachute. This capsule is intended for the SLS rocket, for ISS supplies and Artemis missions.

Different types of engines are effective at different speeds, even on the same rocket, plane, or car. When slowing down, different types of parachutes are effective for different speeds, to avoid the fabric getting ripped apart.

Chapter 7: Improbable Ways to Launch Astronauts Into Space, like Railguns, Elevators, and Nuclear Power

We need better access to outer space, although these improbable ways are unlikely to happen soon.

People dream of making the solar system our next frontier, with livable bases in Earth's orbit and bases spread around the planets and moons. For example, our Moon is the closest, and the Moon has dust water in the shadows of canyons which allow oxygen and fuel. The poles of Mars have ice water, where the Sun does not evaporate the ice. Asteroids are good for mining for construction material and frozen water. Some of the moons of Jupiter have water oceans.

Project HARP 16-inch gun

Getting to orbit: fighting gravity and building up speed:
Let's cover a lot a radical ideas to make getting into orbit either faster or more affordable, including balloons, lasers, space elevators, or slingshots.

A cannon using an exploding powder won't work. The exploding gas can't keep up with the projectile or rocket going Mach 10. The replacement for an exploding gas is a magnetic force from a rail gun. A rail gun can accelerate us at 3 g's for 500 miles and put us in orbit. Maybe a 2nd stage rocket can then push us out of orbit. We'll need to have the rail gun go up a tall mountain so that the reduced air drag in the thin air will not overheat and slow down the rocket, once the rocket is released from the rail gun into the open air.

We can talk about floating a balloon 100 miles up and then using a rocket to get up to speed. But we'll still have some air drag as we're trying to get up to speed, and a balloon will have a large area to cause more air drag. For example, weather balloons do go up to 25 miles altitude, but the balloons don't try to accelerate to orbital speed at Mach 25.

We could rely on a ground laser to heat our exhaust, so we do not need an oxidizer. That might be doable. We need a laser that can focus on the bottom of our rocket and can track us very well.

We could build a cable into space that is more than 3 times the radius of the Earth. That will take some really nice new materials to handle the stresses. But then we are not talking about orbital rocket speeds anymore, just a slow and steady rise on the cable into the great outer space.

We could use nuclear explosions to push us up, but that is a radiation nightmare. Nuclear explosions have potential after a rocket is in Space, but not in the atmosphere. In Space, the nuclear radioactive byproducts can not hurt anyone.

Balloon-rocket hybrid

Concept of Rail Gun for launch off the Moon.

Escaping Earth: using 3 stages or 2 stages and a refueling station in orbit:
Let's make the escaping rocket go really fast, rather than just using most of the fuel just to get off the ground. After we get into orbit, we can go to the rocket fuel gas station, which is orbiting and resupplied that day, and refuel our rocket for our longer journey to the Moon or to Mars. Maybe the fuel for the orbiting gas station can be thrown up into space using a high-g SpinLaunch or a rail gun.

For long distance travel, at some point we must go nuclear:
We could also have an ion rocket engine that is powered by nuclear power, which will take us to Jupiter in a few months instead of 2 years or longer. Ion rocket engines and their very high exhaust velocity are very useful.
We could have hydrogen gas that is heated by a radioactive heat source, called thermal nuclear propulsion.
We could have nuclear fusion in a plasma that is expelled as exhaust.
The movies say in a few centuries we'll have faster-than-light travel. That breaks any design people know about to date.

Concept of space elevator for Earth.

Our future may have all varieties of rockets (liquid, cascaded engines, piggyback), and may even have rail guns, floating blimps, laser boosters, or space elevators.

Future 'Jetsons' Lifestyles, in the Next Solar System Age

Let's jump ahead to the future year 2200 and listen in on a telephone conversation about space travel, which, in the future, probably is a holodeck conversation with virtual 3D holograms of people:

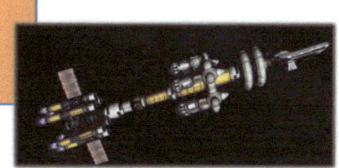

Concept of ion/chemical rocket for distant travel. The ion rocket can be powered by nuclear power.

Daughter on satellite phone: 'Hey, Mom. I'm going to Jupiter today, but I want something cutting edge. What's the best way to get to the orbiting space port? Should I take the **Space elevator**, or the **Rail gun**, or the **Molecular transporter**?'

Mom: 'Dear, if you can't take the **Hybrid rocket**, then the **Space elevator** is slow and reliable. The **Rail gun** is too jarring. The **Molecular transporter** gives me a headache after it rips me apart and puts all my atoms back together again. In fact, people said this molecular transporter was impossible until just recently, and if the power goes out you've been erased. So I'd take the **Space elevator**.'

 Space Port in geo-stationary orbit

The end of the **Space Elevator** is either a heavy off-planet city without the feeling of gravity*, or a Transfer station to next stage of travel:
- Chemical rocket to get to Moon base.
- Combined Chemical and Electrical Ion rocket to get to a Mars base, or a farther planet.

Space Elevator on thick cable

'SpinLaunch' sling, a space catapult

Rail gun launch

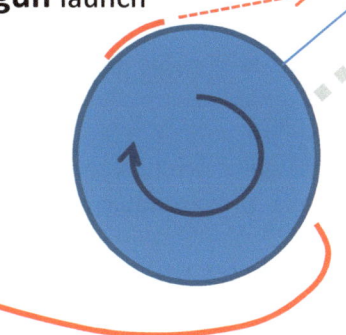

Chemical rocket, vertical launch

Laser heat of exhaust

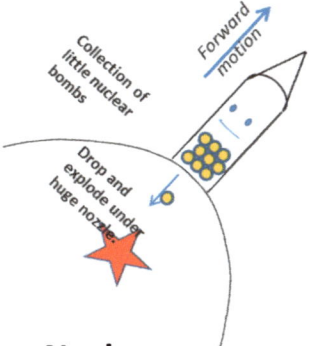

Nuclear blasts

Hopefully we have more choices than chemical rockets in the future, like hybrid rockets, piggyback rockets, space elevators, rail guns, or 'Beam me up Scotty' molecular transporters.

Improbable Ways to Launch Astronauts Into Space, like Railguns, Elevators, and Nuclear Power

Here are some improbable pie-in-the-sky ways to get into orbit.
We need better access to outer space, although these improbable ways are unlikely to happen soon. People dream of making the solar system our next frontier, with livable bases in Earth's orbit and bases spread around the planets and moons. Our Moon is the closest. The poles of Mars have water. Asteroids are good for mining construction material and frozen water. Some of the moons of Jupiter have water oceans.

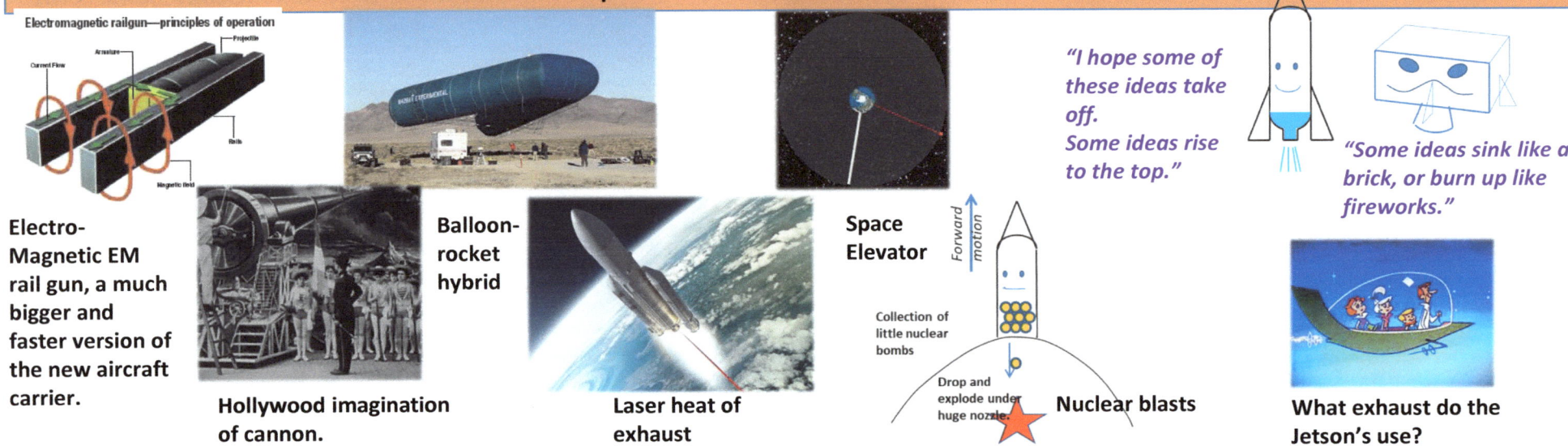

Electro-Magnetic EM rail gun, a much bigger and faster version of the new aircraft carrier.

Hollywood imagination of cannon.

Balloon-rocket hybrid

Laser heat of exhaust

Space Elevator

Nuclear blasts

"I hope some of these ideas take off.
Some ideas rise to the top."

"Some ideas sink like a brick, or burn up like fireworks."

What exhaust do the Jetson's use?

Chemical rockets seem the only practical way to get to space, but rockets are very expensive. Imaginary anti-gravity floating spaceships – somehow presented as lower cost, more reliable methods of the future – just do not seem based in reality, despite pictures in the movies of anti-gravity floating spaceships in 'Star Wars', or pictures of small shuttles going from space to ground in 'Star Trek'.

What are some **improbable** ways to get to space, besides cascaded-engine rockets and piggyback rockets? People are dreaming up many other ways to get things into orbit.
- A cannon, using a rail gun (not a chemical explosion) may get equipment into orbit. A cannon will probably not launch people, because the accelerations would rip people apart even for a 1 mile long cannon, and air drag will dampen all the speed before getting to orbit. A spin launch can get fast speeds, but the accelerations are over 1000 g's and are for non-living supplies only. If we wanted to launch people at reasonable g's, these people cannons, using a rail gun, would be over 500 miles long, even at a force of 10 times the persons weight.
- Floating balloons at the stratosphere that gradually over months pick up speed to get to orbital velocity
- Laser boost, using the heat from the laser built on the ground.
- Space elevators rising up a huge cable to geo-stationary orbit (length of 5 times the radius of the Earth)
- Nuclear heat source to heat exhaust gas or have nuclear explosions directly below the rocket nozzle.

Maybe some improbable scheme will work in the future, to make getting to space a lot less expensive, and maybe Hollywood can claim to be the predictors of the future.

Our future may have all varieties of rockets (liquid, cascaded engines, piggyback), and may even have rail guns, floating blimps, laser boosters, or space elevators.

Dreaming: Other Ways to Launch Astronauts Up Into Space, with Focus on the Improbable

Yes, there is a pathway to new technologies and change, to get into space. The dreams exist, and gradual work is getting done on these potential alternatives. We've already talked about rockets and hybrid air-breathing airplanes. Now let's discuss improbable rail gun cannons, balloons with thrusters, ground lasers heating rocket exhaust, and elevators 5 Earth radii long.

Let's explore the Improbable!

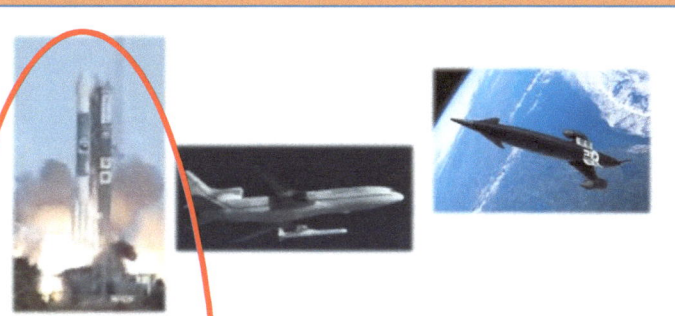

Electromagnetic railgun—principles of operation

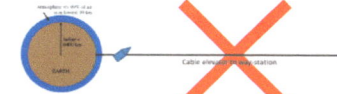

Takes huge ground laser hardware

Not practical, needs 'un-obtainium' cable

Done (practical) — *Research* — *Not practical* — *Improbable* — *Conceptual problems*

Conventional rockets: Hey, we know rockets already work well, even though they are extremely expensive and inefficient.

Piggyback launch: This piggyback launch is already done using smaller satellites for LEO.

Cascaded engines before rockets: Hey, we have the cascaded rocket design, we just need to work out the huge heat and weight issues.

Cannon: Chemical Explosions:
Issues:
- Explosions do not provide fast enough gases to push. Expanding gas can not keep up with the projectile (better to put explosions in rocket).

Cannon: Magnetic rail guns: Conceptually can accelerate the capsule to escape Earth speeds, but now have a host of other issues:
- Air drag,
- Temperature handling
- Finding an Arizona-length rail along a mountain slope.
- Building a power plant

Airship balloon to orbital speed: Float at edge of atmosphere, and then use ion rockets to slowly get to orbital velocity (maybe over months).
Issue:
- Air drag

Laser boost from ground: Use super powerful blasts of light from lasers to heat the air under the rocket, or heat on-board water. The hot gas is now the exhaust.
Issue:
- Building a GigaWatt average power laser.

Space elevator: Slide up and down a wire 5 Earth radii long.
Issues
- There is no strong and light enough cable.

Mothership speed:
- Currently only boost to Mach 1.
- Need to boost to Mach 5 or so to make more than a 10% difference in fuel, when orbital velocity is much larger at Mach 25.

Conventional rockets are the only engineering approach that works so far to get to Earth's orbit. The rocket travels over 700 miles with thrust at 3 g's acceleration for 300 seconds, to get to orbital velocity. The rocket needs lots of fuel and good balancing, no ground rail or cannon needed.

Rail Gun example: launch airplanes on aircraft carriers.

- **EM guns for un-manned objects and short barrels**: Mach 2 bullets (speed of 600 m/s) are shot out of guns and cannons all the time, over a barrel distance of a few meters, and can go up a few km with air drag. However, we are talking fatal accelerations for people, about 10,000 g's.
- **EM guns for manned objects and long barrels**: Electro Magnetic rail guns with much longer barrels (>100km), to keep acceleration below 10 g's.
- **Chemical guns and upper limit to speed**: Chemical explosions in a cannon are not the answer. Atoms only travel 3000 m/s during an explosion, so they can not push against a capsule going up to 4 times faster, at 12,000 m/s.

Our future may have all varieties of rockets (liquid, cascaded air-breathing engines, piggyback), and may even have rail guns, floating blimps or laser boosters.

Success of Rockets for Space: Height and Flight Time

Rockets with exhaust are different than arrows from a bow and bullets from exploding guns and cannons, which are just coasting projectiles. Rockets with exhaust keep steady thrust until orbital speed is achieved.
A bullet going up doesn't have much control, especially when it flies out of the atmosphere. Fins wouldn't work without an air flow, and spin would keep it oriented but not enable any turn.
A rocket can steer the nozzle and keep the thrust going.

"Again, chemical rockets get to space, and other projectiles don't. Projectiles that don't are arrows, bullets or bottle rockets."

Space Rockets, with steady fuel and thrust:

Rockets are proven and effective to get to space due to large and steady thrust. There are no other choices so far that work.

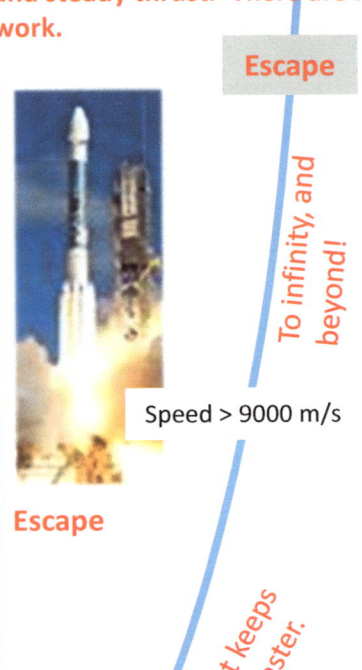

Speed > 9000 m/s

Escape

To infinity, and beyond!

Rocket exhaust keeps rocket getting faster.

Height (km) / time (seconds)

Space Rockets with steady thrust:
Not Ballistic launch

Great performance from steady thrust of rockets:
Oh yeah, payloads, like capsules and satellites, can stay up for years in Earth's orbit, because they are going sideways fast enough to orbit.

Or, if going to the Moon or Mars, the payload does not need to come back down. It has reached a speed of 11000 m/s and escaped the Earth's gravity.

Rocket trajectories still use spin of Earth and orbital movement of Earth through space to help get even more speed relative to Sun.

There are launch dates that work better to get to other planets when the distance is closest.

The Moon stays at the same distance, but we want to arrive at the landing site when there is 'sunrise' at the start of the 14 days of sunlight.

Cannon, with quick bang and ballistic flight:

Cannons on the ground are highly improbable, but the projectile might get to space under a right heavy design that can plow through air drag

height versus time

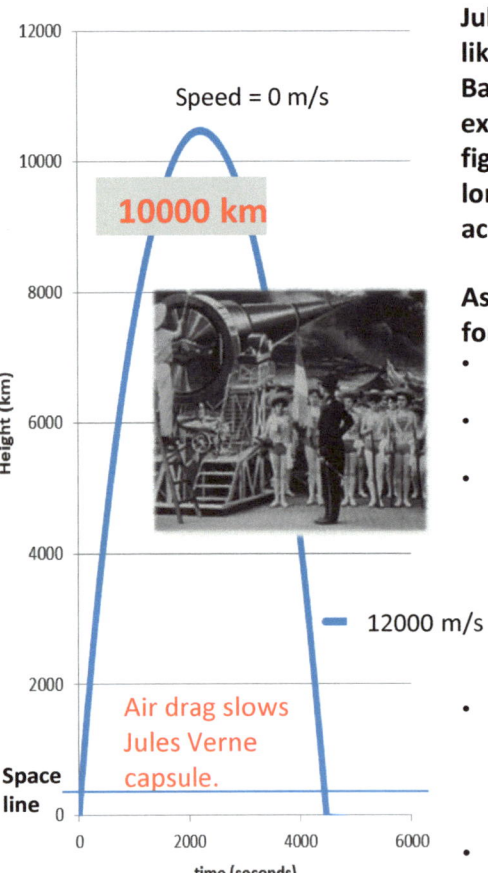

Speed = 0 m/s

10000 km

12000 m/s

Air drag slows Jules Verne capsule.

Space line

Height (km) / time (seconds)

Jules Verne Cannon to orbit, like Jules Verne stories:
Ballistic like bullets, using extremely heavy capsule to fight air drag and extremely long barrel of cannon to accelerate gradually.

Assume optimum conditions for bullets and cannons:
- Use heavy capsule (30,000 kg) to reduce air drag impact
- Use narrow diameter of 2 meters, to reduce air drag
- Rail Gun at 10 g's, for minimum travel distance of 700km, to get to 12 km/sec. Need an electro-magnetic rail gun because the magnetic push can keep up with the speed. The expansion of chemical explosions is not fast enough.
- Heat would melt the capsule. Instead, should release capsule at top of mountain in thinner air (altitude of 10km, 6 miles) to avoid most air drag
- The capsule would have almost no speed, if managed to escaped Earth.

Project HARP 16-inch gun

In 1966, the few inch diameter bullet reached an altitude of 155km. The acceleration was huge, and a 2nd stage rocket would be required to make orbit.

Abandoned HARP gun

Want to get to space and stay there? You need a rocket, with a steady thrust.
A bullet might get to space, but it would have no orbital velocity after the air drag and it would fall back to the ground.

Chemical Cannon: Bogus Impractical Movie Ideas

People write about what they see, so in 1900 rockets were not yet on the scene and science fiction writers did not assume them. In 1900, all the movie script writers had for inspiration were the cannons on the huge Dreadnought battleships of Britain and Germany, which fired a 1000 lb projectile 15 miles and were aimed using binoculars. Liquid fuel rockets didn't happen until the 1920s, by Dr. Goddard. The solid fuel rockets were there but ignored. The rocket equation was not well known yet, although it was discovered already by a school teacher Tsiolkovsky in 1903.

"I don't think Hollywood consulted a scientist back then, in the silent movie days. Explosions in the barrel can't keep up with the supersonic projectile."

Engineering issues ignored by Hollywood scientific advisors on cannons in 1900 are listed below, from least to greatest:

Jules Verne cannon to Moon: a poor and impossible ballistic flight plan

'*A Journey to the Moon*' silent film, 1902

The launch needs an improbably long cannon, and air drag would over heat the capsule.

Moon

Fall from Moon and land back in Earth's ocean.

Earth's ocean

Issue 6: How would they get back?:
According to Hollywood, they just fall from the Moon back to Earth, like a visit to the top of a cliff on Earth. By the way, this wouldn't work … We need another rocket to escape the gravity of the Moon. Nothing falls from the Moon.

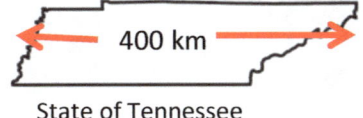
State of Tennessee — 400 km

Ok, I'm up here, now what?

Issue 5: Huge air drag causing heat and melting:
The air drag has lots of friction, and the heat could melt the capsule (10,000 Kelvin).
- One way to design for high heat is to use ceramic tiles, like the Space Shuttle (insulating). Still, tiles can not withstand the huge heat of air density near ground level. If tiles overheat just during breaking for re-entry at low pressure, high altitude, think how hot the tiles would get near the ground, with greater than 100 times the atmospheric pressure.
- The second way to handle heat is a thick shield, designed to burn away (ablative).

Issue 1: Need improbably long cannon:
Estimate a rail length of more than 500 km to stay below 10 g's and still get to escape speed, a length as long as the state of Tennessee, unless you wanted the humans to go splat as a pancake by accelerating faster. This is a similar distance space rockets use to accelerate in the air during a typical launch, except a rail gun does it on the ground.

Issue 2: Gun powder would lose its pressure over such a long barrel:
The explosion of the powder does not even travel that fast, hypersonic, to keep up with the projectile. Need electro-magnetic gun, or multi-explosion barrel.
That said, potentially light hydrogen gas could keep up, if heated to more than 5000 degree F.

Issue 3: No energy after escaping Earth:
The capsule would have almost no speed relative to Earth after escaped Earth. We're talking about the capsule just orbiting the Sun alongside the Earth, even without air drag.

Issue 4: Huge air drag slows capsule:
Unless the capsule is very heavy so force of air drag does not decelerate the capsule much, air drag prohibits this capsule from getting to orbit, with drag coefficient of 0.2. The capsule would slow down. A heavy design with a huge ballistic coefficient might get through.

Movies are fun, and probably show what humans could be and should be doing well before engineers figure it out. However, this Moon cannon idea was before the age of rockets. In the 1960s, rocket engineers did get us to the Moon, just in a smarter practical way.

More Practical Cannon Solution: Electro-Magnetic Rails

Chemical guns have a speed limit at the speed of the expanding gas inside the barrel. Rail guns with electro-magnetic forces can provide the 10 g propulsion system, pushing the capsule faster and faster with magnetic forces and no chemical limit. Stored electrical energy* can be released really quickly to get high power. The closest we have to a railgun now are prototype hypervelocity guns less than 100 feet long (imagine the g's!), or prototype levitating trains.

"Rail guns already launch hypersonic bullets, and launch heavy fully loaded airplanes from an aircraft carrier."

Rail guns and electro-magnetic propulsion

Rail guns are a better solution than gun powder cannons:

Rail guns, not explosive powder, can shoot an object faster and provide steady thrust at any speed.
- With explosive powder, the powder would lose its pressure over such a long barrel, and the explosion speed of the powder does not even travel that fast, to keep up with the projectile and provide pressure.

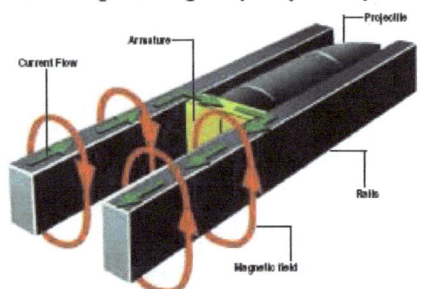
Electromagnetic railgun—principles of operation

⭐ **Home Experiment**: Using rails with electrical current, have metal rod roll along two rails (toy train tracks) by connecting a battery. Electric current causes its own magnetic field and force. The magnetic field created by the current in the rails pushes on the current crossing over.

Electric current

Existing examples of rail guns and electro-magnetic propulsion

Ford Aircraft Carrier: This modern aircraft carrier uses electro-magnetic rail gun boosters to launch airplanes, instead of steam boosters. Rail guns can have custom thrust for different airplanes for less wear, have faster recharge, and are less costly to maintain.

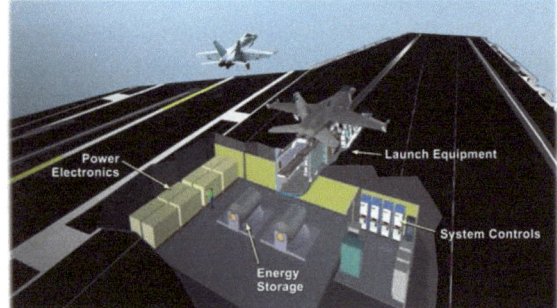

Electro-magnetic gun: for battleship.

Hyper velocity projectiles from rail guns

Rail Guns use large electric currents flowing across the projectile. The large electric current creates its own magnetic field which pushes on the current crossing between the rails across the projectile.

Rail Guns do not use gun powder. The speed is not limited by any gun powder pressure or gas expansion velocity.

Levitating Train prototype: A first case application of electro-magnetic thrust with magnetic fields pulling and pushing things away, scheduled for Japan's Bullet Train.
This type of thrust uses coils and an unwrapped linear motor. Magnets keep getting pulled to the next coil.

Magnetic levitation of trains

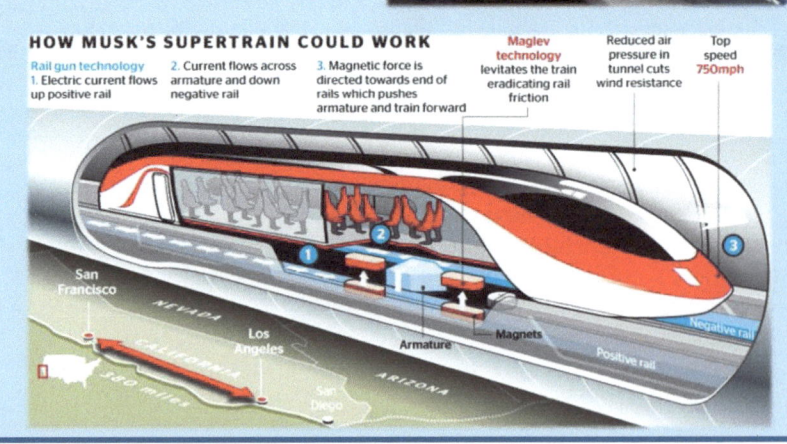

*can store energy in batteries, large capacitors, or superconducting coils.

Rail guns have already been done (airplane launching, super-sonic bullets), but not on a 500 mile scale.

Lay a Long Magnetic Rail-gun Cannon on the Western Side of a Large Mountain, like a Super Pumped Levitating Train

Launch design rules: The launch ramps should end above 5 miles up, to reduce air drag and heat in the thin air, the same altitude as commercial jets. The payload should actually have added weight to break through air drag, which is opposite to a rocket design.
For orbital launches, the launch ramps should face east, to get the extra boost of the Earth's rotation. And, oh, the ramp should be 400 miles long and powered by a huge power plant! 400 miles is similar to the distance a space rocket today uses to accelerate in its first 8 minutes of launch.
A rail gun could replace the first stage with a shorter ramp, where a rocket ignites after Mach 5.

*"Rail guns are possible, but are really impractical for the long launch to space.
The railgun needs to be just as long as the over 5 minute launch into space in a regular rocket."*

Inter-continental launches for Mach 3-5 (hypersonic) travel using 2 mile tube:

2 mile long tube up a mountain, or into the sea.
- Not long enough at 10g's to get into orbit or escape Earth, but long enough to blast from New York to Tokyo.

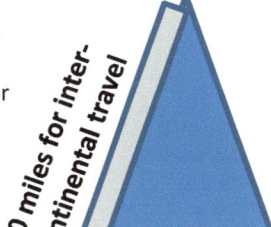

10 miles for inter-continental travel

Height: **5 miles**
Location: Everest, in Nepal, Asia which has same latitude as Cape Canaveral, Florida

Space launches for Mach 25 using 400 mile tube:

More than 400 mile tube up the mountains, for space:

Launch tube from CA or Arizona to the Rocky Mountains

Vacuum in tube***

Turning forces at any sharp bend would kill people**

Height: **2.5 miles**
Location: Rocky Mountains in Arizona, USA
Ka-Boom!

$$velocity = \sqrt{2 \cdot acceleration \cdot distance}$$

Cannon Advantage (rail gun) compared to chemical rocket:
- Can have large mass projectiles

Cannon Disadvantage:
- Expensive and long rail structure
- Huge power station
- Need to launch more than 5 miles up to avoid air drag because have faster speed right out of the barrel in the atmosphere.

Potential launch sites for cannons in the USA, going up mountain ranges*

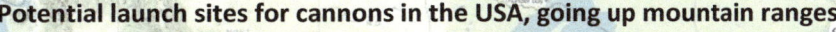

Inter-continental cannon to Asia

Inter-continental cannon to West Coast

Inter-continental cannon to Europe

Inter-continental cannon to East Coast

Space cannon
Arizona into New Mexico
4300 m altitude

Space cannon
Across Tennessee

- Start in a valley, and go up a mountain chain.
- To orbit, launch toward east to use spin velocity of Earth's surface, just like today's rockets.

Mountain

Vacuum tube or launcher

Power Plant

Meteor explodes over Russia due to heating from air drag.

What a glowing 'Ka-Boom' to expect if a short-lived payload is shot out of cannon at Mach 30 at air pressure near ground!

*** To find taller mountains**, rail guns need to be built in Asia or South America, with 7000 m altitude with ½ less air drag.
****Bend** would not work because the small radius of curvature would cause 1000 g's acceleration to turn, crushing people inside, much worse than turning fast in a car.
******Vacuum tube to remove air drag**: We want a vacuum in the cannon, like a vacuum bazooka, or hyper-tube travel, or vacuum pin pong gun.

Cannon length and acceleration: This extremely long cannon to launch humans could probably get to low Earth orbit at 10 g's acceleration. The end of the cannon should be high up where the air is thinner, ideally 5 miles up. There will still be large air drag slowing the capsule down. Of course, using shorter cannons, we could launch non-living things like supplies, at higher accelerations, out of Earth's gravity.
Locations: Possibly the first rail gun for astronauts will happen on the Moon, where gravity is less and chemical fuel is harder to generate.

Would a Rail Gun Work Better on the Moon?

On the Moon, there is plenty of sunlight to charge up the rail gun, gravity is much lower than Earth so the orbital velocity is much lower, and there is no air drag.

"Rail guns are possible, but are really impractical for the long launch to space.
The railgun needs to be just as long as the over 5 minute launch into space in a regular rocket."

The daylight lasts 14 Earth days, so there is plenty of time to charge up batteries using solar panels.

Daylight lasts 14 Earth days on the Moon

Astronauts on the Moon in the 1970s were making Olympic height high jumps, and one astronaut hit a golf ball for miles. So yes, gravity is lower. People dream of doing extreme sports on the Moon because the gravity is so low.

The Moon's surface is mostly the vacuum of Space. So a projectile, like the golf ball, doesn't feel air drag.

NASA astronaut Alan Shepard hitting golf ball on the Moon, which went a few miles with low gravity and no air drag.

But wait, there are other advantages of a rail gun on the Moon. Electricity comes from solar panels, so we don't need to launch fuel from the Earth to then power launches from the Moon.

A rail gun could replace the first stage with a shorter ramp, where a rocket ignites after achieving orbit to return back to Earth.

The orbital speed to stay in low Moon orbit is 1.6 km/s. That is Mach 5 here on Earth. At an acceleration of 3 g's, the rail gun length is about 50km, or 33 miles.

That rail gun is still long, and the fabrication would take a lot of wiring, which needs to be delivered to the Moon from Earth.

Concept of Rail Gun for launch off the Moon.

Let's remind ourselves about the basic length estimates for a rail gun, based on maximum acceleration and desired final velocity.

$$velocity = \sqrt{2\, acceleration \cdot distance}$$

The escape velocity is proportional to the radius of the surface.

$$v_{escape} = \sqrt{2gR}$$

On the Moon, the g is 1/6th that of Earth, and the radius is 1/3rd the Earth, so the escape velocity is about 1/4th the Earth. Instead of 12km/s for the Earth, we have 2.38km/s for the Moon.

To get to orbit around the Moon, we need a rail gun that is 50 km at a human friendly 3 g steady acceleration.

Except for the forbidding vacuum and hot/cold conditions on the Moon, the rail gun on the Moon is more friendly than on Earth.

Cannon length and acceleration on the Moon: A 50 km long cannon to launch humans could probably get to low Moon orbit at 3 g's acceleration.
Locations: Possibly the first rail gun for astronauts will happen on the Moon, where gravity is less and chemical fuel is harder to generate.

Sling Shot to Orbit, for Supplies and Satellites, Not People

Could we just throw things into Space? The basic thing a satellite needs is speed, and speed is not necessarily from a semi-explosive rocket.

A spin catapult can throw objects into space. This spin launch would be a short version of the EM rail gun, and would operate with very high accelerations, over 1000 g's. Due to air drag, the object or payload would probably need extra rocket boost to make orbit. The Spinlaunch could replace the 1st stage of a rocket for delivering supplies to orbit, but not launch people.

A linear rail gun, with 100 miles of length to accelerate a rocket to Mach 5 at 3 g's, would be better for people.

The SpinLaunch concept could be used to launch fuel into orbit, or launch food or supplies into orbit, to be captured by ISS.

The fuel could also be launched using a rail gun with high g's, or most likely using another rocket.

SpinLaunch can not be used to launch people into space, because the accelerations are over 200 times larger than the maximum for human blood flow. A 200 pound human would feel like they weigh over 200 thousand pounds, basically crushing them.

Besides the high g's, the main launch issue is the immediate air drag when the payload is released at ocean level. The payload needs to be heavy and aerodynamic streamlined. Instead of at ocean level, these SpinLaunch sites should be at higher altitudes with thinner air, for example in Colorado or on mountain tops, to reduce air drag. At 5 miles up the air is only 40% as dense which is why climbers need days to adjust to the lower oxygen level, and climbers breath extra oxygen from a tank when at the top of Mount Everest or other high mountain.

Spin launch as a first stage:

'SpinLaunch' sling, a space catapult

Payload at end of spinning arm, which needs to be heavy to punch through the air drag during launch. The payload has a high ballistic coefficient, or ability to plow through air drag, like a bullet.

This high mass design is the opposite methodology compared to a typical rocket launch, where weight needs to be minimized.

The arm can be heavy because its energy after releasing the payload can be recovered by regenerative braking.

The final design will probably have two payloads, one on each end of the arms for balance. The second one will be released a half turn after the first one.

Power: The payload can be gradually accelerated up to top spin speed, so the instantaneous power of the launch device does not need to be huge.

Vacuum: The payload must spin in a vacuum inside the large centrifuge, or the air drag would stop further accelerations and would generate heat.

Acceleration: Electronics can withstand over 1000 g's, and that is demonstrated in 'smart' bullets already.

Design issues:
- Vibrations on the spinning arms due to weight imbalance
- Maintaining a vacuum when payload is release from arm to outside air.

Huge centrifugal acceleration in design at spin speeds:

$$acceleration = \frac{v^2}{R}$$

R = 40 meters
V = 3000 m/s (Mach 9)
A = 22,000 m/s² (2200 g's)

Other slower centrifuges:

Centrifuge for people: The huge 20 G centrifuge at the NASA Ames Research Center, to train astronauts at high g endurance.

Accelerations **longer than a few seconds** at greater than 5 to 10 g's cause blood to not flow through the body, and cause black outs or fainting.

David and Goliath, with sling.

A slingshot uses spin to get the rocket to high speeds before release.

Spin shots are rather common on a grander scale. The Earth's spin is already providing the slingshot to help get to orbit, before fire the last stage engine to get to the Moon.

The Earth's orbit speed also provides energy to get to other planets.

Let's throw stuff into orbit with a sling, like David and Goliath, at least as a first stage.

Sling Shot into Orbit at 2000 g's:
Sideways Turn Needs a Sideways Force

The ridiculous forces to spin something up would rip most things apart. The speed and the short radius of turn or spinning arm gives ridiculous forces for the Spin Launch. Huge sideways forces and accelerations are created. We all have felt sideways forces during a turn, but just not at the magnitude of the Spin Launch. Anytime something turns, there must be a force pushing it to the side.

The examples below all need a force pulling them around a circle, if they are turning.

Possible orbit delivery using spin launch:

The Sling Shot to Orbit
~ 2000 g's

Now we are getting really extreme. The materials pulling the weight around in a circle need to be very strong.

This is no ordinary centrifuge. The accelerations don't stop at 10 g's and then you say time out.

The acceleration gets up to 2000 g's. No human can withstand this force, but supplies can. So this would be a good replacement for a 1st stage of a rocket to bring supplies into orbit.

Comparison accelerations during spin:

Turning around a corner in a car
~ 0.1 g

Those tires need to push sideways on the road to turn the car.

When you are in a car going around a turn fast, can you feel the force push you sideways?

You can feel the sideways force, although you are only going 30 m/s.

Ball on a string
~ 1 g

Pulling on rope to keep ball going in circle.

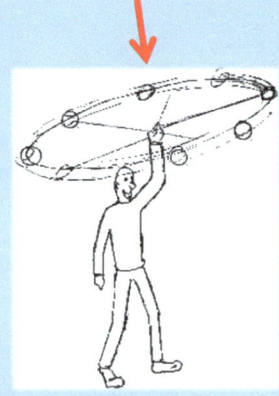

When twirling a ball overhead, the stress can get exhausting constantly pulling the ball in.

You are the force keeping the ball going in a circle.

Earth going around the Sun
~ 0.000001 g

Thank you gravity from the Sun, or Earth and we would be flung away from the Sun, to be a cold barren rock.

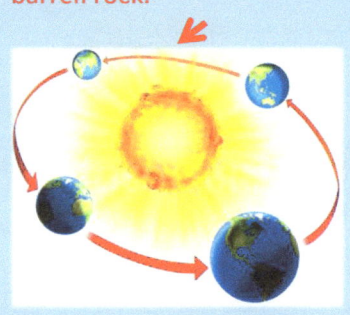

Gravity is pulling the Earth back in to orbit the Sun, even though the Earth wants to go straight.

Gravity between the Sun and the Earth is keeping the Earth going in a near circular orbit around the Sun.

The centripetal acceleration of the Earth toward the Sun is actually a small acceleration, less than 1 millionth of a g, although the force is immense on the huge mass of the Earth.

Spinning rides at the fair
~ 2 g's

Even at the fair, you exploit this sideways force.

The spinning keeps you glued to the wall of the carnival ride.

You are squished against the wall, even though the wall can be up-side-down.

Maybe you are going 10m/s.

Imagine going 300 times faster, where the force to keep you in a circle goes as your velocity squared.

That's more than 1000 g's of force.

You can feel a sideways force every time you turn a corner in a car. If you are going 3000m/s in the Sling Shot, then that force is huge.

Balloon Lift and Ion Thruster: Far Out Dreams

Why demand high power and high thrust launches, with semi-explosive power, to get off the ground and fight gravity?
What about floating up to the top of the atmosphere and gradually picking up speed to orbital speeds?
Building up speed in a balloon in the stratosphere is a long shot, given that the balloon is big and there is still air drag even up high at low pressure. The balloon needs to handle the air drag stresses and the thrust needs to be reasonable.
Let's look at what air drag forces are present even high up. Recall that even the somewhat aerodynamic Space Shuttle gets slowed down 70 miles up in the near vacuum of the mesosphere during re-entry, so, unfortunately, any thrust on the balloon from a rocket or jet engine still needs to beat the air drag force on the Space Shuttle. The Space Shuttle gets about 80,000 pounds air drag force to slow down from orbital speed over two time zones.
What rocket engine could the balloon use? The ion rocket below only produces a few pounds of thrust or force to date.
This balloon probably needs to carry chemical rockets just to get reasonable thrust. In contrast, the beauty of solar powered ion rockets is that it is light, but of course we have not solved the weak thrust issue against the much larger air drag.

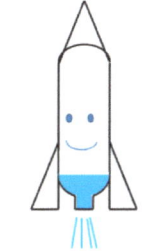

"Go up the slow way, floating on the air for months. The thrust can be much weaker because the air is supporting the rocket."

Airship balloon to orbit, with gradual thrusters:

Don't take 6 minutes to get to orbit, but rather 1 month or longer, using low-thrust ion rocket engines and balloons?

Float to 200 thousand feet (~60 km), and then use ion thruster to accelerate to orbital velocity over a long time. The lift is provided by the air pressure in upper atmosphere and would keep the balloon aloft, giving the weak thrust the opportunity to accelerate the balloon and payload to orbital velocity.

JP Aerospace demonstration of a lifter: push balloon to orbital velocity.

Concept: Airship spirals outward, over a month, as it gradually builds up orbital velocity and can leave the buoyancy and drag of the atmosphere.

What type of strap-on rocket is best to accelerate the balloon?

Fuel/ Oxidizer standard engine:
- If use a chemical reaction rocket, that is just like a ground rocket, and the rocket needs nearly the same amount of fuel.

Cascaded engines:
- If use cascaded engines to grab oxygen in the atmosphere, then the balloon may need to be at lower altitude and have air drag.

Ion engine:
- Ion thrusters have been used for decades as altitude and attitude (angle or orientation) adjustors on satellites, even with low thrust.
- If use an ion rocket, thrust is very low. To get a reasonable thrust at a fixed power, ion rockets only apply a few kilovolts (dc) to accelerate the ions, and the exhaust speed is about 30km/s, or 10 times larger than chemical rockets.
- The thrust depends on the flow rate and available power. A 10 kW power from the solar panels only gives 1 or 2 lb* thrust.
- Ion rockets can have theoretically an exhaust speed approaching the speed of light, but not enough electrical power so very low thrust. The flow rate would be very small to keep the same power level. In contrast, typical chemical rockets use Gigawatts of power over 6 minutes, but an ion rocket to date only uses Kilowatts over years due to limited electric power sources.

Heat from drag

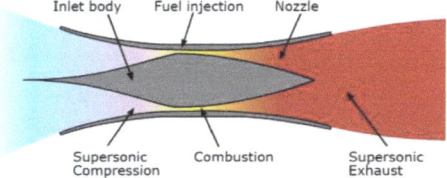

Scramjet engine: use chemical fuel to create the thrust.

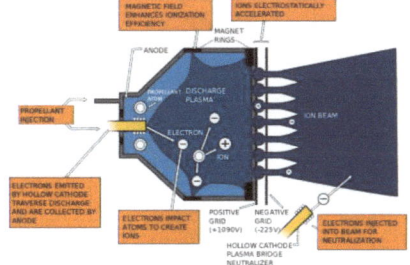

Ion rocket: Electric voltage will accelerate an ion out the back. Solar panels could generate the power to keep the high kV voltage for acceleration.

If we can break the stranglehold of the rocket equation and poor efficiency by floating into orbit, then costs go down. These balloons would be good for launching hardware, not people, into orbit.

Laser Energy From Ground: Far-out Dreams

Maybe some day we'll go to space by heating the exhaust using a laser beam from the ground. The ground laser can heat the ejecting hot water or liquid hydrogen on the rocket. A ground laser avoids a heavy heat source or chemical reaction and fuel on the rocket, but the rocket still needs to carry an exhaust material to get thrust.

"Using lasers from the ground to heat the exhaust gas ... Most scientists would swoon in awe, but so far lasers are completely outrageous."

Ground laser heat may help rocket exhaust as energy source:

Concept of laser beam heating exhaust

Use the heat from the off-board (ground) laser beam to heat air or vaporize water and heat the ejected gases.

Do not need the oxidizer on board

Laser has lots of heat to vaporize gases

Power: 100 kWatt
Super high average power laser beam acts as power source to heat ejected gases. Still, rockets typically use GigaWatts of power during launch.
The heat source could also be a beam of microwave radiation, not just beam of visible light.

Demonstration

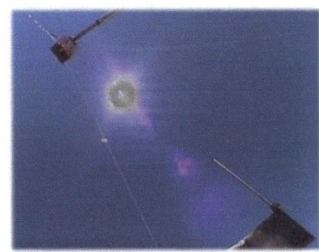

Push upward by heating gas under a disk: Demonstration tests using high power laser.

Spinning Disk: For stability, spin the disk like a Frisbee.

Use heat from a ground laser, not chemical reactions, to eject gases:
- Probably better to use a ground laser to heat liquid or gas in a cavity from the laser. The rocket pumps air into a cavity that gets hot and is ejected. This ejection is similar to how a toy spinning photo-gyro works, with heat from the sun.
- Or, could use a ground laser to provide extra heat to chemical reaction, so molecules leave at even faster exhaust velocity than chemical velocities.
- Use a ground laser to break apart rocket exhaust (H_2O, water molecules), so the lower mass hydrogen H is leaving at a faster exhaust velocity.

Solar Sail: Solar pressure is already demonstrated on space satellites using small sails, but not anywhere near the force magnitude needed to launch off Earth:

Solar sails use force from sunlight, and although the force is extremely weak the sunlight is free.
Unfurl a solar sail to reflect sunlight, but be prepared for long distance very slow trips. This sail has already been demonstrated in space by NASA, with a sail pushed by the Sun (mission NanoSail-D2).

The momentum from sunlight does push slightly after the rocket is in space: the force is extremely weak, but the sail is already out of Earth's gravity.

Rays from the sun keep momentum and push on the solar sail.

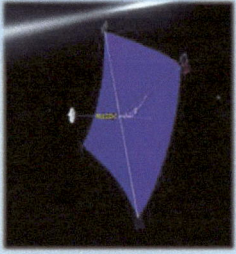
Solar Sail, like ship at sea.

Laser heat is large, but direct force from laser is extremely small:
A laser provides a lot more heat than the extremely small momentum. Heat of laser is good and equals the power of the laser, but force from a laser beam is not practical for launch: we use the laser heat to ejected gases and there is only an extremely weak push from laser pressure itself.

A photon is mostly energy, not momentum, compared to a bullet with mass.
For example, there is ridiculously low direct force from 100 kWatt laser …In terms of direct force, there is something very impractical here, lots of heat but no momentum. The momentum per photon exists but is very weak.

Maybe laser heat can heat up the gas to allow high speed exhaust velocity, instead of or in combination with a chemical reaction. Radiation from the Sun has already been used to push satellites far from Earth.

Laser Energy From Ground: Far-out Dreams

Maybe some day we'll go to space by heating and ejecting hot water or liquid hydrogen on the rocket, heated by a laser beam from the ground. A ground laser avoids a heavy heat source or chemical reaction and fuel on the rocket, but the rocket still needs to carry an exhaust material to get thrust.

"Using lasers from the ground to heat the exhaust gas ... Most scientists would swoon in awe, but so far lasers are completely outrageous."

Laser can really cut metal with near continuous laser pulses

Even the movies assume lasers are only for burning holes.

There are military laser cannons to disable incoming weapons like drones and missiles, typically by blinding the sensors.

Laser can burn holes in thick metal sheets. Laser can burn hole through buildings, like the exaggerated 'Godzilla versus King Kong' movie. Laser typically do not hit us and cause us to fly backwards from the momentum of the hit. Instead they burn a hole through us if they are powerful enough.

Maybe laser heat can heat up the gas to allow high speed exhaust velocity, instead of or in combination with a chemical reaction. Radiation from the Sun has already been used to push satellites far from Earth.

Space Elevator: Far-out Dreams

Let's climb a cable. Remember Jack and the Beanstalk? Instead of climbing to the clouds we could climb a cable or space elevator far into space, into the blackness of space where there is no air. The cable is hanging from a huge space station far away near geo-stationary orbit. This cable can rotate with the Earth if there is a huge weight at geo-stationary orbit, well above low Earth orbit. If the station is a little lower, then the cable can drag at Mach 1 over the Earth.

"Inventing a super strong cable for the elevator ...again, scientists would swoon in awe, if built, but so far a 20 thousand mile long cable into space is completely outrageous."

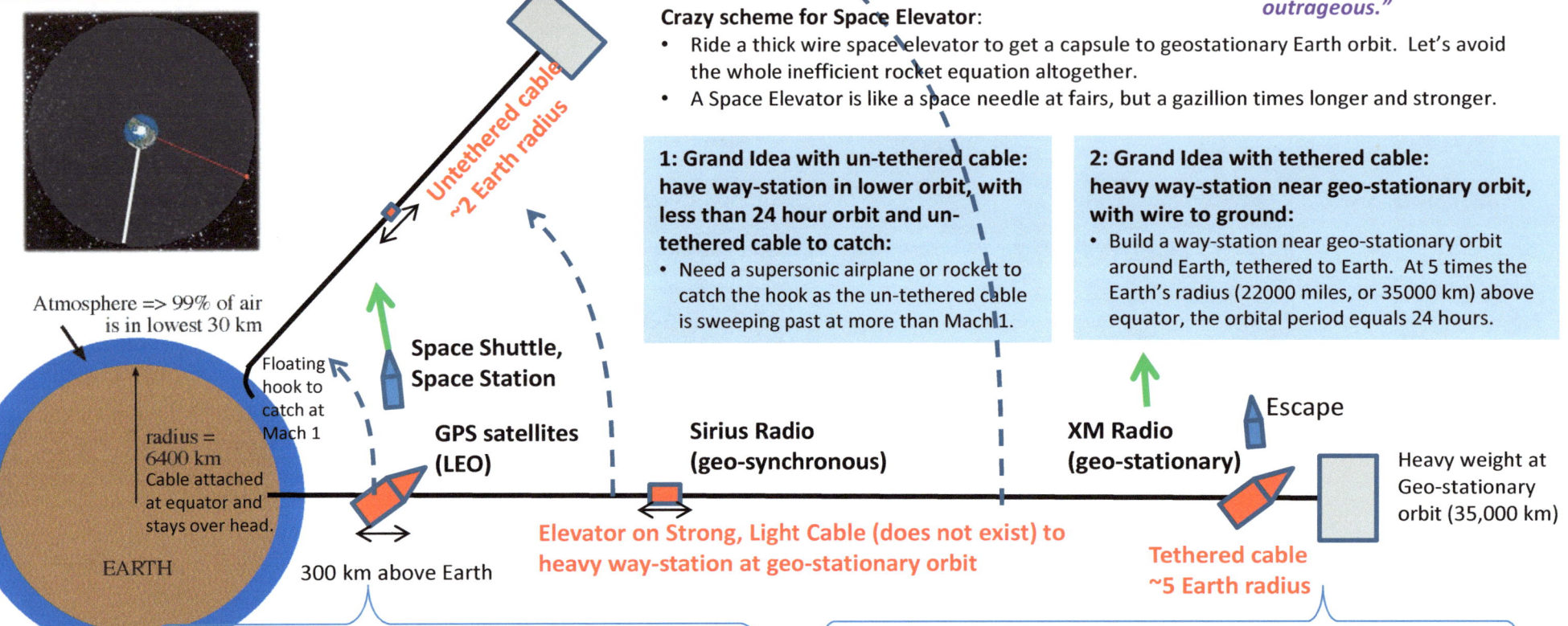

Crazy scheme for Space Elevator:
- Ride a thick wire space elevator to get a capsule to geostationary Earth orbit. Let's avoid the whole inefficient rocket equation altogether.
- A Space Elevator is like a space needle at fairs, but a gazillion times longer and stronger.

1: Grand Idea with un-tethered cable: have way-station in lower orbit, with less than 24 hour orbit and un-tethered cable to catch:
- Need a supersonic airplane or rocket to catch the hook as the un-tethered cable is sweeping past at more than Mach 1.

2: Grand Idea with tethered cable: heavy way-station near geo-stationary orbit, with wire to ground:
- Build a way-station near geo-stationary orbit around Earth, tethered to Earth. At 5 times the Earth's radius (22000 miles, or 35000 km) above equator, the orbital period equals 24 hours.

If only want to go into low Earth orbit, then you are already there using part of the elevator, although not going fast enough:
- *To get extra speed, to launch into low Earth orbit, you still need to use a rocket to speed up the satellite to orbital velocity at your chosen altitude, but can use smaller rocket. One idea is to go higher, and then descend to get more speed. Low Earth orbit has a period of 90 minutes, and the cable tracks the Earth at 24 hours.*

- *To launch a rocket from geo stationary orbit to escape Earth, can get the rocket on an elevator to a way-station, at the 5 times the Earth's radius altitude, then the energy to escape Earth is reduced to just 4% of the energy at the Earth's surface. That sounds very enticing.*

Engineering Needs:
- Un-obtainium: Super light, super strong cable.
One candidate:
- Cable made from carbon nano-tubes.

Heavy way-station at end of tethered cable: Our cable and a satellite stays over the same square inch of land, so we want a 24 hour period for our elevator cable. Orbit period around Earth depends on altitude. To make orbit period equal to one day, need to go out to geo-stationary orbit, at 22000 miles. If any closer, or less radius, then the satellite would move too fast and wrap the cable around the Earth.
Planet of choice location: Possibly the first Space elevator will be created on the Moon, where the gravity is less.   https://en.wikipedia.org/wiki/Geostationary_orbit

If we can make some un-obtainium wire — a light weight and super strong wire — then this space elevator is possible.

Space Elevator: Far-out Dreams

How would we build this Space Elevator on Earth? Are other planets with lower gravity and less air and a faster spin a better fit? Is the Earth, Moon or Mars a better fit for Space Elevator or Rail Guns?

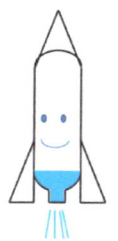

How would we even build this cable into space? Really the cable is just hanging from a very heavy space station in geostationary orbit.

This cable can rotate with the Earth if there is a huge weight at geo-stationary orbit, well above low Earth orbit.

The cable is actually not something that is holding the space station in, and in fact is just dangling from the heavy space station. That space station is already in a stable orbit. For geo-stationary orbit at the right distance from Earth at 5 radii, the orbital period is 24 hours so the space station just stays over the same spot on Earth. So the space station is the 'rock' that we are building off of.

The cable will need to be thicker high up at the space station, because that is where the tension is from supporting the weight of the lower 20000 miles of cable.

How would we install this cable in space from Earth?

We'd need thousands of rockets to bring the cable up to the space station and then reel it down. And we'd need to build the heavy space station as well.

Maybe after the upper part of the cable is in place, we could fire up cable strands from the ground to connect to the dangling cable in mid distance.

Possibly we could send a very thin cable up from ground to the space station. Then we can gradually use this cable to pull up thicker cables.

"Inventing a super strong cable for the elevator ...again, scientists would swoon in awe, if built, but so far a 20 thousand mile long cable into space is completely outrageous."

Earth application: Would this space elevator be better on the Earth, or is a rail gun better on Earth?

Earth is harder for a rail gun, because there is air drag and because gravity is larger. On the other hand, a rail gun is almost do-able. Nothing is suspended in space, and we build a 400 mile long rail that gradually goes up a 5 mile mountain.

So a space elevator makes more sense for the Earth, because gravity is large and the spin rate is relatively large, so the elevator is 'only' 5 Earth radii long. But a space elevator is still almost impossible to build.

Moon application: Would this space elevator be better on the Moon, or is a rail gun better on the Moon?

The gravity of the Moon is only 1/6th of Earth's gravity, so it is relatively easy to blast off the Moon. Also, the Moon has no atmosphere so a rail gun is a much better candidate to launch rockets off the Moon, rather than a space elevator.

The Moon also rotates very very slowly, because it is tidally linked to the Earth. The Moon always keeps the same side facing Earth, with a 28 day orbit. For the tethered space elevator, that means that a space elevator orbiting the Moon would need to be at a very high orbit to keep the 28 day orbital period. Probably instead we'd use an untethered cable, just to keep the cable length shorter. We'd still need a rocket to catch the orbiting cable, and airplanes are not available without an atmosphere.

A rail gun makes more sense for the Moon, with low gravity, low spin rate, and no air drag.

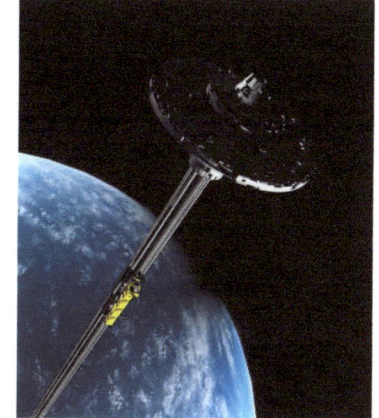

Concept of space elevator for Earth.

Mars application: Would this space elevator be better on the Mars, or is a rail gun better on Mars?

The gravity of the Mars is only 1/3rd of Earth's gravity, so it is also relatively easy to blast off Mars. Also, Mars has some but little atmosphere, so air drag for a rail gun is also low and good. Because the day period is about the same as Earth at 24 hours, the space elevator does not need to be as long, and a space elevator is more practical.

This tethered space elevator cable is just dangling from the Space Station in geo-stationary orbit.

A Proposed Mars Transfer Vehicle, an Orbiting Gas Station

Can sling shots or rail guns supply an orbiting gas station? This station is not launching a human up because the accelerations are huge, but we can refuel rockets and just launch supplies into orbit. Let's launch the fuel into orbit to assemble or refill a fully charged rocket to then blast to escape Earth's orbit and head to Mars.
Where's the closest gas station in space? Let the rocket re-supply itself with fuel in LEO, to go much faster to the Moon or Mars, before the rocket escapes Earth's orbit. Just adding 4 km/second speed to the rocket can shorten the trip to Mars by months. Below is a description of the shorter timeline to get to Mars if we can throw fuel into orbit.

Most 9 month estimates of the time to get to Mars assume that we have a 3 stage rocket and that most of the original fuel is used up just launching into orbit around Earth. Then the remaining fuel would get the last stage to 3 km/sec speed. We break that paradigm if we add more fuel when the rocket has already achieved orbit. Currently all we have for transportation is the technology of rockets to launch fuel and supplies, and that is expensive. The rocket to leave Earth is now more expensive because multiple rockets are required to launch the fuel into Earth's orbit. SpaceX plans to use supply rockets to get fuel to an orbiting fuel station.
As a better solution or technology, rather than rockets, the fuel could be launched more cheaply with higher g's. For example, a high-g launch for the fuel could be a shorter EM rail gun or a sling shot catapult.
There are also other approaches to get to Mars quicker, instead of just a fuel re-fill, so an orbiting gas station around Earth isn't the only idea out there. An ion rocket can also accelerate the rocket over a month to get to Mars in 3 months instead of 9 months. Also, luckily, we don't need to carry much fuel to slow down to land on the Mars surface. The atmosphere of Mars can slow down the rocket using air drag instead of requiring retro rockets, even at 1% of the Earth's atmospheric pressure.

Orbiting gas station, with many deliveries of rockets to supply fuel.

Get a fuel re-fill in orbit from an orbiting gas station.
Send up fuel and oxidizer into Earth orbit, to be used for another rocket to fly to Mars more quickly than 9 months.

Fuel deliveries, using high-g rail guns or spin launches instead of rockets.

Hyper velocity projectiles from rail guns to throw fuel up into orbit?

High-g Spinlaunch to throw fuel up into orbit?

If we can find a low cost way to launch fuel and oxidizer into orbit, just by themselves using a rail gun, then the human launches can be more efficient. The fuel and oxidizer can be launched using high-g rail guns or spin catapults, and without people these launches are allowed to exceed a 10 g limit.
https://en.wikipedia.org/wiki/Orion_(spacecraft)#/media/File:Orion_docked_to_Mars_Transfer_Vehicle.jpg

To shorten travel time around the solar system, let high-thrust chemical rockets kick-start the flight, and then refill the high-thrust chemicals with fuel already launched into orbit.

Summary: What Improbable Alternatives to Rockets are People Looking At?

> Whatever alternatives people think about to replace rockets – such as long rail guns, balloons, lasers, space elevators, or nuclear heat or explosions – it is a healthy exercise to challenge the inefficiency of today's rockets.
> For example, trains challenged horse pulled carriages across country in the 1850s. Cars with batteries or combustion engines challenged horse pulled carriages in the cities in the 1910s. Dirigibles with propellers challenged hot air balloons in the 1910s. Airplanes challenged ocean steam ships and air dirigibles in the 1930s. Jet planes challenged propeller combustion engine airplanes in the 1950s.

The good old rocket: What are the big advantages of our current rockets, over alternatives? -Alternatives are alternatives or runner ups for a reason. **The good old chemical rocket provides semi-explosive thrust for minutes to get to fight gravity and orbit in space.**
- A typical chemical rocket works well. Air drag issues have been overcome, gradual accelerations have been designed, and the rocket can be custom designed for different payload weights and different orbits. Unfortunately, rockets are still expensive and every launch is a big deal.

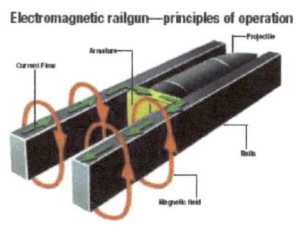

Rail gun

Push balloon to orbital velocity

Use ground laser to heat exhaust gas

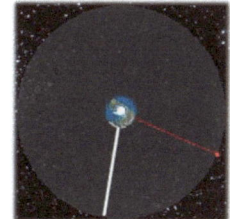

Climb up a geostationary elevator cable

Improbable 1: Rail Guns: How about rail guns using electricity to launch stuff into orbit, like a cannon? -The acceleration can happen over 100s of miles, but the spacecraft still needs a rocket section afterwards to get through the air drag.
- Yes, but need a very long rail gun (500 miles) if stick to less than 10 g's acceleration, just like the distances a rocket travels through air during thrust and acceleration during launch to orbital velocity. Moreover, a rail gun needs to place the end of the launch tube in the low pressure of the upper atmosphere to minimize air drag.
- Rail gun idea works a lot better on the Moon (still 100 miles long), where gravity is 1/3rd Earth, and there is no water to make liquid fuel to launch a chemical rocket. There is plenty of sunlight available to use solar panels to charge up batteries to use for a rail gun.

Improbable 2: Balloons: What's wrong with using a balloon to float to the top of atmosphere, and then gradually accelerate to orbital velocities? -Air drag.
- Well, there is air drag as the balloon is getting accelerated. Ion rockets have the potential to be very efficient due to the high exhaust velocity, but the typical weak thrust on an ion rocket needs to be large enough to counteract air drag, which will be 1000s of pounds, and weak thrust means a long time to build up the velocity.

Improbable 3: Laser Heating: If laser beams have very little pressure, how can they help rockets? -Laser heat from the ground can heat the exhaust gas without a chemical reaction, if the laser is powerful and well aimed.
- Laser beams have little physical pressure, even for high energy beams, but they have huge energy or heat. The laser can heat up the gas in the rocket, for high speed exhaust, as long as there is still a supply of exhaust gas on board.

Improbable 4: Space Elevators: Can space elevators work, 22000 miles long? - Hang a cable from a heavy satellite in space. We need an extremely strong but lightweight cable, and we need a way to launch the cable to assemble the elevator.
- Space elevators could be great. Do away with rocket launches from ground. Have an elevator go up and down the elevator cable like a very tall building, only this cable is 22000 miles, 5 times the radius of the Earth, to geo-stationary orbit.
- Unfortunately, this elevator idea needs a very light and very strong cable, which is not yet able to be built, that is, 'un-obtainium'. People are thinking about wires made from carbon nanotubes, if scientists and material engineers can make carbon tubes meters or kilometers long.

What's Not Going to Space? Need Lots of Energy and Steady Thrust

Let's look at various projectiles, and see if they've gotten to space: Projectiles just coast after the initial thrust.
Bullets are blasted from cannons, and the air drag and high-temperature melting stops them from getting out of the atmosphere.
Water bottles with air pressure just don't have the energy to go more than 1 km up.
Toy chemical rockets are not designed for high performance. Toy chemical rockets don't have much fuel (low mass ratio), and the chemical reaction of the less-expensive type of solid fuel (gun powder) used does not have the highest exhaust velocity.

Hyper-sonic projectile

Evel Knieval: Test firing a steam rocket, to cross a canyon

Poseidon get-out-of-water blast from steam, before chemical ignition

Not Space Rocket 1: Have bullets gone into outer space? -By definition, bullets have a quick large initial push, and then they coast, unlike a rocket which keeps a steady thrust using exhaust. Fast bullets launched from ground level would just overheat and slow down due to air drag.
- No, a regular bullet speed is only Mach 2 or so just leaving the barrel, and air drag quickly slows the bullet down and it falls.
- A hyper-sonic very heavy bullet out of a tank cannon might reach Mach 8, but that is still not fast enough, when need Mach 25 for orbit. The bullet needs to be very heavy and withstand all the air drag and the heating. Some Mach 8 bullets are made with very heavy uranium. The bullet heats up, air drag slows it down, and it falls. With the heavy metal, the heat on the surface can quickly spread to the middle.

Not Space Rocket 2: Has a water bottle rocket gone into space? -No, the energy of compressed gas is not enough, and the thrust does not last long enough.
- No, even at a very high pressure of 500 psi, the exhaust speed of the water is too slow (80 m/s), and is no match to the exhaust speed from a chemical reaction (3000 to 4000 m/s). Water also runs out too quickly.
- On the brighter side, high pressure steam has more hope, but still not as much energy as a chemical liquid or solid fuel rocket. The dare-devil Evel Knievel did fly across a canyon in a steam powered rocket (although he drifted back into the canyon when his parachute deployed too early).

Not Space Rocket 3: Has a toy Estes or Quest solid fuel rocket gone into space? -No, the mass ratio is only 1.1.
- No, the mass ratio of a toy rocket does not allow enough continuous thrust and not enough fuel. A typical toy Estes solid fuel engine is only a small fraction of the hardware dry mass of the rocket. That low fuel mass means that the final rocket speed will not get much faster than its exhaust speed of about 1000 m/s, which is not enough to go to outer space (need 8000 m/s for low Earth orbit, or need 1500 m/s just to go straight up and down to 100km without air drag).
- Estes rockets are designed for safety, and oohs and ahhs, and to stay within visual range for easy recovery.
- Also, the toy Estes rocket would have no stability in space because fins would not work. Fins need the drag from flowing air. Space rockets need vectored nozzles instead.

Rocket engineers go back to chemical reactions to launch into space because chemical reactions have lots of energy and it works.

Chapter 8: Where Does Nuclear Power Fit In?

Nuclear fusion or fission has about 1000 times more energy than chemical reactions, and obviously needs to be harnessed somehow for deep space missions if humans are to stay in the outer solar system or especially to visit other stars. Starlight won't be around to power solar panels in deep space.
The nuclear energy can be used for propulsion, and for electricity to power the electronics and the life support system of the rocket.

Electronics and Life Support, from steady nuclear generator to generate a moderate few kiloWatt of electricity over a decade:

Let's say we are at the outer solar system, with little solar heat, and we plan to stay there for years. Where is the power coming from?

Batteries will have long drained out. Our chemical fuel will be gone, unless we can find methane and oxygen on some moon or asteroid, which people are trying to do.

Solar panels will not work well, because the Sun is just a tiny dot with very little heat this far away. Recall that those outer gas planets are near absolute zero temperature.

So we need nuclear power for these outer planets. Nuclear power can provide electricity for decades, and provide its own heat to help keep the satellite warm.

Thrust, after achieving orbit, from accelerating exhaust using huge nuclear power of 100 MegaWatt to 10 GigaWatt:

Strangely, thrust from nuclear power is not going to be larger than a chemical rocket, at least with current technology. The thrust from nuclear power will last more than 1000 times longer than a chemical rocket, and the exhaust velocity can be 10 to a million times faster than a chemical rocket. But the instantaneous thrust will not be more than a chemical rocket, which probably still makes chemical rockets the go-to solution for launching a rocket off a planet against the force of gravity.

Let's look at a sports analogy. Chemical rockets run a sprint, and Nuclear rockets would run a marathon. A nuclear powered rocket will not get a rocket to launch against gravity from the ground, but a nuclear powered rocket could get the rocket to go much faster when already in outer space.

Ion rocket approach:

The thrust can come from an electric ion rocket. The heat source from the nuclear reaction will generate the electricity, and the electricity will power the ion rocket, which accelerates ions out the back using an electric field like in old TV screens. The ions are recombined with electrons after the ions leave, so there is no electric attraction between the rocket and the exhaust after the exhaust leaves.

Current chemical rockets use 10 GigaWatts to get off the ground, and even nuclear power stations sprawling on the ground do not generate 10 GigaWatts. So nuclear power will not be used to launch off the ground. That kind of instant power belongs to the chemical rockets.

Rockets already in space can use less thrust and less power, without fighting gravity, and the stored energy in nuclear reactions is 1000 times more powerful than any stored energy in a chemical reaction. So a nuclear reactor can power an ion rocket for years in outer space. The nuclear and ion rocket still need some gas to shoot out the back, so we still are limited by the gas supply.

Thermal nuclear propulsion approach:

We could have hydrogen gas that is heated by a radioactive heat source, called thermal nuclear propulsion. There is no conversion to electrical power.

Fusion in a gas approach:

We could have nuclear fusion in a plasma. That plasma is then expelled as exhaust. There is no conversion to electrical power. The plasma is the exhaust.

Explosion approach:

The thrust can come from exploding tiny nuclear bombs out the back end of the rocket.

"Movies always assume energy is always available for space travel for year long missions. Well, that means nuclear power at least, like fission or fusion.

Sometimes movies assume something even more glorious, like anti-matter, but we won't discuss that here. We don't know how to make large amounts of anti-matter and we don't know how to contain it."

When space craft get far away from the Sun, the solar power from solar panels is very small. It is better to use a hot fission source to power the electronics. If we want to have continuous propulsion during the mission, nuclear power offers much more energy for the weight. There are many ways nuclear energy is being considered to help the thrust of space craft.

Where Does Nuclear Power Fit In?

Nuclear fusion or fission has about 1000 times more energy than chemical reactions, and obviously needs to be harnessed somehow for deep space missions if humans are to stay in the outer solar system or especially to visit other stars.
The nuclear energy can be used at extreme powers for propulsion, and at low powers for electricity to power the electronics and life support system of the rocket.

"Movies always assume energy is always available for space travel for year long missions. Well, that means nuclear power at least, like fission or fusion.

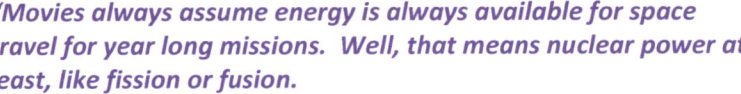

Real nuclear power:

Nuclear power for submarine:
~4GigaWatt of heat and 300MegaWatt of power using nuclear fission heat, to heat water to turn a generator and steam engine.

Nuclear power for electricity on satellites:
~1kiloWatt power using nuclear fission heat, to heat thermoelectric crystals with no moving parts.

Nuclear power station in Seabrook New Hampshire:
~1.2GigaWatt power using nuclear fission heat, to heat water to turn a generator and steam engine.

Science fiction nuclear power in the movies (that is, not real yet):

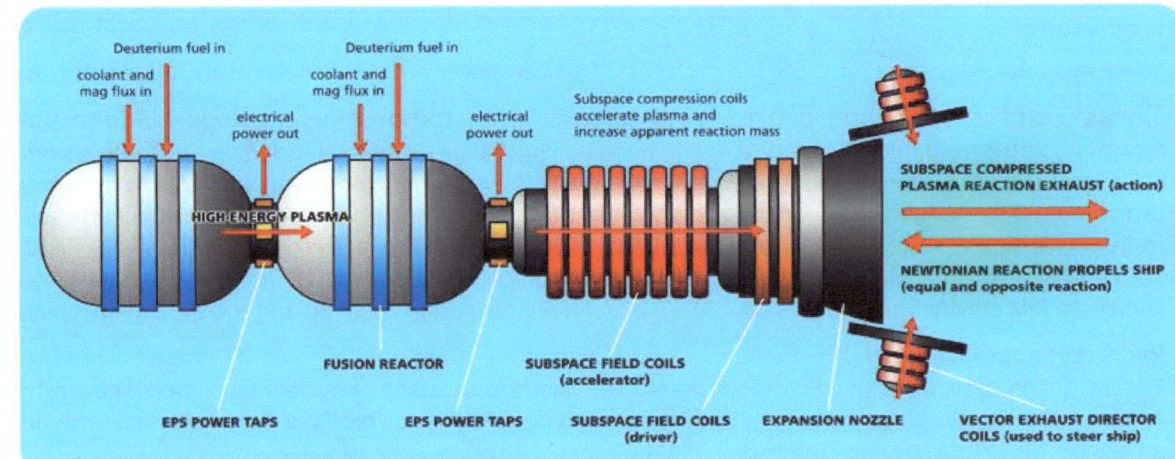

Science Fiction fusion impulse engine:
The movies with Star Trek impulse power using fusion: Can it produce 100's of GigaWatts?
100's of GigaWatts are necessary to move around a solar system in weeks.

- We've already had a few KiloWatt nuclear power on spacecraft, but only for electricity for sensors, communication, and some heating. A few kW power source can also supply a very weak ion rocket, much less than 1 pound.
- The movies, like Star Trek, assume in the future we will have 100's of Giga Watts or more of fusion power for the impulse engines. That power of course is nothing compared to the warp drives, which use anti-matter / matter annihilation for heat.

Chapter 8A: What Nuclear Power Energy Sources are There for Electricity?

Nuclear power is probably necessary for long term space travel, simply to have power for the electronics and maybe to keep the spacecraft warm. So, with current technology, we use nuclear power only for electricity at a few kiloWatts and we depend on chemistry for rocket thrust at GigaWatts to get off the Earth.

If spacecraft always stay close to the Sun or a star where the sunlight is bright then, yes, maybe we just use solar panels. But the outer planets are far from the Sun where the sunlight is dim. Also, when landing on a planet, the planet rotates and the spacecraft is blocked from the Sun by nighttime, just like on Earth.

Nuclear power of electronics, using nuclear heat for either thermoelectric power or a Stirling engine

Mars Curiosity rover and satellites are powered by a radioisotope thermoelectric generator.
The heat from a nuclear reaction causes a temperature drop across a crystal, which makes a voltage with no moving parts.

Mars base is probably powered by Stirling engine, or piston based generator.
The heat from a nuclear reaction heats steam, which pushes a piston and spins a generator.

Nuclear thermal (steady heat): Do you want to go nuclear for electricity, not thrust, where the radioactive material just serves as a heat source?
- Well, nuclear power in outer space is already typically done to power the satellite's electronics, at least as a power source for electricity on satellites that can't get enough electric power from solar panels, far out in the solar system.
- For a thermoelectric generator, the nuclear heat will power a thermo-electric ceramic to generate a voltage. This heat conversion is the same idea as camp generators with no moving parts (no spinning generator, instead using a heat gradient across a ceramic) to charge your cell phone while camping.
- Power conversion from nuclear heat can also come from the Stirling engine. This is similar to a nuclear power plant, where heating a gas turns a generator. The gas would be closed cycle and cooled by the planet.

History and Future Use of Nuclear Power for Electricity

We already use nuclear power for spacecraft, from the Voyager spacecraft from the 1970s to the Mars rovers.
Heat from nuclear power can be used to create electricity.
Approach 1: The heat can power a radioisotope thermoelectric generator. This is just a heat gradient across a thermocouple crystal, which makes a voltage with no moving parts.
Approach 2: The heat can also power a spinning generator, with steam or some other liquid to boil, like power plants here on Earth. This spinning generator is a 'Stirling' process.

"Nuclear power is dangerous, but it does have the absolute best energy to mass. Nuclear power with fission is already used to generate electricity in space, like the Voyager satellite in the 70s, still kicking."

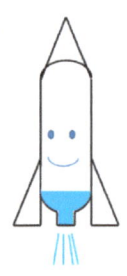

Thermoelectric generators using a crystal and temperature gradient

Nuclear Reactors using hot steam or hot gas and spinning turbines

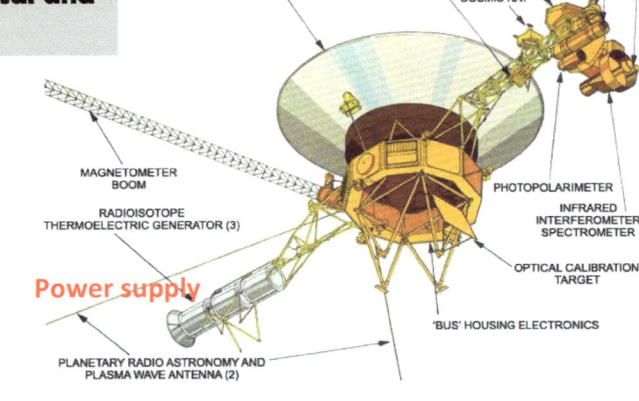

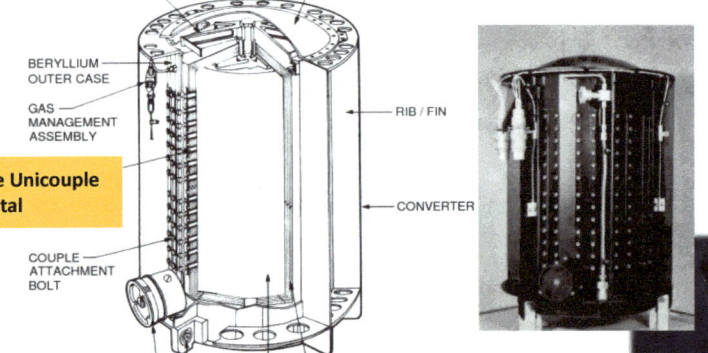

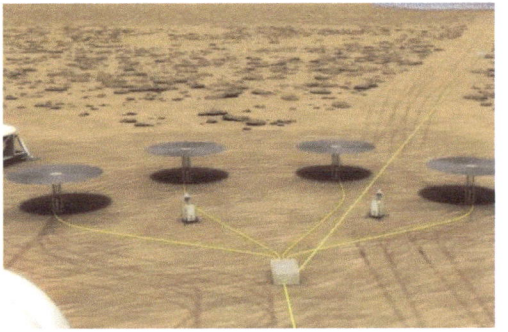

Rovers and electric power:
Mars Curiosity rover is powered by a radioisotope thermoelectric generator (RTG), using plutonium-238.
The nuclear heat helps keep the rover warm, as well as provide about 100 Watts of electrical power due to the thermal gradient.

Space nuclear thermoelectric generator:
Voyager spacecraft, using thermoelectric generator for 100s of Watts for decades. The crystal thermocouple is made of Silicon Germanium.

Campfire thermoelectric generator:
You can power a cell phone from a camp fire using this effect.

Nuclear power on Mars for bases:
KRUSTY (kilopower reactor using Stirling technology) can be used on Mars to provide electricity during nighttime or dust storms.

The pictures shows a concept of 4 KRUSTY generators with heat radiators on Mars.

Stirling technology means spinning a generator using a heated gas or liquid flowing through a turbine.

DARPA has a program to get nuclear propulsion out of Earth's orbit by 2025.

Chapter 8B: The Dream: Most Ideal Travel Profile to get to Other Planets in Our Solar System or Stars

We basically want a rocket that can keep 1 g of thrust throughout the entire flight to the other planet within our solar system or get to other stars, and we'll depend on some form of nuclear power to enable that thrust.
Let's ignore the fact that we will need a steady 10 GigaWatts of power to accomplish this.
Let's ignore the fact that for current chemical rockets we can only get 1 g of thrust for a few minutes, not days or a year.
Let's back away from any real implementation of a dream technology to get the thrust, and just assume we can get 1 g of thrust for a long time. At this really high level of conversation regarding flight times, we don't even need to know the technology for the thrust, we just need to know that we have waved a magic wand and the thrust exists.
To get the flight time, that is a simple calculation. With a steady 1-g thrust, what is the rocket timeline now? Within the solar system, we need 1-g thrust only for a few hours to get to planets in a day or so. Between stars, with a steady 1-g thrust will get us to near the speed of light in a year. So travel to a star 10 light years away would be about 20 years, not 1000 years using current chemical technology.

Within the Solar System: Travel times at 1 g steady thrust, the dream

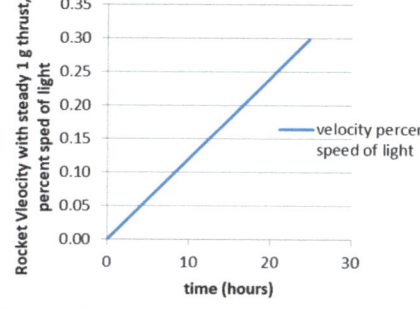

1 day to the planets at 1 g

Solar System ideal travel time of hours with make-believe steady 1-g thrust:
At a 1 g steady acceleration, the rocket would get to most every part of our solar system with one day.
If nuclear power can make this dream a realty, then we can keep the dream of convenient travel to Mars and Jupiter alive.

Outside the Solar System: Travel times at 1 g steady thrust, the dream

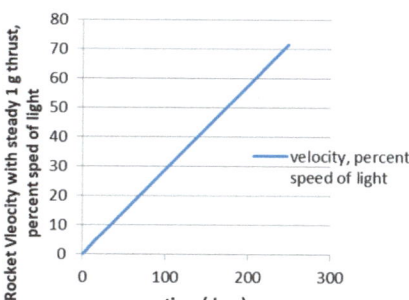

20 years to closer stars if get to half the speed of light at 1 g

Let's assume we have a rocket that can always travel with a thrust that creates 1 g of acceleration. This is conceptually possible with fusion power.
If we are only considering travel within our solar system, then trips to the outer planets can take weeks instead of years. So there is a more grounded reason to pursue nuclear power for thrust, where we are 'shooting for the planets' instead of 'shooting for the stars'.
Now, no nuclear power is yet invented to use nuclear power directly for thrust. For fission power to heat the regular exhaust, or nuclear thermal propulsion, we are still only talking about exhaust velocities on the order of chemical reactions. For fission power converted to electricity to power an ion rocket, then we can get faster exhaust velocities. For fusion power where the nuclear reaction products are used as the exhaust, then, yes, they have fast exhaust velocity, but we don't have a way to control their direction except from some extreme large magnetic fields. Also, we are asking for 10s or 100s of GigaWatts from a smallish rocket. That of course has not been developed.
Nuclear power is probably necessary for long term space travel. So, do we use nuclear power only for electricity and depend on chemistry for thrust? Do we make more powerful nuclear reactors to get a reasonable thrust, meaning typical extreme rocket thrust? No matter what we do, we still need to eject something, so the thrust will only last as long as our tank of material to eject. With nuclear power for thrust, a steady power is available over months or years. Regarding the exhaust, we are better off ejecting stuff with extreme exhaust velocity but at low mass rate, so we keep our exhaust 'stuff' for as long as possible and we get the most momentum change.

Star ideal travel time of 10's of years with make-believe steady 1-g thrust:
At a 1 g steady acceleration, the rocket would get to about 50% of the speed of light in 200 days. Trying to go faster than that would just use lots of energy, and the rocket would be fighting relativistic effects. So the rocket can just coast after it gets to 50% of the speed of light.
At 50% of the speed of light, a star 10 light years away would take about 20 years.
If we had energy to throw away, then we can keep accelerating to close to the speed of light, but the thrust necessary would be larger and larger.

With potential 1-g thrust using fusion, convenient solar system travel would be possible, and star travel would take 20 year. But within current technology limits, not 1 g steady thrust, we're talking 1000 years to get to neighboring solar systems using ion rockets and nuclear power. We're either talking hibernation, or more than 30 generations of people during the trip.

The Dream: Most Ideal Travel Profile to get Around our Solar System, with 200 MegaWatts of Power

Let's assume we have some magic wand and we get nuclear thermal power of exhaust gas or we get fusion power to directly create the exhaust gas, without melting our rocket. Now we can get an almost feasible 200 MegaWatts of power and exhaust velocities about 0.01% of the speed of light. This is all a direct heat transfer to the exhaust gas, without any intermediate step of generating huge electricity.

Probably we do not use conversion of the heat to electricity, because then we don't get the 200 MegaWatts of power for an ion rocket. Regardless, let's assume 200 MegaWatts of power. What is the rocket timeline now to travel around the solar system?

Let's look at ways we can travel with different power sources between stars, with fusion power, with solar panels, or with standard chemical rockets. Note that none of the possible technologies has 1 g acceleration or thrust for any long period of time. The thrust is only 10s of pounds force, but for a steady long time.

If we are only considering travel within our solar system, then trips to the outer planets can take weeks instead of years. So there is a more grounded reason to pursue nuclear power for thrust, where we are 'shooting for the planets' instead of 'shooting for the stars'.

Now, no nuclear power is yet invented to use nuclear power directly for thrust. For fission power to heat the regular exhaust, we are still only talking about exhaust velocities on the order of chemical reactions. For fission power converted to electricity to power an ion rocket, then we can get faster exhaust velocities. For fusion power where the nuclear reaction products are used as the exhaust, then, yes, they have fast exhaust velocity, but we don't have a way to control their direction except from some extreme large magnetic fields. Also, we are asking for 10s or 100s of GigaWatts from a smallish rocket. That of course has not been developed.

Weeks and Months of Travel to Other Planets in Our Solar System
using high power nuclear engine, or using low power solar panels, or using coasting from a chemical rocket launch.

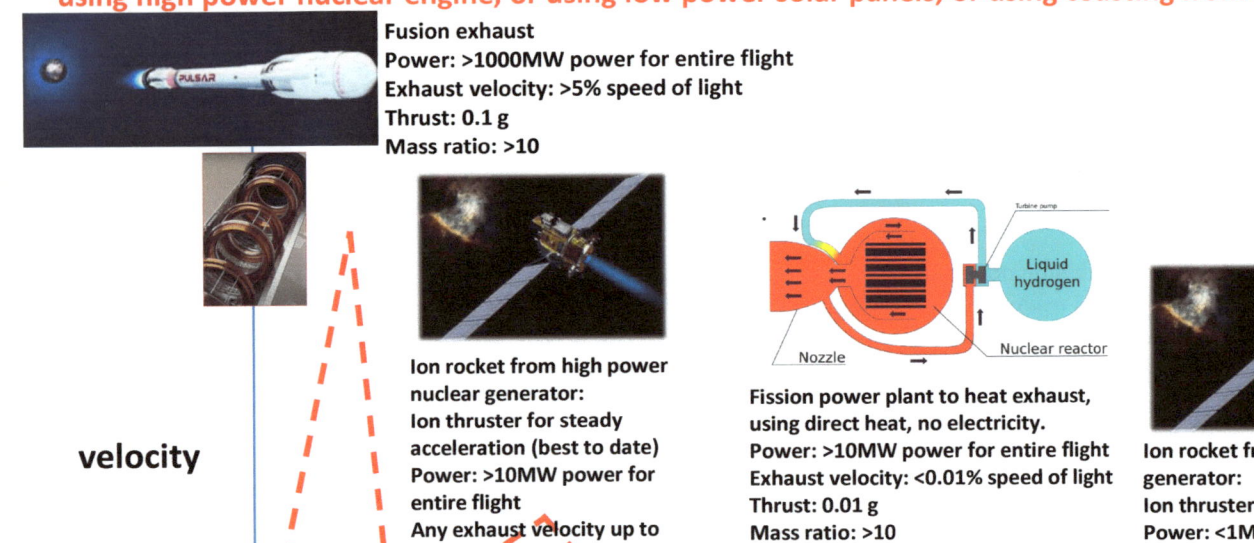

Fusion exhaust
Power: >1000MW power for entire flight
Exhaust velocity: >5% speed of light
Thrust: 0.1 g
Mass ratio: >10

Ion rocket from high power nuclear generator:
Ion thruster for steady acceleration (best to date)
Power: >10MW power for entire flight
Any exhaust velocity up to speed of light, depends on voltage
Mass ratio: >10

Fission power plant to heat exhaust, using direct heat, no electricity.
Power: >10MW power for entire flight
Exhaust velocity: <0.01% speed of light
Thrust: 0.01 g
Mass ratio: >10

Ion rocket from solar panels or low power nuclear generator:
Ion thruster for steady acceleration (best to date)
Power: <1MW power for entire flight
Any exhaust velocity, depends on voltage
Mass ratio: >10

Chemical rocket, with quick thrust and then coasting
Power: >1000MW power for a few minutes at launch
Exhaust velocity: <0.01% speed of light
Mass ratio: >10

velocity — Earth — weeks — **Time to Mars** — months — year

Using chemical rockets, we're talking 1 year to get to Mars, 6 years for the right orbit to get to inner planet Venus, and 10 years to the outer planets. Better to use ion rockets and nuclear power. We're either talking hibernation, or a long trip.

The Dream: Most Ideal Travel Profile to get Between Stars, with 100 GigaWatts of Power

Let's assume we have some magic wand and we get fusion power to directly create the exhaust gas for many, many years. Now we can get >100 GigaWatts of power and exhaust velocities about 10% of the speed of light. What is the rocket timeline now to travel between stars?

Let's look at ways we can travel with different power sources within our solar system, with fusion power, with solar panels, or with standard chemical rockets. Note that none of the possible technologies has 1 g acceleration or thrust for any long period of time.

If we are only considering travel within our solar system, then trips to the outer planets can take weeks instead of years. So there is a more grounded reason to pursue nuclear power for thrust, where we are 'shooting for the planets' instead of 'shooting for the stars'.

Centuries and Millennia of Travel to Other Stars
using high power nuclear engine with fusion, or using lower power exhaust from fission and heat, or using coasting from a chemical rocket launch.

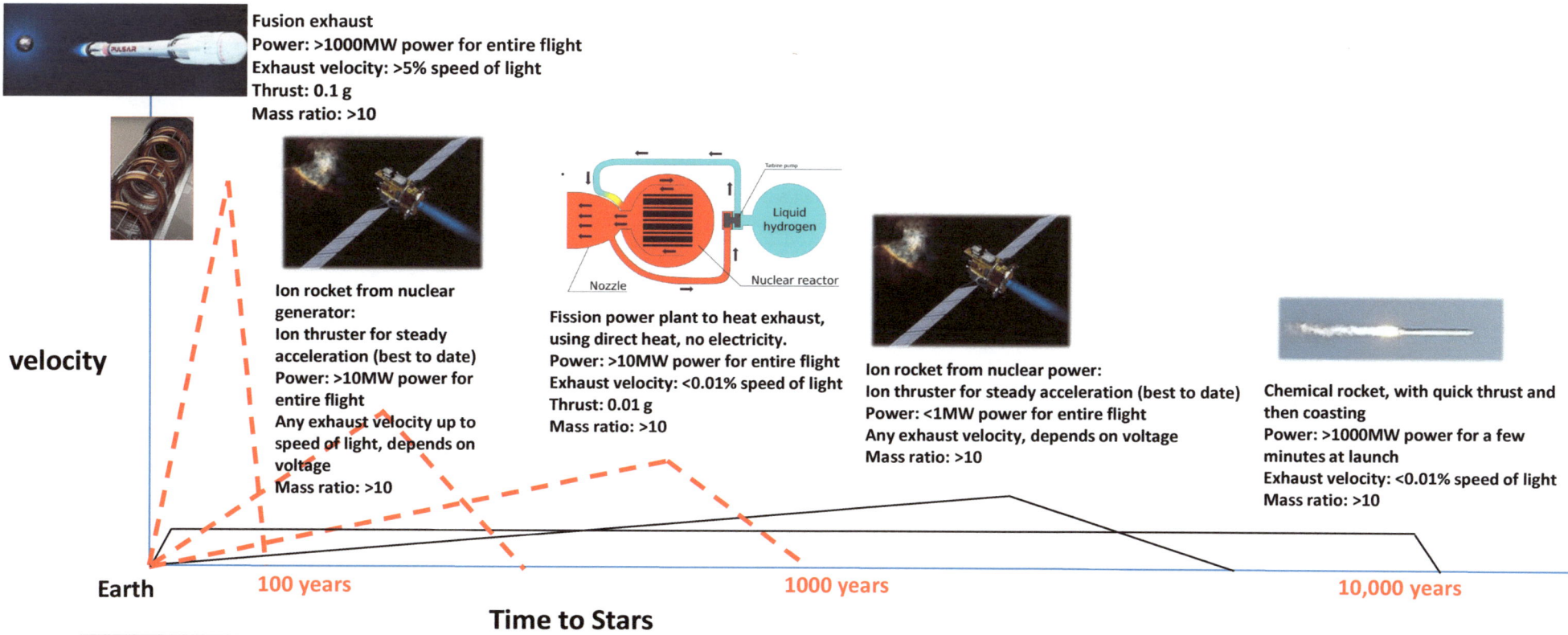

Fusion exhaust
Power: >1000MW power for entire flight
Exhaust velocity: >5% speed of light
Thrust: 0.1 g
Mass ratio: >10

Ion rocket from nuclear generator:
Ion thruster for steady acceleration (best to date)
Power: >10MW power for entire flight
Any exhaust velocity up to speed of light, depends on voltage
Mass ratio: >10

Fission power plant to heat exhaust, using direct heat, no electricity.
Power: >10MW power for entire flight
Exhaust velocity: <0.01% speed of light
Thrust: 0.01 g
Mass ratio: >10

Ion rocket from nuclear power:
Ion thruster for steady acceleration (best to date)
Power: <1MW power for entire flight
Any exhaust velocity, depends on voltage
Mass ratio: >10

Chemical rocket, with quick thrust and then coasting
Power: >1000MW power for a few minutes at launch
Exhaust velocity: <0.01% speed of light
Mass ratio: >10

We're talking 1000 years to get to neighboring solar systems using ion rockets and nuclear power. We're either talking hibernation, or more than 30 generations of people during the trip.

Faster Travel Between Planets: Chemical and Electric Thrust

Rockets don't need to just passively coast between planets. Instead, there can be a constant thrust from an ion rocket boosting the speed*, powered by nuclear power or solar panels with a can of compressed gas to heat for exhaust – ion or chemical rockets, or any rocket, still needs to eject something.

Chemical rockets with fast burn rate work best to get high thrust and escape Earth, and ion rockets with low mass rate work best for a steady lower thrust to keep increasing speed. The final rocket velocity is determined by exhaust velocity, where ion rockets clearly win, not instantaneous thrust (see next chapter, 'Thrust and Rocket Speed').

Cascaded chemical / electric rockets:
1. Chemical rocket provides larger and initial starting push against gravity
2. Nuclear / Ion rocket provides steady inter-planetary push, with more efficiency and faster final rocket speed with a steady build up.

Different rockets and designs for trips to Mars:
Supply ships that can take a long slow time:
- Use chemical rocket only: 7 months. The rocket gets a starting speed using a 10 minute chemical reaction and then coasts the rest of the way, like today.
- A solar sail could also help by reducing the fuel requirement, but the flight time is not much reduced because light has little momentum and sails provide only a little thrust.

Passenger ships with impatient people:
- Use chemical and nuclear/ion rockets: 3 months or less. The chemical rocket will get the rocket either off the ground, or up to a reasonable speed right away, to greatly shorten the trip time. The ion rocket will provide a continuous boost in speed over weeks or months, in a more efficient way. Then the ion rockets provide retro-thrust to slow down over an equal time and match the speed of the planet, if there is no atmosphere to slow down using air drag around the planet.

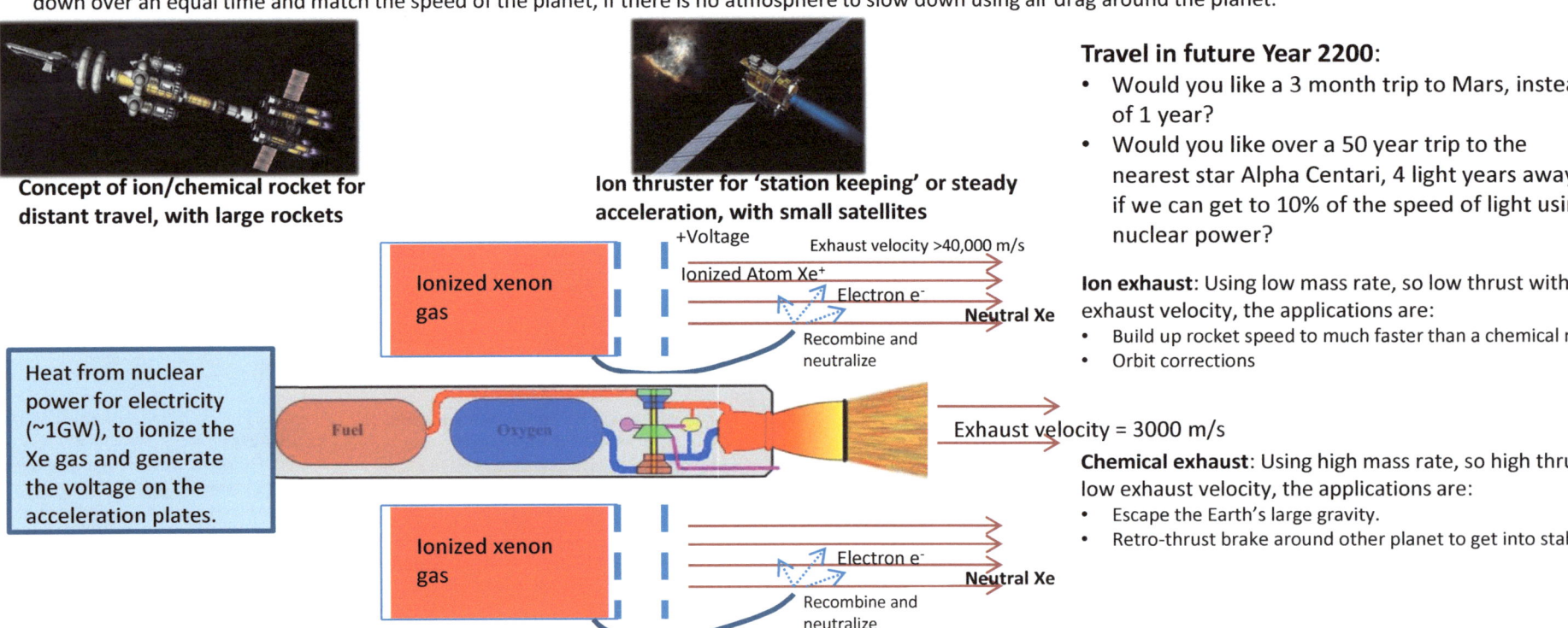

Concept of ion/chemical rocket for distant travel, with large rockets

Ion thruster for 'station keeping' or steady acceleration, with small satellites

Travel in future Year 2200:
- Would you like a 3 month trip to Mars, instead of 1 year?
- Would you like over a 50 year trip to the nearest star Alpha Centari, 4 light years away, if we can get to 10% of the speed of light using nuclear power?

Ion exhaust: Using low mass rate, so low thrust with high exhaust velocity, the applications are:
- Build up rocket speed to much faster than a chemical rocket.
- Orbit corrections

Chemical exhaust: Using high mass rate, so high thrust with low exhaust velocity, the applications are:
- Escape the Earth's large gravity.
- Retro-thrust brake around other planet to get into stable orbit.

Heat from nuclear power for electricity (~1GW), to ionize the Xe gas and generate the voltage on the acceleration plates.

Combined chemical and ion thrust to first get off the ground and then keep accelerating for months.

*https://www.nasa.gov/centers/glenn/technology/Ion_Propulsion1.html

To shorten travel time around the solar system, let high-thrust chemical rockets kick-start the flight, and then switch to the gradual thrust of ion rockets to exploit their huge exhaust velocity.

Difference Between Energy and Power

There is a huge difference between energy and power. Chemicals have moderate energy, and huge power because they react so quickly together. The energy gets released very quickly to create huge power. Controlled nuclear reactions have huge energy, but only moderate power, because we are trying to avoid an explosion. We all know that splitting atoms or combining atoms releases huge energy, but we don't want to do it too quickly or there will be an explosion. Power is what is needed to get huge thrust (against gravity), not energy. Of course, energy is what is needed to keep the power and thrust going over a long time.

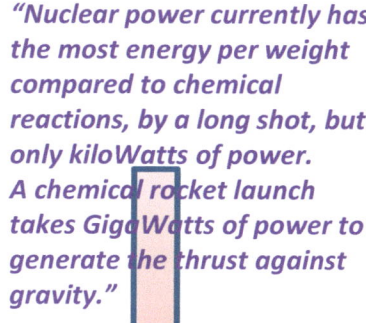

"Nuclear power currently has the most energy per weight compared to chemical reactions, by a long shot, but only kiloWatts of power. A chemical rocket launch takes GigaWatts of power to generate the thrust against gravity."

- Energy (blue)
- Power (orange)

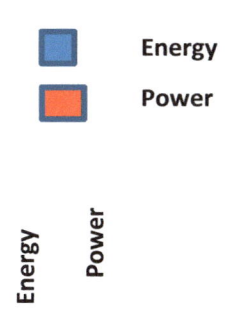

Compressed Air
Application:
Toy bottle rockets

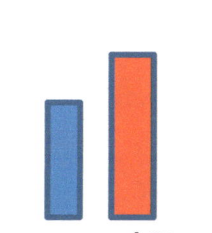

Compressed Steam
Application:
Short flight rockets, like Evel Knievel's launch across a canyon.

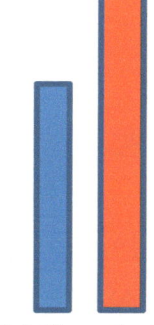

Solid Chemical Fuels
Application:
1st stage thrust of a space rocket, because the energy is strong and is released very quickly.

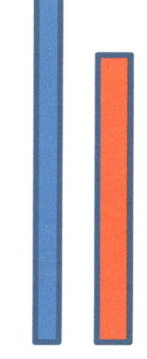

Liquid Chemical Fuels
Application:
2nd and higher stage thrust, because there is more energy than solid fuels, even if it can't burn as quickly.

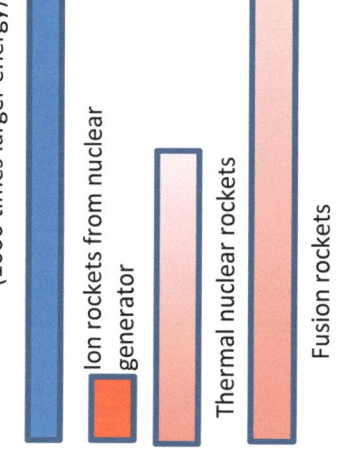

(1000 times larger energy) — Ion rockets from nuclear generator — Thermal nuclear rockets — Fusion rockets

Nuclear Fission (decay) and Fusion
Application:
100 year long power for electronics. Maybe power for ion rockets with low to moderate thrust while already in space.

Compressed air is easy to pump up, and the energy can be release quickly for bottle rockets. But the total energy of the compressed air is very small compared to chemical reactions.

Compressed steam has more energy than compressed air, and compressed steam can be released very quickly to get large power. But still this total energy and power is much less than chemical reactions.

Solid fuel has a strong chemical reaction, like dynamite. The energy density is moderate for a chemical reaction. The big advantage is that it only takes a large surface area to get a huge burn rate and a huge power. There is simplicity in using the solid fuel to get thrust.

Liquid fuel has the best energy, but the ability to mix the fuel with the oxidizer is limited by fuel turbo pumps. So liquid fuels have more energy than solid fuels, but less power or less burn rate.

Nuclear material has 1000 times larger energy than any chemical reaction. But we can't extract this energy quickly except by a nuclear explosion, which we don't want.
- With current ion rockets, the nuclear energy is extracted very slowly to generate electricity. The nuclear fuel can last 100s of years, but we can't use it to launch off the ground because we can't extract the energy that quickly.
- With research and hope and thermal propulsion or fusion rockets, maybe we'll get more power and thrust.

To use some fuel for thrust, there needs to be a lot of energy released very quickly, that is, there needs to be a technique to get huge power from the fuel. Chemical fuels are semi-explosive, so chemical fuels are great to get thrust at launch.

Nuclear Propulsion that Starts with Electricity

Want low power electricity? Let heat flow across a crystal. Heat from nuclear power can be used to provide a heat difference across a crystal and provide voltage for an ion rocket with no moving parts. This is almost practical for low power and low mass rate and low thrust.

Want stronger power electricity? Let heat create steam. The heat from nuclear power can also heat steam and turn a turbine. This voltage will power an ion rocket.

"The heat from nuclear reactions can generate electricity in two ways. One is the temperature gradient across a crystal, which is not very efficient, less than 5%, but it is free. The other way is the way 20% of US power is generated using hot steam and generators, which is more than 30% efficient."

The voltage from any electric generator will power the ion rocket. The gas needs to be ionized, and a high voltage needs to be applied to the acceleration grid to accelerate the ions. The gas can be ionized from the electric power.

For a thermoelectric generator, the inside of the satellite can be heated by the nuclear power, and the outside of the satellite is the absolute zero of outer space. That temperature difference just begs to create a temperature gradient.

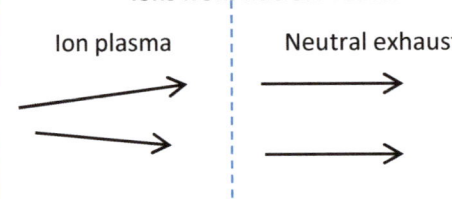

Gas used for exhaust | Ion plasma | Neutral exhaust

Voltage to accelerate the ions from nuclear reactor

Practical but weak

Nuclear Heat flow across a thermoelectric crystal to generate a voltage and electricity, to power an ion rocket, for 1 kiloWatt

Almost practical

Nuclear Reactors using hot steam and spinning turbines to generate electricity, to power an Ion Rocket, for more than 1 MegaWatt

Thermoelectric generator: You can power a cell phone from a camp fire using this effect.

Nuclear fuel rods

Turbine for the hot steam

Generator: Make the generator spin, and it will give electricity

Standard steam and spinning generators, with heat from nuclear power.
- The nuclear fuel rods will heat steam. This steam will spin a turbine and a generator.
- The voltage from the generator will power the ion rocket.

Thermoelectric crystal: A heat flow across a crystal will generate a voltage, called the 'Seebeck' effect. Interestingly, the reverse also works: a voltage across the crystal will cause a temperature gradient.

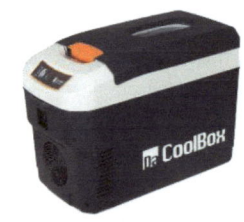

Thermoelectric refrigerator: Refrigerator in a car, using an applied voltage across the crystal.

Nuclear heat, in this case fission, can create electrical power and can power an ion rocket.

Nuclear Propulsion using Direct Heating of Exhaust

Heat from nuclear power from fission can be used to heat the exhaust once in orbit, which is almost practical for low power and low mass rate and low thrust. NASA has a research program, DRACO, to demonstrate this direct heating of exhaust. Heat creates this fast exhaust. Months of travel time can be taken off the trip to Mars, with just a small 10s of pounds of steady thrust over weeks and months.

Almost practical

"Nuclear power can just be a heat source to heat the exhaust gases. Now half upper stage weight will be gone, because we don't need an oxidizer.

This is a really basic and strong idea that will be tested in orbit in a few years.

This heat source idea is simple heating from a well known fission material, not some as-yet-not-invented fusion idea."

Nuclear Heat to directly heat exhaust gas for low thrust: Nuclear Thermal Propulsion

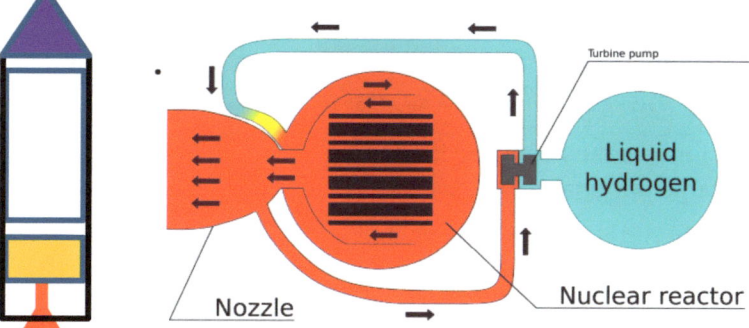

Hydrogen liquid storage, no oxidizer, for use as exhaust gas.

Uranium rods and radioactive decay provide heat, like power plants.

Hot hydrogen exhaust

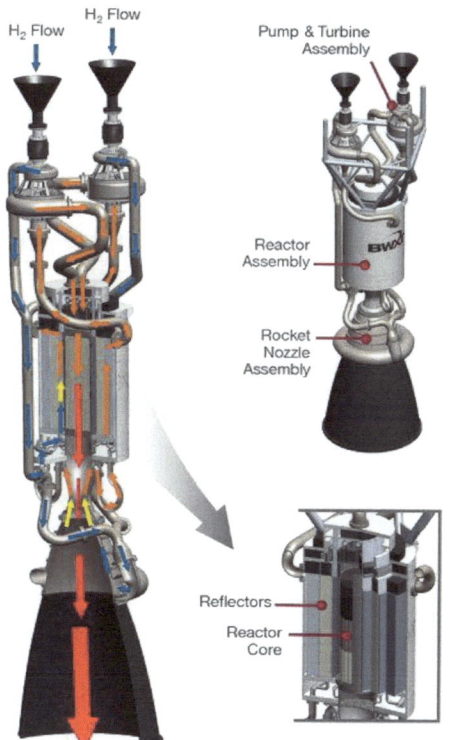

The nuclear heat concept is just another way to get hot gas to use as exhaust. Don't use chemical reactions to get heat. Instead use nuclear reactions to get heat. Both chemistry and nuclear heat obey Newton's laws: once the store liquid for the exhaust gas is gone, there is no exhaust and no thrust.

The hydrogen exhaust gas is heated to over 4000 degrees F by flowing over the hot fission material. The heat is limited by the melting temperature of the fission radioactive material and the support structure. The hot gas would not be hotter than a chemical reaction, or the support metals around would melt and the nuclear material would also melt.

The exhaust is just hot hydrogen, not combined with O2. The hydrogen H2 is 6 times lighter than water exhaust from H2 and O2, so the exhaust speed is much faster. Also, the thrust lasts twice as long as a chemical reaction, because there is no need to carry an oxidizer (no Liquid Oxygen LOX). The thrust would be low and long from the steady heat, to avoid a runaway nuclear reaction. This is comparable to an Ion Rocket engine, although the support materials need to withstand extreme heat. Trips to Mars or the Moon would be cut in half. Nuclear thermal propulsion was even considered in the 1960s for the Apollo program. Refer to 1960s NASA program NERVA (Nuclear Engine for Rocket Vehicle Applications).

Here are ways to test of this nuclear thermal propulsion: 1) lower grade nuclear sources can be used, and 2) exhaust testing can be done on the ground.

Concept drawing of heating H2 gas using nuclear core, from Popular Mechanics.

Development of Thermal Propulsion:
NASA aims to launch a nuclear-powered spacecraft, known as DRACO (Demonstration Rocket for Agile Cislunar Operations), into Earth's orbit either by late 2025 or early 2026.

Nuclear heat can directly heat a gas, and the hot gas is the exhaust.

Nuclear Propulsion using Fusion

Only fission – splitting atoms – has been used in satellites in space for electricity, like for the Voyager spacecraft. In the future, fusion – combining atoms – can also play a role. Fusion has a much higher energy for the weight because we are using light hydrogen atoms to get similar reaction energies.

Heat from nuclear power from fusion can be used to heat the exhaust once in orbit. The heat source can be an extremely hot fusion reactor.
If the nuclear fuel is just heating the exhaust, then we have a super powered ion rocket. Maybe we'll get a MW as power.
If the nuclear fuel is also the exhaust, then in space we have much more energy and power, and our rocket is like a hot rod. Trips around the solar system could have continuous 1 to 2 months of thrust, with only months to travel to the outer solar system instead of years. With nuclear reactions, we can potentially get 100s of MW as power.

*"Fusion power is the dream of power generation, which has more energy per weight than fission. Independent of the weight advantage, many national labs are building test cases of fusion reactors, either by using electric currents and heat in a donut-shaped Tokamak or by using laser pulses to compress heavy hydrogen spheres.
The purpose is to get the hydrogen gas at a high enough pressure and temperature, like in the Sun, to combine."*

Okay, nuclear fusion has not been developed yet for a steady power supply. But it is the promised land for unlimited power, and it has been demonstrated for extremely short times in large national labs.

Fission combines some really light atoms already like hydrogen and helium, for about the same energy that is extracted per reaction from splitting some really heavy atoms like plutonium.

Research stage

Nuclear Heat to directly heat exhaust gas for low thrust: Fusion reactor where the fusion heat is transferred to a different exhaust gas

Nuclear Heat to create the exhaust gas for low thrust: Fusion reactor where the fusion daughter products are exhaust gas

Tokamak fusion reactor
Hot plasma gas that undergoes nuclear fusion of hydrogen atoms. The heat can be transferred to a different exhaust gas for the rocket propulsion.
A fusion reactor can have less shielding when in space.

Magnetic coils to direct exhaust out the back
The hot exhaust will be so hot that we want to use magnetic walls, instead of melting metal.

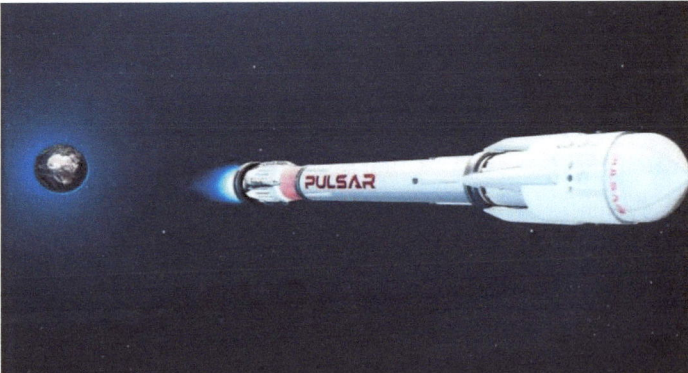

Potential fusion power enabling faster travel in the solar system.
Trip times can be reduced by more than half to Mars and to Jupiter, using the long term power from a nuclear heat source to expel the exhaust.

Nuclear heat can directly heat a gas.

Nuclear Propulsion using Heat or Electricity

Here is some history of improbable ideas for nuclear power for thrust in space – powering ion rockets or direct explosions for thrust - and more probable nuclear power for electricity. After all, we already use nuclear power for some satellites, which can last for 100s of years. Nuclear fusion or fission has about 1000 times more energy than chemical reactions. If a satellite is going to the dark outer gas planets, away from the Sun, then solar panels are not so effective. The Sun is just a dot without providing much solar heat. These outer gas planets certainly know they are not getting much solar heat: these planets are very cold.

Almost practical

Nuclear Heat for electricity or low thrust:

Electric power from radioactivity for a low thrust ion rocket, and just for electricity:
Let's recall that nuclear power plants are highly effective here on Earth. A large percentage of the USA's grid power comes from nuclear energy, about 20%. Out in space we would not need all the heavy shielding, and there would be a huge penalty for that extra shielding weight.
Satellites are already using nuclear power to get a few kiloWatts of steady power out in space, using the heat from the reactions to create a voltage.
This heat can be used to heat a liquid which turns a generator, or can be used to heat a thermoelectric crystal which generates a voltage due to a temperature gradient.

"Nuclear power can either be fission, which we currently use in power plants, or fusion, which we want to use in power plants."

Fission power (splitting atoms):
Fission is used as a controlled heating mechanism for nuclear power stations. This steady power is just like a nuclear power stations for powering cities. Isotopes of uranium and plutonium will split their nucleus and give off heat. A few kiloWatts have been produced using nuclear power in space, using thermoelectric crystals.

Fusion power (combining atoms):
Fusion power happens inside the sun, but has not yet been harnessed for electricity in a controlled way.
Fusion power can potentially get the hydrogen atoms close together a few different ways. One way is a tokamak, in the shape of a donut, running a strong current through a plasma gas of hydrogen inside a magnetic field, which holds the current together. Magnetic rings are around the plasma. Another way is to zap a hydrogen pellet of heavy hydrogen with a strong laser beam, pulsed from all sides, to get compression. This form of nuclear power is still in development.
One large Tokamak is at ITER in Europe, which is an international effort. One pulsed laser fusion location is at Lawrence Livermore National Laboratory in California.

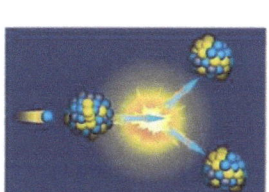
Fission
Atoms are heavy uranium and plutonium that split

Nuclear fuel rods

Nuclear power plant

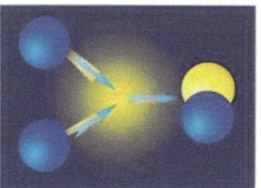
Fusion
Atoms are light hydrogen that combine

Tokamak fusion reactor
Still in the research stage in France at ITER, with loop of hot plasma.

Laser fusion reactor
Still in the research stage in California, with laser pulse compression of hydrogen pellet.

Nuclear power plants on the ground can also be nuclear power ideas for space.

Nuclear Propulsion using Explosions

Here is one idea to get thrust from explosions of fission bombs. The energy can be used for propulsion. Explosions from nuclear fission with high power can launch the rocket, or more likely propel the rocket after it achieves orbit.

Here is also another idea for infinite exhaust for fusion. Out in interstellar space, a fusion reactor can scoop up interstellar dusk as it flies along. That is, create exhaust from fusion of interstellar dust for high power for travel once away from Earth – yes, even the vacuum of solar space or interstellar space has proton dust to scoop up.

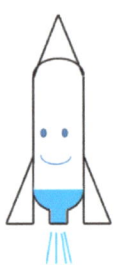

"Does dropping little nuclear bombs under the nozzle sound like a good idea?
Also, maybe we can get an inexhaustible supply of hydrogen from out space just by scooping it up as the rocket flies along."

Really impractical so far

Nuclear Explosions for thrust:

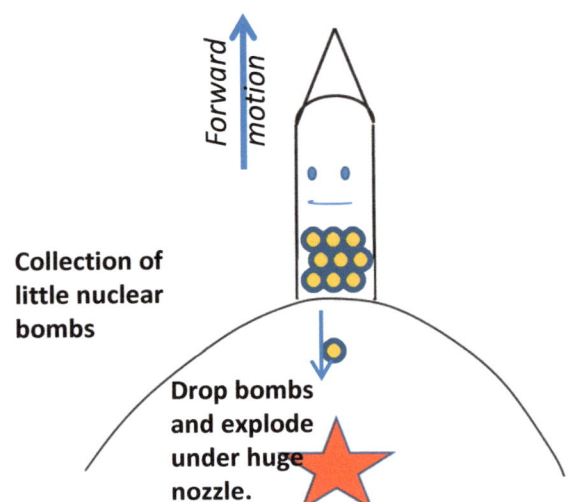

Idea 1: Launching from the ground, with many explosions below the rocket.

- The idea is to explode small nuclear bombs just below the rocket. There is huge energy below the rocket bowl. Nuclear explosions have more than 1000 times more energy per mass than chemical explosions, which sounds great for rockets.
- Unfortunately, there is also huge nuclear fallout of radioactive dust and gamma rays which can cause cancer and failed organs for millions of people below or down wind. So these explosions would be done after the rocket is in orbit from a chemical launch.

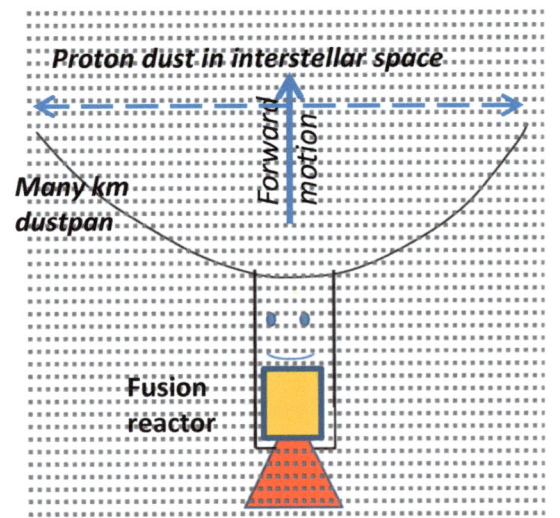

Idea 2: After get to space, then can have interstellar space travel by fusing proton dust into helium in space.

- The idea is to grab hydrogen atoms from the near vacuum of interstellar space. There is typically 1 proton per cubic centimeter everywhere in the interstellar universe, or the vacuum of space.
- The rocket would use nuclear fusion of these proton atoms, collected from interstellar space like a dust pan, while moving.
- The rocket needs a 'dust pan' more than 1 km wide, to collect enough protons to accelerate a reasonable size rocket

Nuclear explosions could propel a rocket after in orbit. Nuclear explosions for launching from ground might give enough heat to launch a rocket from the ground, but the radiation fallout would be atrocious.
For interstellar travel for fusion in space, there is still proton dust to collect in empty space, which can be compressed and fused for heat and ejected.
DARPA has a program to get nuclear propulsion out of Earth's orbit by 2025.

Nuclear Propulsion using Explosions

Here is some history of using nuclear explosions for thrust in space. Mostly this idea of bombs for thrust was considered after WW2, when nuclear bombs were getting developed.
We certainly do not want explosions anywhere near Earth, with all the radio-active fallout. Explosions near the upper atmosphere can also cause a huge electromagnetic burst, which disables nearby electronics, as the nuclear radiation hits the particles in the atmosphere.

Really impractical so far

"Nuclear power is an offshoot of the development of nuclear bombs in WW2. It is a very successful offshoot, but this history does demonstrate that nuclear energy is huge.

Fission has been the offshoot with many electric power plants.

Fusion is still just for big explosions, but the dream is to make better power plants using steady heat from fusion."

Nuclear Explosions for thrust:

Fusion bombs under a nozzle for high instantaneous thrust:
The idea for nuclear explosions under a rocket nozzle as thrust was pushed by Dr. Teller after the WW2, as a spinoff of civilian uses of the nuclear Manhattan project. The hot gasses from the explosion, and the gamma rays, can push up on the nozzle and cause thrust. Hydrogen fusion bombs would be lighter, so that would be the preference, but uranium fission bombs also have a lot more energy than chemically explosions too.
If nuclear explosions are used during launch from the Earth's surface, there would be large nuclear fallout issues, that is cancer and deaths, so probably the initial launch would be chemical reactions and nuclear explosions would only be used after the rocket is in space.
A better spinoff of nuclear energy is nuclear power stations here on Earth, and this other idea of rocket thrust really did not go anywhere.

A little nuclear bomb history

Dr. Teller is credited for proposing the above fusion power and H-bombs after the Manhattan project.

Dr. Teller also proposed using nuclear explosion to clear trenches for building canals. He did not fully understand the nuclear fallout issues. All the ground around the canal would have been radiative. All the rocks and dust blown into the air would be radioactive. It is far better to simply used a large amount of regular chemical explosives like dynamite.

<u>Fission bomb history, in the 1940s:</u> In history, the bombs that fell on Japan were atomic fission bombs, which breaks uranium and plutonium nuclei apart to create energy. The few spare neutrons from each splitting of the atom will collide with another atom and split that too, in a run-away chain reaction called an explosion.

Atomic bomb in WW2 using fission.

Atomic bomb explosion over Japan.

<u>Fusion bomb history, in the 1950s:</u> Fusion or hydrogen bombs do the opposite of a fission reaction, of combining two H atoms to create energy also called an explosion. There is more energy released in fusion than in fission, which makes modern fusion bombs much more powerful. For fusion, it is very hard to get hydrogen atoms close enough together to combine, which can combine their heavy nuclei into a heavier atom (helium) and release energy. The fusion bombs accomplish this by surrounding the hydrogen with a fission atomic bomb, causing a hybrid explosion. The gamma rays from the initial explosion of the outer atomic bomb provide enough pressure to compress the inner hydrogen, which then get their hydrogen nuclei so close together that they undergo fusion for a much bigger bang.

Stars easily get hydrogen atoms close enough together for fusion due to the huge pressures and temperature due to gravity near the center of stars.

Hydrogen bomb after WW2 using fusion.

Hydrogen bomb explosion over Marshall Islands in the Pacific.

Nuclear bombs were a solution looking for a problem after WW2, from construction to space propulsion. So far the only use of run-away nuclear reactions is a bomb.
The other civilian idea for nuclear power plants have been a huge success. Nuclear power plants on the ground can also be nuclear power ideas for space.

What Nuclear Power Energy Sources are There for Thrust?

Nuclear power is probably necessary for long term space travel. So, do we use nuclear power only for electricity and depend on chemistry for thrust? Do we make more powerful nuclear reactors to get a reasonable thrust, meaning typical extreme rocket thrust? No matter what we do, we still need to eject something, so the thrust will only last as long as our tank of material to eject.

With nuclear power for thrust, at a fixed power level, we are better off ejecting stuff with extreme exhaust velocity but at low mass rate, so we keep our 'stuff' for as long as possible.

| Nuclear electricity to power an ion rocket | Nuclear direct heating of exhaust gas | Nuclear fusion, where radioactive products are the exhaust | Nuclear micro explosions for thrust |

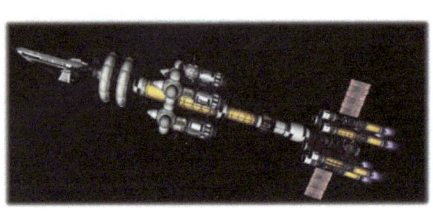
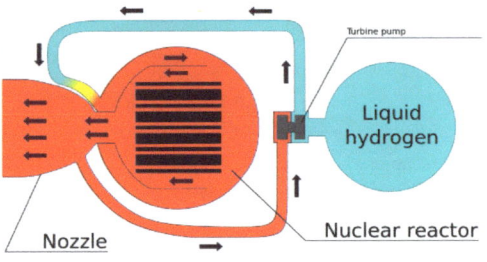
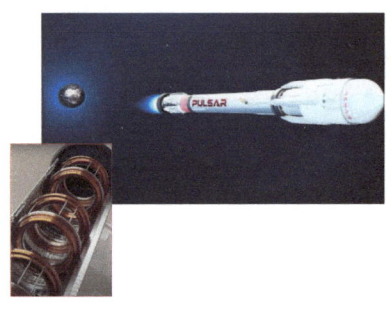
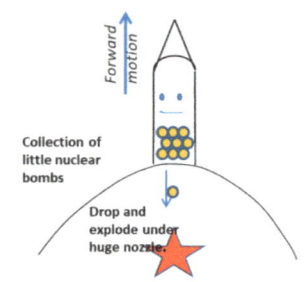

Concept of direct nuclear / chemical or ion / chemical rocket for distant travel

Concept of direct heating of exhaust gas passing over a hot fission source.

Concept of nuclear fusion reactor where the fusion daughter products are exhaust gas

Concept of using exhaust gas from nuclear explosions

Nuclear thermal (steady heat): Do you want to go nuclear for electricity for thrust, with the radioactive material just serving as a heat source to power the ion rocket?
- If there is a very large heat source, then we can get more electricity from the heat than just electricity to power electronics. We can also power an ion rocket.
- We'd probably use a Stirling engine to get the most electricity, similar to a nuclear power plant.

Nuclear thermal (steady heat): Do you want to go nuclear for thrust, with the radioactive material just serving as a heat source?
- For nuclear thermal to act as thrust, we need a bottle of some atom that can get heated up by nuclear rods and ejected as exhaust, without a chemical reaction. This is not a nuclear explosion. The nuclear rods have limited heat from steady and slow nuclear reactions instead of quick and near-explosive chemical reactions .
- The temperatures of the exhaust gas are still close to chemical reaction temperatures, so the main advantage here is not carrying liquid fuel, and the higher speed of light hydrogen exhaust instead of heavier O2 exhaust.

Nuclear fusion: Do you want to go nuclear for thrust, with the radioactive material or daughter products as the exhaust gas?
- If the daughter products of fusion are the exhaust out the back, then the exhaust velocity can be 10% of the speed of light. That means that the rocket can get faster than 10% of the speed of light, over time.
- Probably a very large magnetic field is necessary to deflect the charge exhaust out the back.
- Of course, we are talking power levels that are much larger than large nuclear power plants on Earth.

Nuclear explosion: Do you want to go nuclear, with the explosion variety?
- Nuclear explosions, no different than bombs dropped during a war, would create radioactive dust and fall-out, which is bad for people near the launch and even far away from launch, because the radioactive dust would drift far away in the upper atmosphere. Explosions would work after the rocket was safely in space.
- Well, there are rocket failures during launch and we certainly don't want scattered radioactivity and genetic mutations in people for hundreds of years.
- Similarly, people once proposed using nuclear bombs to blast away large amounts of earth to make large canals, and again the danger of radioactive fallout made people see the fallacy of their ways.

Here are the various ideas for nuclear power for thrust space.

Chapter 9: Thrust and Rocket Speed, the Quick Estimates

Here are some basic rules of thumb to get a fast rocket. These conceptual rules or observations are great to use to predict which rocket will go faster and higher.

Impulse of the fuel:
What is the relationship between the total momentum change of the fuel, or the 'impulse', and the final speed of the rocket?

Ignoring gravity, the final speed of the rocket does not depend on the instantaneous thrust. The final speed is the product of the instantaneous thrust and the time duration of the thrust, which happens to be the 'impulse'. So the rocket could have a slow burn rate and still get to the same final speed, because the time duration is longer.

When it comes to real space rocket design, we do care a lot about instantaneous thrust for the first stage. The first stage is all about getting off the ground with the full weight of the rocket, and the thrust needs to be a few times the weight of the rocket. That means burning a lot of fuel very quickly to get a very fast flow rate and large thrust.

"Aah, the secrets of the trade, shed weight and have fuel with fast burn rate and fast exhaust velocity."

Rocket equation:
The prediction for the final rocket velocity is given by the iconic 'rocket equation'. This equation only depends on exhaust velocity and mass ratio. The burn rate is not included because a longer weaker thrust over a long time duration have the same impact as a shorter stronger thrust over a short time duration, assuming there is no gravity.

The actual performance of water bottle rockets, of toy chemical solid fuel rockets, and of real space rockets can all be compared by using this simple 'rocket equation'.

- Let's compare a bottle rocket to a space rocket. A bottle rocket does not have more mass ratio, or more exhaust velocity than a real space rocket, so there is no competition. Good. Space rockets do get into space after all. The exhaust velocity of water out of a bottle rocket is about 30 m/s, pushed by air pressure. The exhaust velocity of chemical reactions out of a space rocket can be 4000 m/s. So we expect chemical reactions to have a huge advantage.
- Let's compare a bottle rocket to a toy chemical rocket. A bottle rocket can have more mass ratio than a toy chemical rocket, but the exhaust velocity is much less. So a toy chemical rocket wins.

The rocket equation predicts that multiple stages provides a big help to get the final payload up to a much faster speed.

Basic fuel energy consideration:
The rocket can not do more than it has energy for. The energy in a birthday balloon will not lift a space rocket. The speed (kinetic) energy and the gravitational potential energy can't be more than the starting chemical energy. Also, the fuel needs to burn quickly to get the instantaneous thrust to beat the weight of the rocket on Earth.

Impulse, or momentum transfer:

$$impulse_{fuel} = mass_{fuel} v_{exhaust}$$

Rocket Equation for final rocket velocity:

$$v_{rocket} = v_{exhaust} * \ln(mass\ ratio)$$

We always care about the impulse of the fuel. That is another parameter that means high energy density, or high specific impulse. For space rockets or water bottle rockets, we need the rocket equation and the rocket equation says that the final velocity is mostly dependent on the exhaust velocity, not the flow rate or even the mass ratio.

Thrust and Rocket Speed, the Quick Estimates

Here are some basic rules of thumb to get a fast rocket. These rules are great to use to predict which rocket will go faster and higher.

The goal of rocket design is to do the following:

1. **Shed weight as you go**: Shed the hardware weight as you go, typically by dropping stages in a 2 or 3 stage rocket, or using boosters.
2. **Be light**: Little weight in hardware, relative to the fuel weight
3. **Fast exhaust**: Get a fast exhaust speed of whatever the rocket is spitting out to get thrust (hot gases, water). This exhaust speed is mostly fixed by chemistry, the energy of the chemical reaction.
4. **Low acceleration**: Do not exceed the force and acceleration that a human can take if there are astronauts (less than 10 g's, or get squished like a bug at higher forces).
5. **Avoid air drag**:
   - **Narrow diameter rocket**: Minimize air drag, if launched from the ground.
   - **Avoid high speeds at low altitude during launch**: Reduce air drag in the more dense air closer to ground. If most speed is obtained after rocket rises above atmosphere, then air drag is not a huge effect.

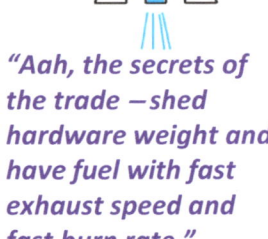

"Aah, the secrets of the trade — shed hardware weight and have fuel with fast exhaust speed and fast burn rate."

There is the 'Rocket equation' to predict an upper limit for how fast the rocket will be going after all the fuel is used up, based on fuel to hardware mass ratio and exhaust speed. The 'Rocket equation' has been used ever since the 1940s.

Cartoon of a 3-stage rocket, with exhaust gases

Velocity of exhaust gasses which allows faster rockets →

30 m/s*	200 m/s	1000 m/s	2000 m/s (1000 – 4000 m/s)	>40,000 m/s	>400,000 m/s	300,000,000 m/s speed of light
High Pressure Water Rocket	High Pressure Air Rocket	Hot Steam Rocket	Chemical rocket	Ion rocket using heavier Xenon atoms	Ion rocket using lighter Hydrogen atom	Nuclear explosions / Anti-matter – regular matter annihilation

Water has slow exhaust, but lots of mass, so go up a few 100 feet.
Water rocket

Pressurized air has a faster exhaust than water rocket, but air has little mass, so go up less. Air exhaust is close to the speed of sound.
Steam rocket

Hot Steam worked for Evel Knievel to cross a canyon, but not as much total energy as a chemical rocket.
Space chemical rocket

Chemistry is your sweet spot for typical toy chemical rockets and space rockets.
Ion rocket

Ion Rockets with large exhaust velocity seem a good choice to go between stars, because the rocket can build up speed to a much higher final velocity, based on rocket equation (huge momentum change for a very small mass). For example, an Ion rocket shortened the travel time to Jupiter in the Dawn mission.

The fuel can be anything that is ejected at some exhaust speed.

*m/s = meters per second. 1 meter is about 3 feet.

Exhaust speed and shedding weight are the key to getting speed and thrust. Water rocket exhaust velocity is only 30 m/s, but chemical rocket exhaust velocity is more than 2000 m/s, up to 4000 m/s for hydrogen fuel. To get even faster exhaust speed and rocket speed, we need to go to ionic rockets, but then the stream of ions is too small to get much thrust.

Thrust, Burn Time, and Final Rocket Speed

To get to the same speed, do you want to accelerate fast for a short time, or accelerate gradually for a long time? Out in space it does not matter, a quick or long duration. The final rocket velocity is the same, whatever your choice for exhaust flow rate and acceleration profile, for the same amount of fuel.

Final rocket velocity does not depend on the thrust or the exhaust time (burn time) exactly, but instead the product of the two.

Thrust and time

Final rocket velocity does not necessarily get faster when the thrust is larger but short. The final rocket velocity is thrust times the burn time, not just thrust.

For example, a moderate thrust of 2 times the weight (2g) for long time of 10 seconds will provide the same final rocket velocity as a stronger thrust of 10 times the weight (10g) thrust for a shorter time of 2 seconds.

Rocket Equation for final rocket velocity:
$$v_{rocket} = v_{exhaust} * mass\_change\_factor$$

Notice that the rocket equation does not directly use thrust, or directly use burn time. Instead, the rocket equation reduces the momentum change to just the exhaust velocity times a mass ratio factor.

The rocket equation is the basic way to estimate any rocket final velocity, without air drag or gravity. We just need to know two things:

1. **Exhaust velocity of the fuel**
2. **Mass ratio**: ratio of starting and ending mass of the rocket, after the fuel is burnt off

The exact details of the exhaust velocity and the masses are just particular to a type of rocket.

The burn rate does not matter, except burn rate must generate enough thrust to counter-act gravity during launch.

Same final rocket velocity with same impulse or amount of fuel

Thrust versus time curves, with rocket velocity change, for long thrust and for short thrust.

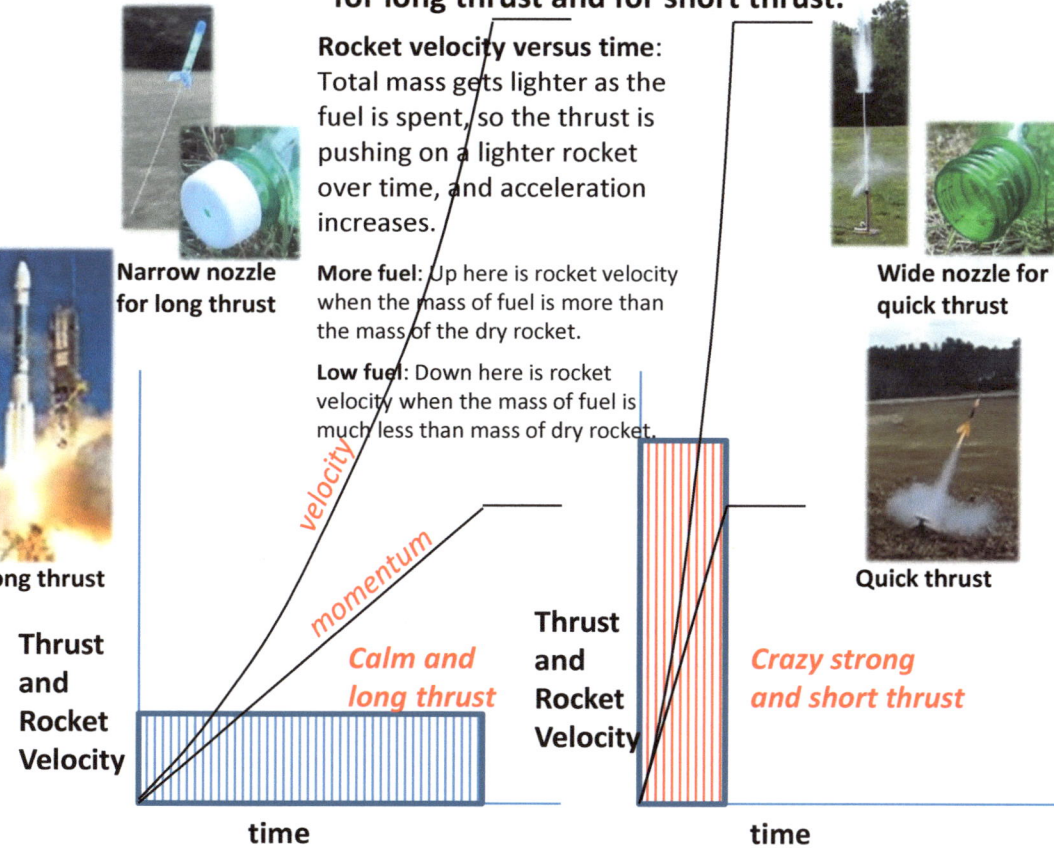

Rocket velocity versus time: Total mass gets lighter as the fuel is spent, so the thrust is pushing on a lighter rocket over time, and acceleration increases.

More fuel: Up here is rocket velocity when the mass of fuel is more than the mass of the dry rocket.

Low fuel: Down here is rocket velocity when the mass of fuel is much less than mass of dry rocket.

Long thrust — Narrow nozzle for long thrust — *Calm and long thrust*

Quick thrust — Wide nozzle for quick thrust — *Crazy strong and short thrust*

Thrust and rocket velocity versus time:
Area under the curve is the total change in momentum of the rocket, which gives the final rocket velocity.

*momentum change = thrust * time = mass * final velocity*

Same energy for both fast burn and slow burn, and same final velocity.

Force and time examples:
Think about a race between a super-charged race car and a small under-powered car. Both accelerate to 60mph, and stop going faster, or else they are speeding. The race car has the power and torque to go from 0 to 60 in 3 seconds. The under-powered car has weaker torque and takes 10 seconds. But both get to the same speed.

Think about the opposite, the reverse deceleration to stop a car, going from 60 to 0 mph. You can decelerate gradually over 100 meters, or suddenly over 1 meter. The 100 meters is a gradual stop and lower force. The 1 meter sudden stop is a crash, where the force is huge. Both have the same velocity change and momentum change. One hurts, and has much more force!

Thrust and Final Velocity, at Different Burn Rates

The thrust magnitude is part of the rocket design. There is only so much fuel. There can be different burn rates of the same amount of fuel.

Out in space without gravity, or moving sideways to gravity, we can burn the fuel slowly or quickly to get low or high thrust. A rocket can accelerate fast or slow and still reach the same speed when all the fuel is gone, just depending on the burn rate.

On Earth with gravity, we need to burn the fuel quickly to get high thrust. Rockets fighting gravity need a thrust 3 or 4 times the weight of the rocket, so that most of the energy of the fuel goes into the final speed instead of just causing the rocket to hover over the ground.

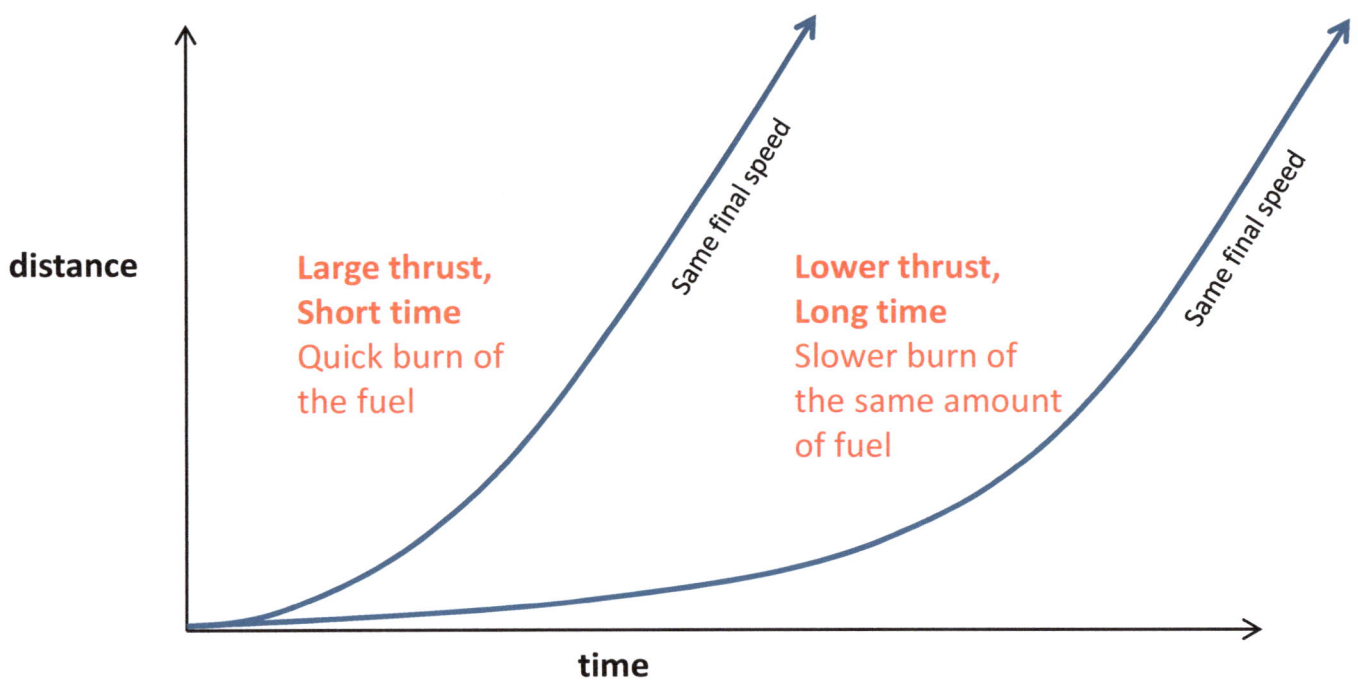

Out in space, the rocket that burns its fuel more quickly with more thrust and same amount of fuel will reach the same final rocket speed as a rocket that burns its fuel more slowly and has less instant thrust but for a longer time.

When gravity is not part of the picture, that same final velocity is true.   When thrust is so large that gravity is just a small part of the picture, then the same velocity is almost true.

When gravity is similar to thrust, when the low thrust case is about the weight of the rocket, then we really want more thrust. Then burn rate is not just some secondary consideration, it is necessary to have a sizable burn rate.

Missile rockets can use large thrust, and space rockets use lower thrust compared to the weight.

Thrust is just the burn rate, but the final rocket velocity is determined by the amount of fuel, not the burn rate.

Example: Nozzle Size for Space Rockets

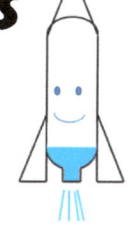

Space rockets and water bottle rockets have the same physics about thrust. Some large space programs have used only a few rocket engines, each of which are very large, and some space programs have used many smaller engines. Both get the same total thrust. Although all solutions get the thrust, there are cost, nozzle aiming, and turbulence considerations as well. Many rocket engines, or an array of engines, are necessary in order to roll and pitch to get the right path to orbit. In contrast, a water bottle rocket does not need to have any particular flight path, and there is no control feedback anyway, so one nozzle will do. A large nozzle with more flow rate just means the thrust is much larger than the weight of the rocket, just using that one rocket engine.

 "Space rockets can have a design with only a few large nozzles."

 "Space rockets can also have a design with many smaller nozzles."

The rocket launch needs a thrust greater than the weight of the rocket. Space rockets have 3 g's of acceleration and use 2 or more rocket engines, each of which is a medium nozzle compared to the weight of the rocket. Independent aiming of many engines allows the rocket to roll and pitch to get the right path to orbit. Missiles can have 50 g's of acceleration, without people on board, and effectively have wide nozzles.

Patriot missile, a military rocket:
A single engine with a thrust much larger than the weight of the rocket. Maneuvering is accomplished by fins in the air stream, not by nozzle aiming.

SLS rocket, a space rocket, 2020s:
A few engines, each with large flow rate and a few million pounds thrust.

SpaceX, Falcon Heavy, a space rocket, 2010s:
More engines, each with less flow rate but more ability to handle one engine that does not work. Many engines have potentially lower costs from economies of scale. Smaller engines are also less susceptible to turbulence issues.

Larger wide nozzle for bottle:
large flow and large thrust
Thrust ~ 120 lb-force

A wide nozzle can just be the open bottle.
More water flow coming out of a wide hole means there is more force, and the rocket can lift larger water weights.

Medium nozzle for bottle:
medium flow and medium thrust
Thrust ~ 15 lb-force

A medium nozzle is a fancier adapter cap on bottle.
The narrower bottle neck has o-ring seals.

Smaller narrow nozzle for bottle:
small flow and small thrust
Thrust ~ 2.7 lb-force

A narrow nozzle can just be a bottle cap with a narrow hole drilled into the center.
Less water flow coming out of narrow hole means there is less force, and the rocket can not lift larger water weights.

Even though the thrust from Space Rockets is huge, the mass is also huge, so the acceleration is about 3 g's.

Acceleration of Water Rocket for Wide Nozzle

Bottle rockets lose water weight and accelerate even faster during the thrust. For bottle rockets, there is no throttling the thrust, or constraining the acceleration to a human friendly 3 g's. From Newton's 2nd law, the acceleration is force/mass. So as the fuel leaves and the rocket gets lighter, then the acceleration increases.

Multi-stage space rockets also show the extra acceleration as the fuel for that stage gets used up, as the rocket gets lighter. Each lower stage is the dominant mass of the rocket so the lost fuel really changes the acceleration.

"Rocket gets lighter as water or fuel is ejected. The same exhaust force pushing against something lighter causes acceleration to ramp up."

Water Bottle Acceleration, Single Stage

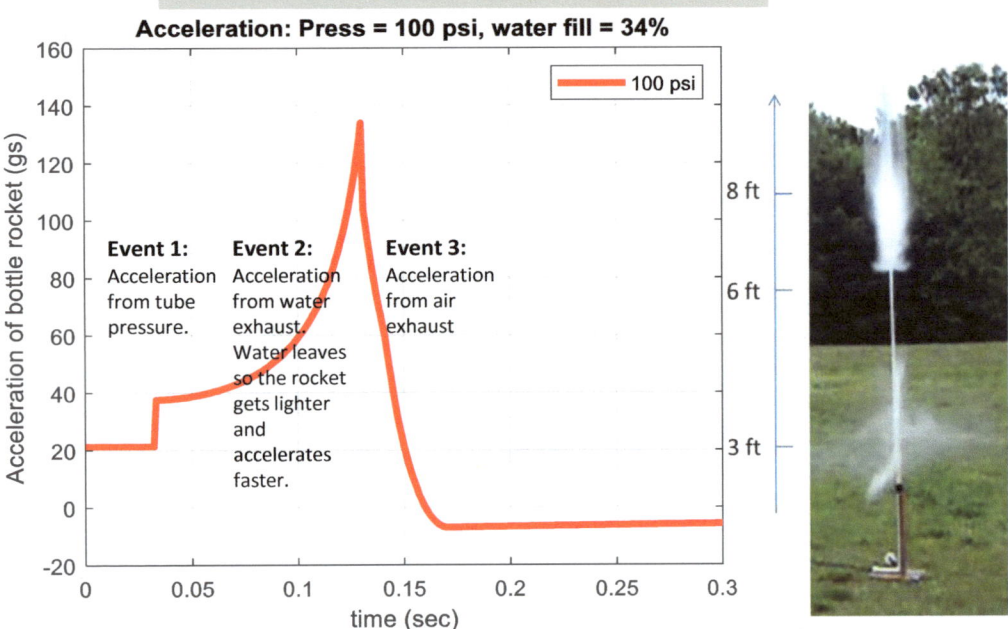

Acceleration of water rocket during thrust as water is leaving

Event 1: Tube Push Mass of rocket and fuel does not change due to tube push, so have constant acceleration.

Burnout of water: Main Engine Cut Off (MECO)

Burn-out of air

Coasting under gravity: Negative acceleration even though rocket is still traveling up: Air drag (about 2 g's) and gravity (1 g) are slowing rocket down.

What a water launch looks like, with high pressure and wide nozzle, at 50 g's.

The acceleration of the first stage of the bottle rocket has the same behavior as a space rocket first stage, although the acceleration is 10 times larger because the mass is much less.

Space Rocket Acceleration, with Multiple Stages

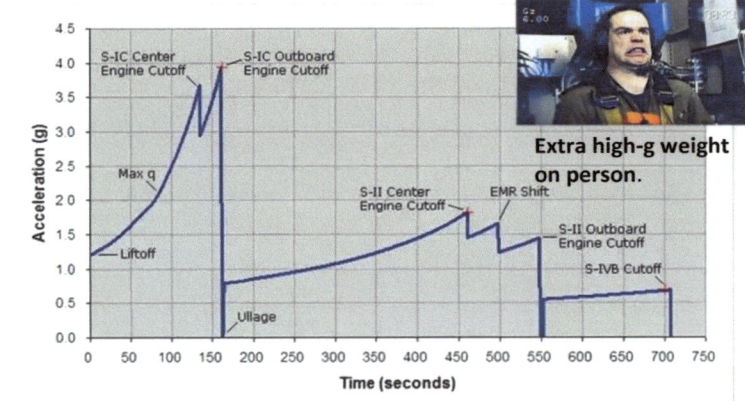

American Apollo space rocket, chemical thrust with multiple stages

Space rockets keep acceleration below 4 gs, and acceleration goes up as the fuel mass burns away if the thrust remains the same.

Extra high-g weight on person.

American Apollo space rocket.

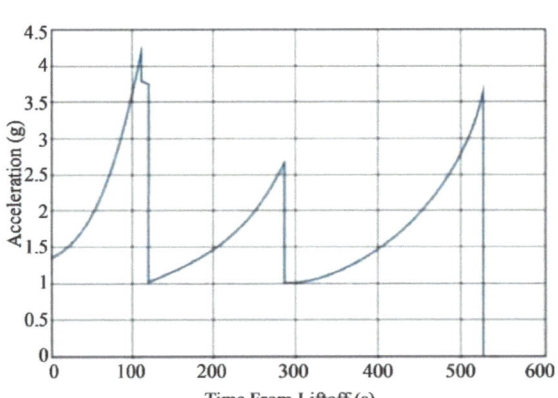

Russian Soyuz space rocket, chemical thrust with multiple stages. The Russian rocket has larger acceleration and a shorter timeline.

Russian Soyuz space rocket

- **Force and accelerations occur for all stages of the launch: air tube, water expelled, and air expelled.**
- **Notice that the acceleration is greatest right before all the water is gone, when a nearly constant water exhaust is pushing on a much lighter rocket with barely any water in it.**

Rocket Speed Estimates Using the Iconic Rocket Equation

Want to know a rocket's final speed? Fortunately, we have a short equation that predicts just that.
The rocket equation is the basic way to estimate any rocket final velocity, the upper limit without air drag or gravity or any force except for the thrust. We just need to know two things:
1. Exhaust velocity of the fuel
2. Mass ratio: ratio of starting and ending mass of the rocket, after the fuel is burnt off

The exact details of the exhaust velocity and the masses are just particular to a type of rocket fuel.
The burn rate does not matter, except it must generate enough thrust to counter-act gravity during launch.

"I'm very predictable …too predictable. I predict an upper limit to rocket performance, which no one likes. Do you want to be told you can't do better?
I need an injection of new ideas."

This rocket equation is a solution to the rocket's final velocity from the thrust and exhaust time given before, after all the fuel is exhausted.

Rocket Equation for final rocket velocity:

$$v_{rocket} = v_{exhaust} * mass\_change\_factor$$

$$v_{rocket} = v_{exhaust} * ln\left(\frac{M_{fuel} + M_{EmpyRocket}}{M_{EmptyRocket}}\right)$$

The 'mass_change_factor' is the Natural log of mass ratio

Saturn V, 3 stage   1st stage launch   Rocket booster falling away

Mass Ratio of wet rocket hardware mass with fuel over dry rocket hardware without fuel, or 'Mass start over Mass end'.
- **1-stage limitations**: There is a limited mass ratio for 1-stage rockets, because keep all the hardware – fuel tanks, engine weight, outside structure – even after most of the fuel is gone. One stage rockets with limited mass ratio can not achieve enough rocket speed to make orbit.

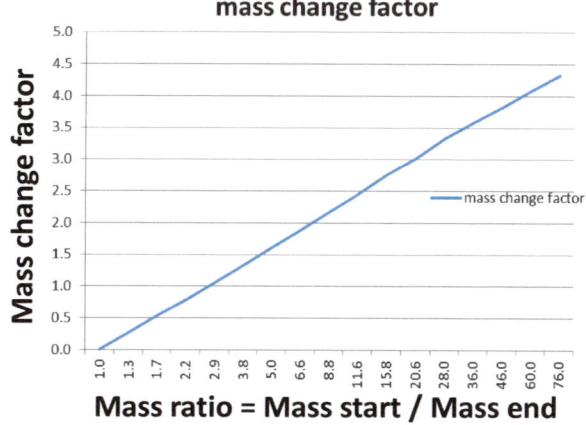

Mass ratio = Mass start / Mass end

How to use rocket equation for multiple stages:
- Treat each stage as a single stage with all the upper stages considered to be the payload, contributing to hardware.
- Add all the rockets velocities of each stage together to get the final velocity.

Breaking the rocket equation, NOT!
- The rocket equation is a tyrant. The final rocket velocity depends on the exhaust velocity and very weakly on the mass ratio, which just makes rockets very inefficient. Exhaust velocities are stuck around 3000m/s in chemical reactions, and the mass ratio per stage can only practically be increased to 20 per stage, which means 95% fuel and 5% hardware.
- Multi-stage rockets are an improvement, dropping dead weight from lower stages, but the rocket is still very inefficient and expensive.

Why use 2 or 3 stage rockets, rather than 1 stage? -The rockets can obtain orbit, and can be smaller or can go faster and higher.
1. **Orbit:** A 1-stage rocket can not get a high enough mass ratio to get to orbit in Earth's gravity.
2. **Smaller Rocket**: For same payload, multi-stage rockets can have much less mass and fuel to get the same final velocity: that is, use a much smaller rocket using 2 or 3 stages instead of 1 stage. It is easier to design a smaller rocket with reasonable lower mass ratios per stage, instead of a larger rocket with a single very high mass ratio. Multi-stage rockets easily can get mass ratios of >30:1, because the rocket discards metal structure as it flies along.
3. **Go Faster and Higher**: For same payload, don't try to get smaller, but instead use the same total large mass rocket with 3 stages to go faster, more efficiently, and escape Earth's gravity.

The rocket equation, using only exhaust velocity and mass ratio, provides a first estimate of final rocket speed: it is simple and terrifying.

Faster Exhaust Speed Makes a Faster Rocket

The exhaust velocity is determined by the energy of the fuel; that is, the energy in the compressed air in water rockets, or the energy in the chemical reaction in chemical space rockets. For good reason space rockets use chemical reactions. Rockets need the highest energy and exhaust velocity, with the most fuel.
The exhaust velocity determines the rocket final velocity.

A water rocket is not as efficient as a chemical rocket because the exhaust velocity is 60 times smaller.
Exhaust velocity for a water rocket is proportional to the square root of the pressure.

There is a lot more energy in chemical reaction, compared to compressed air (another reason why your car uses gasoline and not compressed air)

Chemistry allows fast exhaust velocity

"For rocket speed, need fast exhaust and a rocket mostly made of fuel, or high mass ratio."

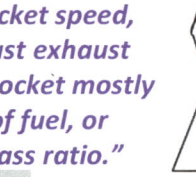

Water Rocket

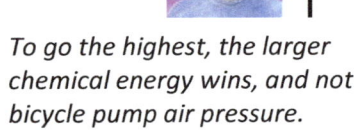

Toy Chemical Rocket

Space Chemical Rocket

To go the highest, the larger chemical energy wins, and not bicycle pump air pressure.

Delta II rocket: chemical reaction (heating) of kerosene and liquid oxygen to make hot steam

Lower exhaust velocity (although feels fast watching launch), although reasonable mass ratio.

Higher exhaust velocity, but Low mass ratio because it is a toy

Highest exhaust velocity, and High mass ratio

Water Rocket, single stage:

Water Exhaust velocity at 100 psi ~ 40 m/s
Full to Empty Mass ratio ~ 6
V rocket final ~ 70 m/s (130 mph)

Toy Chemical Rocket, single stage:

Exhaust velocity ~ 1000 m/s
Full to Empty Mass ratio ~ 1.1
V rocket final ~ 100 m/s (200 mph)

Space Chemical Rocket (first stage):

Hot Exhaust velocity ~ 2300 m/s to 4400 m/s
Full to Empty Mass ratio ~ 10
V rocket final 1st stage ~ 5300 m/s (~12000 mph)

$$v_{rocket} = v_{exhaust} * ln(mass\ ratio) = v_{exhaust} * ln\left(\frac{M_{fuel} + M_{EmpyRocket}}{M_{EmptyRocket}}\right)$$

Rockets that use chemical reactions give much higher exhaust velocities than air pressure, and much higher energy per pound, so performance is more energetic.

Upper Limit to Rocket Speed Using Energy, Not the Rocket Equation

Let's talk about energy, not forces or momentum. The rocket can not do more than it has energy for. For example, the energy in a birthday balloon will not lift a space rocket. The energy from burning a chocolate cake will not lift a human.

Forget the rocket equation (for the moment)! Using energy estimates, let's get the upper limit to the rocket velocity after all the fuel is gone by.

Chemical energy beats compressed air energy per weight, easily.

Liquid Chemical Energy Density

High: $\frac{E}{mass} = 23\ MJoules/kg$

Compressed Air Energy Density

Low: $\frac{E}{mass} = 0.1\ MJoules/kg$

Wood	Coal	Compressed gas	Compressed steam	Rocket fuels

X	X	Maybe	Maybe	Yes
Wood will not burn fast enough to eject much exhaust rate	Coal will not burn fast enough to eject much exhaust rate	Compressed gas can release quickly, but there is not enough energy stored.	Compressed steam can release quickly and has more energy than compressed gas, but there still is not enough energy stored.	Rocket fuels are a chemical reaction. Rocket fuels have huge energy for the weight, and the energy can be released in a semi-contained explosion. The highest known energy per weight is the combination of H and O.
Applications: Household heat and steam trains	Applications: Household heat and steam trains	Applications: Toy bottle rockets to go up 1000 feet	Applications: Evel Knievel steam rocket to go up 2000 feet	Applications: Space rockets

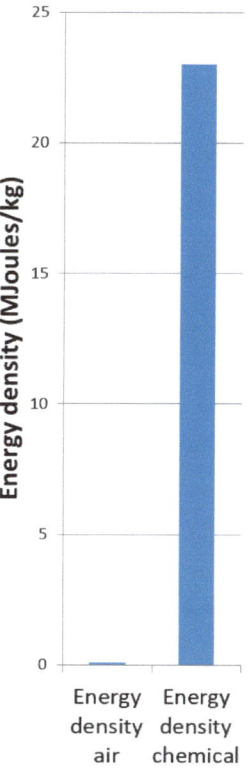

Energy per weight:
More energy per unit mass means better rocket performance.

Quick burning:
Just as important, the energy needs to be able to be released very quickly to get huge power and thrust, which eliminates burning wood or coal.

Where does the energy go?
At minimum, the energy in the fuel must equal the kinetic energy of the satellite and the gravitational potential energy to raise the satellite.
At maximum, the energy in the fuel must be about ½ the energy of the total rocket mass raised into orbit, with kinetic energy and gravitational potential energy.

An energy analysis is a very crude estimate of the potential for the fuel, because the mass and velocity is changing all the time as the rocket is thrust into orbit.

Without knowing the exact details about forces, energy always gives an upper limit to performance. Burn rate is also important if fighting gravity.

- **Compressed air has too little energy to get to Space.**
- **Thank goodness that chemistry has so much energy. That's why we can get into Space, against gravity.**

Chapter 10: Hardware to Visit Other Planets and Moons

What's the right hardware plan to get to the Moon, and then to Mars? Let's talk about habitats, fuel, and rockets to return back to Earth. The main questions are, one, do we have an orbiting return rocket with fuel, or do we land everything, and, two, do we have separate rockets for supplies versus a rocket that can return to Earth.

These mission discussions and design options can take decades, can involve many rocket iterations of trial and error, and can involve billions of dollars.

<u>Let's look at a Moon mission:</u> For the Moon with weak gravity and no atmosphere, there are two effective hardware approaches to land and then return home to Earth. In the Moon's weak gravity, it takes about the same energy either to keep an orbiting fuel station around the Moon for the return home with extra hardware, or to slow down all the hardware and land that fuel on the Moon and then launch it back into orbit with less hardware.
The specialized return rocket, the command module, does not need to land on the surface. In the Apollo missions, the return Command Module also had the heat shields to withstand air drag returning to Earth. Those shields are extra weight and special features that do not need to land on the Moon and could just orbit.

<u>Let's look at a Mars mission:</u> The best hardware plan to land on Mars is still getting debated, with multiple supply rockets and astronaut rockets, and whether to use orbiting fuel stations or not. The gravity is stronger on Mars compared to the Moon, so it takes more fuel and energy to escape Mars. In higher gravity, landing the fuel for the return trip seems silly. A one way trip can land a lot more habitat on Mars, without carrying fuel for re-launching, so maybe it is better to have custom one-way rockets for deliveries and a few separate return rockets for astronauts every 2 years when Mars is closest to Earth.

<u>Venus, Jupiter, and Saturn are just out of the question for people right now because it takes so long to get there.</u>

The mission plan to visit another planet or moon depends on many things, and the rocket equation provides a lot of rough estimates:

1. **Does the destination have an atmosphere to help slow down?** -An atmosphere allows air drag to slow the rocket down and land on the surface either with parachutes or much small rockets. Without an atmosphere, extra fuel needs to be launched from Earth to match the orbital speed of the destination.
2. **Does the destination have strong or weak gravity when launching back up?** -It is obviously easier to visit a destination with weak gravity. The rocket is not accelerated as much toward the destination planet/moon, so slowing down to land takes less rocket retro thrust. When it is time to leave, the rocket also needs less rocket thrust to escape the planet/moon. Again, when there is a stronger gravity, all this extra fuel needs to be launched from Earth.
3. **Is there a plan to deliver a habitat and supplies in a separate rocket, that does not need to return to Earth?** -A one way trip would allow the most stuff (living quarters, food, oxygen, extra fuel) to be brought to the destination planet/moon.

All these secondary rockets for landing and taking off again, with their own fuel, are part of the original payload of the primary rocket as it leaves Earth.

Mostly we consider launching a rocket which has everything it needs to land on the planet and then have the capsule return to Earth. This is the most challenging case. A less challenging solution, which may be necessary, is to launch a few rockets, where only one of the rockets needs the extra fuel for the capsule on the next rocket to return to Earth.

A planet with a large-ish gravity (like Mars) has its own mission plan to land on its surface, which is more challenging than landing on a planet with low gravity (like the Moon). Do we land the return capsule and fuel, or let it orbit? Do we have two separate rockets, one for 1-way trips for supplies and habitat only and one for the return capsule?

> The rocket equation shows that the pros and cons of an orbiting fuel station around the Moon and Mars are different. In the weak Moon gravity, we could keep the return-to-Earth fuel in orbit and save the fuel to get it off the Moon, or we could avoid the extra orbiting hardware and land the fuel on the surface.

What Planets or Moons Should We Visit?

We want to visit a planet or moon that is close, that can support life, and that actually provides a benefit to science or mining.
Let's expand the planet discussion from Book 1 Chapter 3.

Let's consider the Earth's Moon. -3 day travel time.
The gravity is weak, at 1/6th Earth's gravity, and there is no atmosphere. Here it is a toss up whether we want an orbiting fuel station for the return trip or just land everything. There is no convenience of air drag to slow the rocket down for the descent onto the Moon's surface, but on the other hand the gravity is not strong. Having added hardware for an orbiting fuel station also takes mass and extra fuel, which compensates for the fuel to slow the rocket down to land and to then escape the Moon for the return trip.

Let's consider Mars. -9 month travel time.
Mars has moderate gravity, at 1/3rd Earth's gravity. Probably we do not want to land a heavy rocket on the surface. We'd to need to launch it back into space. An orbiting fuel station around Mars is a good idea. To save rocket fuel, it is better to not land and better to keep the larger living quarters and fuel necessary to escape the planet and return to Earth in orbit around the planet/moon.

The planet is far away, with a long travel time of 9 months or longer. We need a larger capsule for the travel time for both sanity of the passengers and extra food and oxygen supplies.

This living quarters for travel is a sizable fraction of the total payload launched from Earth, so to land the traveling living quarters (a command module) on the Mars surface and back takes most of the rocket energy. It is better to have the traveling living quarters orbit the planet, and have only the permanent habitat land on Mars.

Mars lost its oceans about 3 billion years ago. The planet is too small for its iron core to retain its heat, and the weak gravity and loss of magnetic field can not stop the atmosphere from being stripped away by the solar radiation.

Let's consider Venus. -5 year travel time, using sling shots
The planet is closer to the Sun, with a travel time of 2 to 7 years, depending on how much the reverse sling-shot effect off other planets is used to slow the space craft to achieve a slow speed for orbit around Venus.

Venus is hotter than Mercury, at 800 degree F on the surface. Venus is full of greenhouse gases CO_2, and the atmospheric pressure is 100 times higher than Earth's pressure. Metals melt on the surface, and the pressure crushes satellites. So we can not land there. A Russian probe landed in 1982, and survived for 1 hour. A USA satellite orbited the planet, the Magellan probe, in 1990.

Venus might have had oceans 4 billion years ago, but the Sun gradually got brighter and the ocean evaporated and the planet is too close to the Sun. Venus had runaway greenhouse. Oceans evaporated and the ocean is no longer absorbing the greenhouse gas CO_2.

Let's consider Jupiter. -6 year travel time, using sling shots
Jupiter is a gas giant, so there is no surface to land on. All we can do is orbit the planet and land on Jupiter's moons, where 4 of the Jovian moons are larger than Earth's Moon but still have low gravity. The moons Ganymede and Europa are believed to have a water ocean under the ice crust.
Jupiter is a gas planet, but it still is 300 times the mass of Earth. Hence its moons can be rather large.

Let's consider Saturn. -8 year travel time, using sling shots
The Cassini launched to Saturn's moon Titan in 2005. There was a soft landing and pictures using Huygen's probe. The probe battery life lasted for just a few hours. Cassini discovered hundreds of methane lakes.

Venus:
Toxic, super hot, and super high pressure
No structured magnetic field on surface, about 0.001 Gauss, less than 1/100th the Earth's magnetic field.
- Gravity: 1 earth
- Huge atmospheric pressure from gravity, so solar wind not strong enough to sweep away atmosphere due to larger gravity.
- No magnetic field implies no conductive gasses or no iron core.

Mars:
1% Earth's atmosphere, but at least has water on poles.
No structured magnetic field on surface.
- Gravity: 0.37 earth
- The no magnetic field and the low gravity means the atmosphere can be swept away by the solar wind (electrons, protons, alpha particles, gamma rays).

 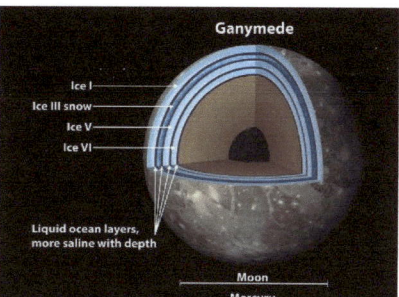

Jupiter: **Ganymede, a moon of Jupiter**
All gas, so maybe land on a moon like Ganymede and Europa.
Average magnetic field of 4 Gauss on surface.
- The large magnetic field may be due to a rapidly spinning metallic hydrogen core.

The rocket equation shows that the pros and cons of an orbiting fuel station around the Moon and Mars are different. In the weak Moon gravity, we could keep the return-to-Earth fuel in orbit and save the fuel to get it off the Moon, or we could avoid the extra orbiting hardware and land the fuel.

Returning from the Earth's Moon which has Weak Gravity and No Atmosphere

What needs to be launched to build a lunar base on the Moon?

What does a lunar base require? - Food, oxygen tanks, batteries, solar panels, computers, suites for exploring, return rockets. There is no going to the hardware store if we forget to bring anything. We can't call for an emergency evacuation. If anything fails, we better have a backup.

Let's look at the lunar lander from the 1970s. This lander was only supposed to support astronauts for a few days.

Here were some of the requirements for the Lunar module:

Astronauts need oxygen to breath, and a way to filter or recycle the carbon dioxide the astronauts generate.

Astronauts need water to drink and food to eat. The food is dried and then mixed with water. In the long term, fresh food is needed to keep people healthy.

There needs to be a power supply for the electronics. Fuel cells using the liquid hydrogen were mostly used. Solar panels are also on the sides of the module.

Thick enough walls are needed to protect astronauts from the radiation from space. Unlike on Earth, there are no magnetic field or atmosphere on the Moon to block solar radiation of electrons from the Sun.

Moderate temperatures are needed inside the module for the comfort of the astronauts. Heat actually takes a lot of energy.

The lander needed the ability to re-launch off the Moon to return back to the Command Module. The return rocket used hypergolic fuel because of its reliability, which self ignites simply by mixing fuel and oxidizer. There was only one rocket engine for blast off, and if that engine failed then the astronauts die. Only the astronaut up in the orbiting command module would return home.

Unknown before the start of the Apollo program, there needs to be a method to clean the inside of the module from all the lunar dust. This dust is very fine grains of dirt that have been resting of the lunar surface for billions of years, and this dust collects over all the suits and control panels.

Return rocket with fuel for rendezvous

Landing rocket with radar sensors and rocket engines and fuel.

Lunar module on the Moon in the 1970s

All the issues that the 1970s lunar modules have will be much larger for the upcoming Artemis program lunar base, with astronauts staying for months at a time.

Returning from the Moon which has No Atmosphere

What does a lunar lander need to launch off the Moon's surface to get back to the orbiting command module? The command module has the fuel to return back the Earth.

Let's look at the lunar lander from the 1970s. The lunar lander only needs to reach the orbiting command module and then it is abandoned.

This landing was only supposed to support astronauts for a few days. The landing was in the middle of the Moon's daylight. Sunlight is on for a long 14 days, but we don't want to be in the cold during the 14 day night. The astronauts also could see what they are doing.

Most of the power for the 3 days came from hydrogen fuel cells. Still, in daylight, the lander can get some power from solar panels, even though the early solar panels in the 1970s were much more expensive and were only 10% efficient.

Lunar lander returning to the command module, with the two astronauts on board
Lunar lander blasted off the Moon using hypergolic fuel. Lander to heading back to the command module to link up, and then discard the lunar lander.
The lunar lander is the most successful and famous single-stage-to-orbit rocket ever built, but on the Moon. Of course, the Moon has 1/6th the gravity of Earth.

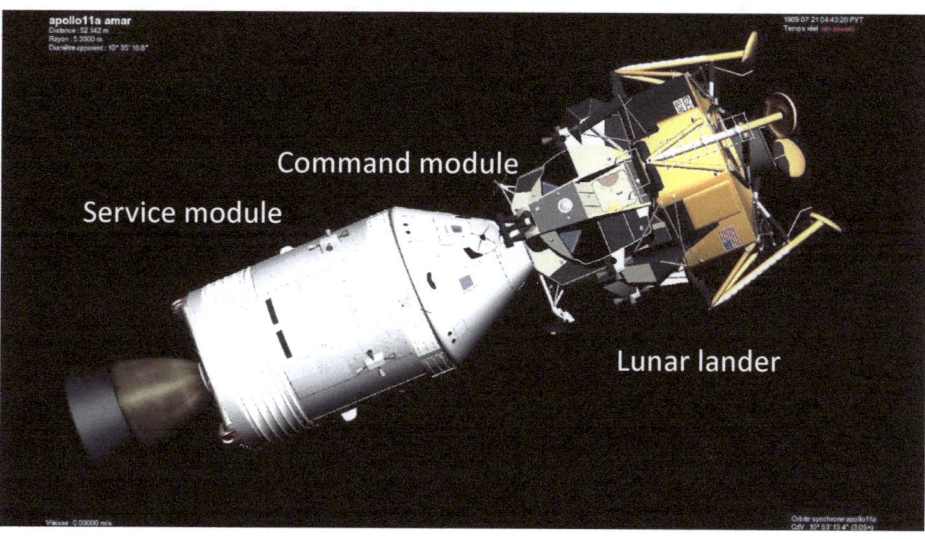

Mating the command module and the lunar module
Like any connection of space craft, the two are connected at a hatch door.
The only part that makes it back to ground is the conical crew command module.

The 1970s Lunar Module separated from the orbiting Command Module. This Lunar Module then landed on the Moon for 3 days, and blasted off to re-connect with the Command Module. The Lunar Module was then abandoned, because it was unwanted extra mass, to eventually crash into the Moon.

Returning from Moon which has No Atmosphere

Why even consider the Moon? The lunar base is practice for the base on Mars, so we should perform the same type of hardware plan that will be required for the Mars mission. Basically, the trip to the Moon takes 3 days, and the trip to Mars takes 9 months. If something goes wrong, the Moon is closer. Also, for 3 days the in-flight living quarters can be lightweight, cramped and tolerable. For a 9 month journey, maybe the astronauts would want more elbow room with some larger and heavier living space.

For the Moon with weak gravity and no atmosphere, the orbital command module is optional. It takes about the same energy either to keep a fuel station for the return home orbiting the Moon with extra hardware or to slow down and land that fuel on the Moon and then launch it back into orbit with less hardware.

The plan for a lunar base is to also have an orbiting module, partly to practice what will be required for Mars.

Lunar base for Planned Artemis Moon missions, 2020s

Possible lunar landers for 2025, with vertical solar panels at the poles

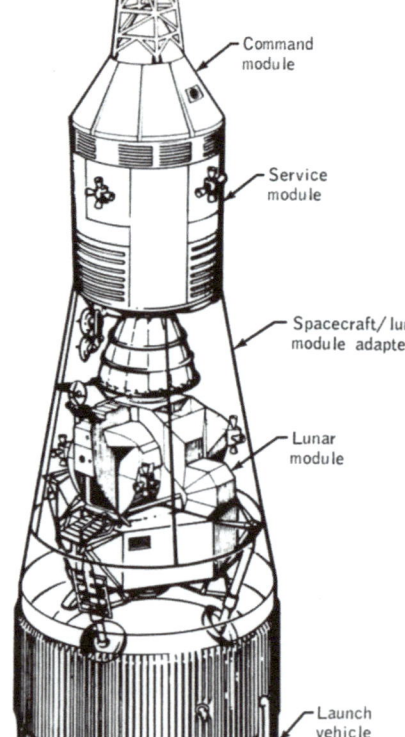

Previous Apollo missions, 1960:
Three astronauts went, two landed and one stayed in orbit. Various mission parts all stacked up, like astronaut's command capsule, service module, and lander.

Electrical Power for everything, like computers, lights, communications, conversion of water into air and fuel:
Power could be solar panels which last for decades if not covered in dust. Power could also be fuel cells, combining H and O, which is limited by the H or O brought from Earth. Power could also be a small nuclear reactor, which also can last for decades and works day and night. Regardless, solar panels will be part of the solution. Here are some considerations.

Solar panels and batteries will help during the 14 Earth day sunlight part of the lunar day, but then it is dark for 14 straight days. The Sun on the Moon does not set for 14 days. For short missions, we should land at 'sunrise' and stay 14 days until 'sunset'.

Fortunately, the poles have the advantage of steady solar power day or night, if a rosary of solar panels is formed for 10s of miles around, with vertical walls to face the Sun.

Unlike the Earth, the Moon only tilts 1.5 degrees on its axis relative to the Sun, so the poles get sunlight year round.

Water for drinking, breathing oxygen, and fuel:
The poles have frozen water. The H2O can be used for water, for fuel, and for breathing.

Lunar Rover Vehicle or Cars to go farther away from base camp with limited oxygen tanks:
Rovers help get around and carry more oxygen, or carry cargo like science experiments.
One person walking is not going to go very far with a ½ hour supply of breathing oxygen in a tank. One person on a rover, powered by solar panels and a battery, can go a lot farther.

The rocket equation shows that the pros and cons of an orbiting fuel station around the Moon are a wash compared to landing everything. In the weak Moon gravity, we could keep the fuel in lunar orbit for the return to Earth and save the fuel to get it off the Moon, or we could avoid the extra orbiting hardware and land the fuel.

Hardware to Return from the Moon which has Weak Gravity and No Atmosphere Drag

The performance of each stage of a multi-stage rocket can be predicted by the rocket equation. The rocket equation is used to cascade all the separate sections to complete a mission, from launch from Earth to the possible return to Earth. We start with the payload, topmost lightest section, which is the habitat and maybe a rocket capsule to return to Earth. We keep working backwards to see how much fuel and stages are required to get that topmost section off Earth.

Let's explain the cascaded rocket equation, which is like the multi-stage explanation a few pages before.

$$v_{rocket} = v_{exhaust} * ln\left(\frac{M_{fuel} + M_{hardware}}{M_{hardware}}\right)$$

At the beginning of the launch, the mass of the hardware includes everything. It includes the 1st stage hardware, and all the upper stages including the upper stage fuel. The upper stages can also have the payload, rovers, return vehicles.

When estimating the size of the rocket, we need to start at the most upper stage and see what its requirements are. That will determine the payload weight, and the payload weight will determine the lower stage requirements.

For example, like the Apollo missions, let's say we want a small rocket to launch off the surface of the Moon and head to a command module, which then returns to Earth. That lunar rocket and command module need to be launched off Earth.
On the very top, the command module needs to have enough fuel to escape the Moon's orbit and return to Earth. The mass of the capsule returning to Earth with its necessary fuel is all part of the payload launched off the Earth.
The lunar module needs enough fuel to land on the surface of the Moon. The lunar module also needs enough fuel to then rise off the Moon's surface and get back into the orbit of the command module. So the cascaded rocket equation would first start with the total mass of the launch rocket from the surface. Then that would determine the total mass of the rocket to land on the Moon.
For the lunar lander, the fuel to land on the Moon is determined by the necessary rocket velocity for retro-thrust in the opposite direction as the orbiting command module. Luckily, the Moon's gravity is not large and the orbit velocity is much less than the orbit velocity of a satellite around Earth. That determines the mass ratio of the whole lunar module landing on the Moon.
For the lunar lander, the re-launch fuel to rendezvous back with the command module has the same mass ratio as the landing, but some mass is left back on the lunar surface, such as the habitat supplies, and there is no landing fuel to consider, so the fuel amount is less to launch then to land.

This total mass of the lunar module and the return capsule is the payload that needs to be lifted off Earth. This payload mass determines the total mass of the 3 stage rocket to deliver this payload to the Moon.

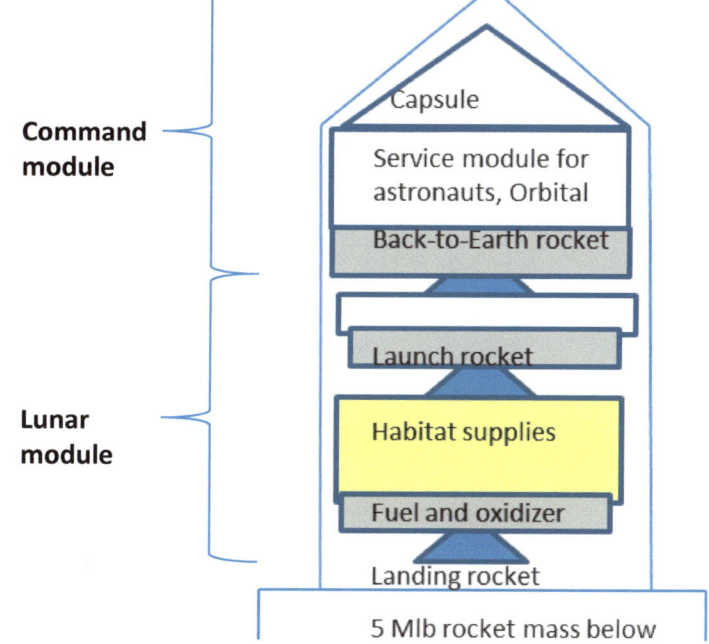

The rocket equation reveals that the pros and cons of an orbiting fuel station around the Moon are a wash compared to landing everything. Start from the weight of the last payload and work backwards to get the first cut at a rocket and mission design.

Choices: Returning from the Moon which has Weak Gravity and No Atmosphere

We need to custom design the mission to the Moon based on close orbit, weak gravity, and no atmosphere. For the Moon with weak gravity and no atmosphere, it takes about the same energy either to keep an orbiting fuel station for the return home orbiting the Moon with extra hardware, or slowing the return fuel down and landing that fuel on the surface of the Moon and then launching it back into orbit with less hardware.
The plan for a lunar base is to also have an orbiting module, partly to practice what will be required for Mars.
Below is a comparison of the mass of stuff that can be landed on the Moon out of a 69 klb total payload on top of a 3-stage rocket, for the case of supplies only with no return, the case of 'land everything and return' and the case of 'have an orbiting command module', all based on the rocket equation

Land everything, one way.

Land habitat of 49,000 pounds.
Need second rocket to deliver people.

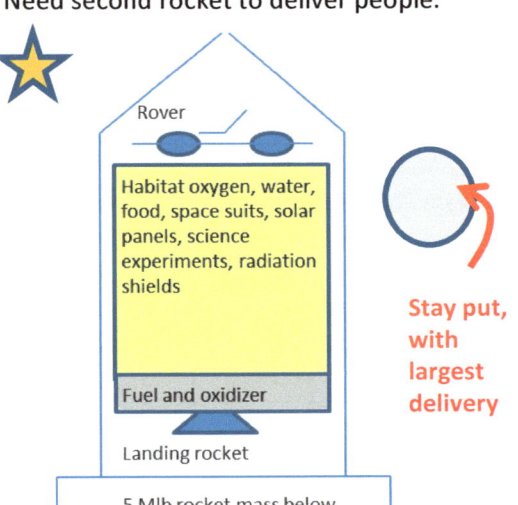

Stay put, with largest delivery

Pro:
- Get the most habitat on the Moon without concerns for life support of astronauts or for the return trip. Another rocket can bring the astronauts.

Con:
- Need another trip to bring the astronauts, but that is required anyway, especially for the goal of future colonization of Mars.

Land everything two way, re-launch, then return home with bare essentials.

Land habitat of 25,000 pounds.
Directly launch back to Earth with no orbiting station around the Moon.

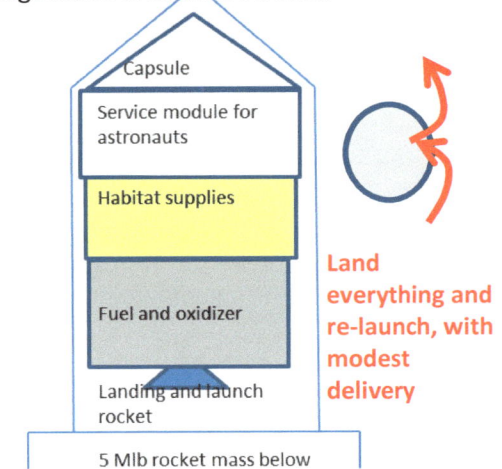

Land everything and re-launch, with modest delivery

Pro:
- Less parts, less complicated.
- Avoid the extra hardware of an orbiting station.

Con:
- The Moon has no atmosphere, so fuel is needed to slow down and land on the Moon. However, because the Moon's gravity is weak, there is not much fuel needed.

Keep separate orbiting fuel station (command module) and separate lander, and return home.

Land habitat of 25,000 pounds.
Launch back to orbiting fuel around the Moon, and then escape the Moon to Earth.

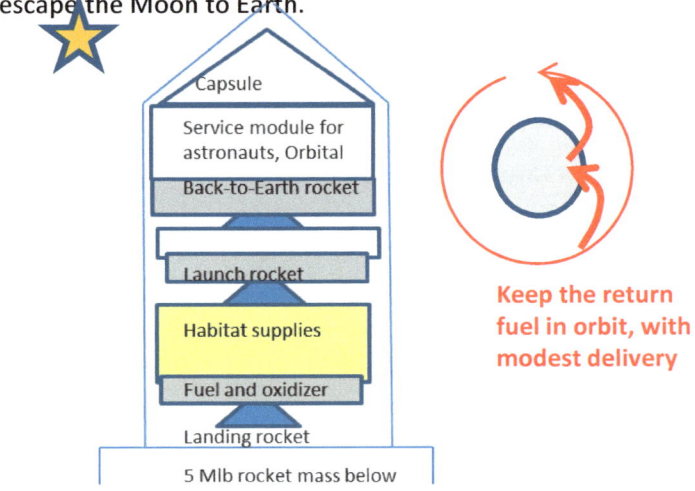

Keep the return fuel in orbit, with modest delivery

Pro:
- Avoid slowing down and lifting fuel off the gravity of the Moon. Instead, keep the fuel moving in orbit around the Moon.
- The Command module had the heat shield to withstand the hot air drag returning to Earth, and this added weight has no reason to land on the Moon.
- This mission imitates the required mission for Mars with higher gravity, which makes it good practice.

Con:
- More complicated.

Supply rocket: The rocket equation shows that landing hardware only one way, no return trip, has a big mass advantage.
Astronaut rocket: When also have astronauts and need to return to Earth, the rocket equation shows that the pros and cons of an orbiting fuel station around the Moon are a wash compared to landing everything. Because of the weak Moon gravity, we could keep the return-to-Earth fuel in orbit and save the fuel to get it off the Moon, or we could avoid the extra orbiting hardware and land the fuel.
Message: Because this Artemis moon base is practice to go to Mars, we should use both the 'land everything' for the one-way habitat and the 'keep orbiting fuel station' for the two-way return trip.

Choices: Returning from Mars which has Moderate Gravity and an Atmosphere

We need to custom design the mission to Mars based on its far orbit or distant location, moderate gravity, and atmosphere of the planet.

For Mars with stronger gravity and a slight atmosphere, it takes less energy to keep a fuel station for the return home orbiting the other planet, rather than landing that fuel on the surface of the planet and then launching it back into orbit.

Even though Mars has an atmosphere and can slow the landing rocket using air drag for free, it still takes a lot of energy to launch back up. So it is a better idea to have an orbiting fuel station.

This simple comparison based on the cascaded rocket equation shows that more material for a Mars habitat can be delivered if 2 or more rockets deliver the hardware, one way, and only one rocket delivers the astronauts.

Below is a comparison of the mass of stuff that can be landed on the Moon out of a 96 klb total payload on top of a 3-stage rocket, for the case of supplies only with no return, the case of 'land everything and return' and the case of 'have an orbiting command module', all based on the rocket equation:

Land everything one way, and don't return home.

Get a 74,000 pound habitat on Mars

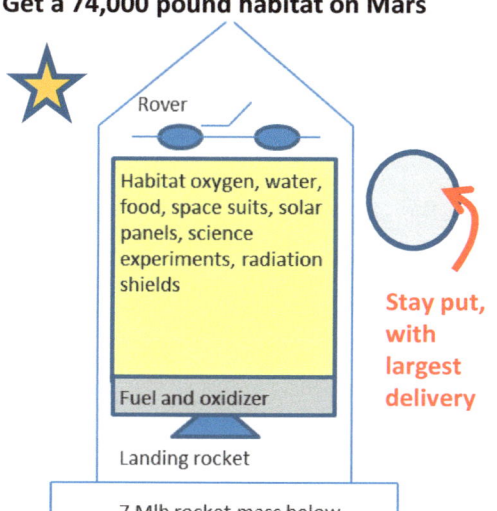

Stay put, with largest delivery

Pro:
- Get the most habitat on the Mars without concerns for life support of astronauts or return trip. Another rocket can bring the astronauts.

Con:
- Need another trip to bring the astronauts, but that is required anyway to bring enough hardware to Mars.

Land everything two way, launch from Mars and return home with bare essentials.

Get a 4,000 pound habitat on Mars

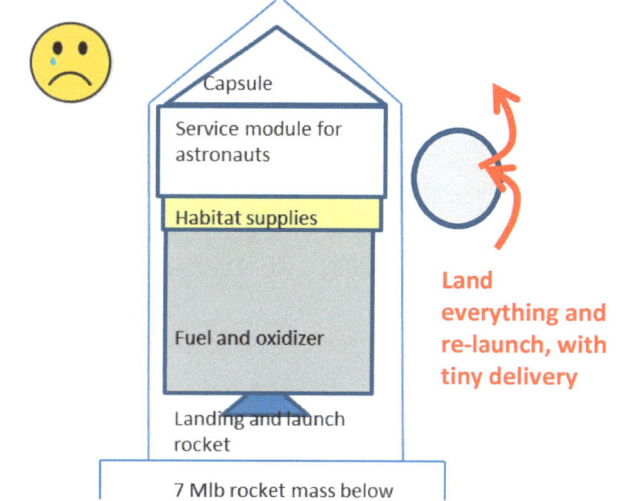

Land everything and re-launch, with tiny delivery

Pro:
- Less parts, Less complicated.
- Avoid the extra hardware of an orbiting station.

Con:
- Very little hardware is left on Mars.
- Mars has a larger gravity, so a lot of fuel is needed to launch back up to orbit Mars and return to Earth.

Keep separate orbiting fuel station (command module) and separate lander, and return home.

Get a 28,000 pound habitat on Mars

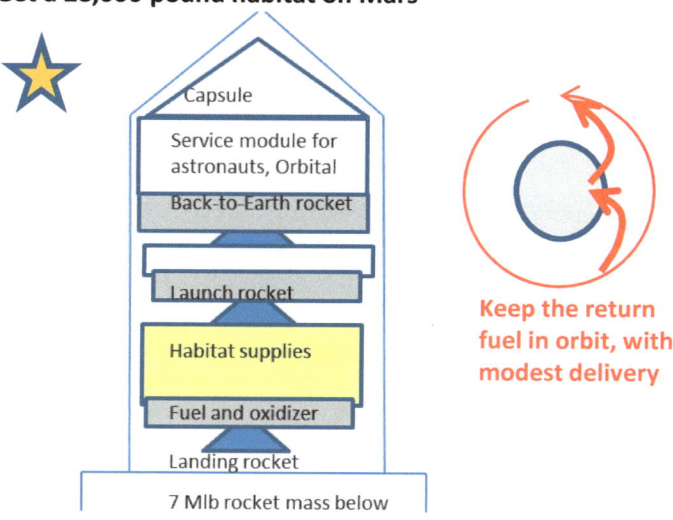

Keep the return fuel in orbit, with modest delivery

Pro:
- Avoid slowing down and lifting fuel off the gravity of the Mars. Instead, keep the fuel moving in orbit around the Moon.
- The Command module had the heat shield to withstand the hot air drag returning to Earth, which can also be used to withstand the Mars air drag.

Con:
- More complicated.

Supply rocket and separate astronaut rocket: Either do a one way trip to get the most habitat to Mars with two or more rockets, or use an orbiting fuel station. The idea of landing the return fuel is the worst option.

Message: The rocket equation can be used to show that we only want to land what is necessary in the stronger Mars gravity, and we keep the return-to-Earth fuel in orbit.

Chapter 11: Summary of Existing and Improbable Ways to Get to Space

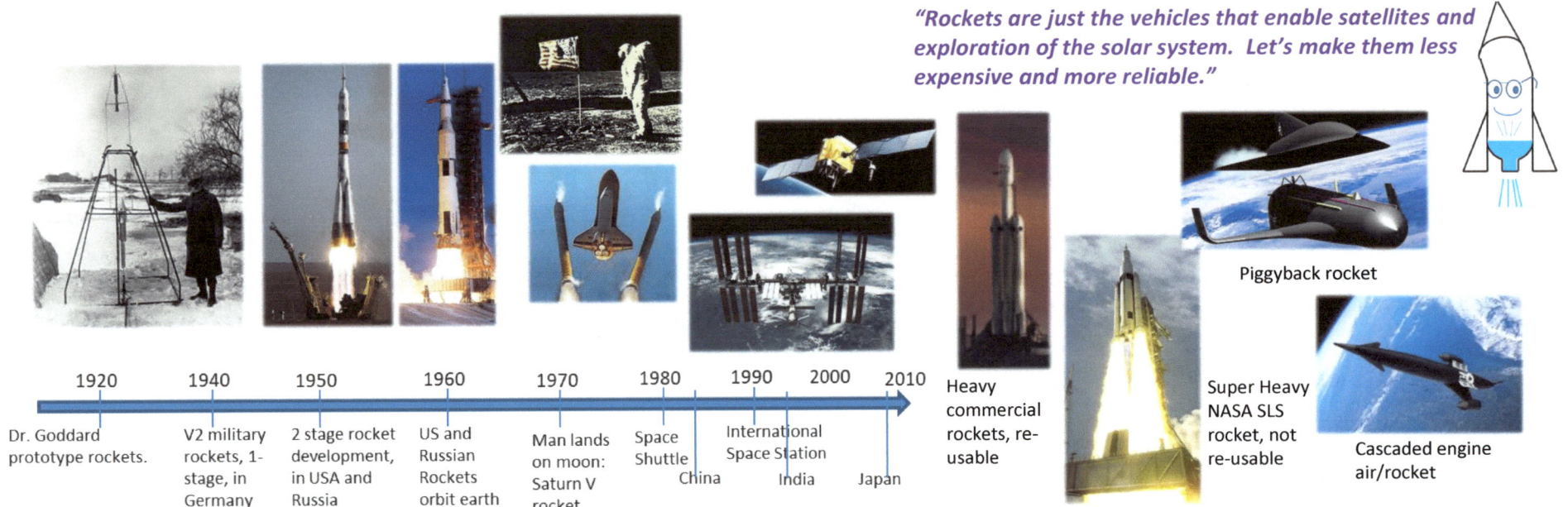

"Rockets are just the vehicles that enable satellites and exploration of the solar system. Let's make them less expensive and more reliable."

Timeline: 1920 Dr. Goddard prototype rockets. | 1940 V2 military rockets, 1-stage, in Germany | 1950 2 stage rocket development, in USA and Russia | 1960 US and Russian Rockets orbit earth | 1970 Man lands on moon: Saturn V rocket | 1980 Space Shuttle | 1990 International Space Station China | 2000 India | 2010 Japan | Heavy commercial rockets, re-usable | Super Heavy NASA SLS rocket, not re-usable | Piggyback rocket | Cascaded engine air/rocket

There you have it, we've introduced toy bottles and chemical rockets, the ways rockets work using fuels and thrust, the history of rocket development due to the Space Race, the recent commercial and military uses of rockets, and some improbable other techniques to get to space like cascaded engine types, rail guns and space elevators. In the future there might even be strong ion rockets using nuclear power to shorten the time to get around our solar system.

We're now just starting the age of space tourism. Would you be brave enough to get in a capsule and say 'Light this candle', like the early astronauts? It has taken a lot of trial and error to develop the rocket technology, for stable fuels, cryogenic liquid fuels, efficient nozzles and reliable fuel pumps, high temperature materials, non-flammable materials, well insulated electronics, nuclear fuel cells, solar cells, space suits, and air and water filters for the astronauts.

You can launch toy rockets in a local park or field by building water bottle rockets, or buying a toy chemical rocket starter kit.

If you *get* Newton's laws, then you are doing great. Newton's 2nd law is that force = mass*acceleration, so the exhaust thrust or force will accelerate the rocket. Newton's 3rd law is that for every force (Action) there is an equal and opposite force (Reaction), so thrown out exhaust will push the rocket the other direction.

As an accepted part of current lifestyles, the satellite payloads in rockets have helped the digital age. We have launched satellites for communication, GPS, earth monitoring, weather forecasting, and for science. Rockets also have kept alive the dream that humans may live on other planets.

Unfortunately, rockets are still far far too expensive, a 1000 times more expensive than an airplane ride per pound of payload. The cost and efficiency are poor. If we could instead design and treat a rocket like a run-of-the-mill bus or airplane ride to space, that would be great. Improvements are on-going. People are succeeding at more mass manufacturing, 3D printing of rocket engines, and re-usable rocket stages that land and are re-filled with fuel.

Going beyond rockets to more far-out concepts, let's get out there and break the limitations of the rocket equation and try other things, like cascaded air-breathing engines, or piggyback launches from supersonic airplanes, or rail guns. If we take hints from the movies, then we'd already have imaginary anti-gravity devices, and anti-matter engines with matter/anti-matter reactions powering the flight such as 'Star Trek'. But we don't, yet.

And what about hovering? Beautiful pictures of quiet spacecraft hovering over land in the movies can not be hovering peacefully because of rockets. We need Newton's 3rd law of Action and Reaction. But we all want hovering spacecraft.

Rockets are in a Wild West new era of development, with both NASA and commercial companies doing the innovating.

Main Achievements for Ways to Get to Space

Many technical hurdles had to be jumped over to get successful space flights. The rocket industry has been around for more than 60 years. People keep achieving better communication, better science, and better defense, so steady effort has been done.

"A lot of good history has been done to make rockets reliable."

Fuels, Solid and Liquid, that burn smoothly, quickly, with fast exhaust speeds

Nozzles and Exhaust, with high temperature handling and converging/diverging design to get the gas to flow in all one direction

Pasting the solid propellant into the booster: Inner surface area gives the flow rate and thrust, developed for the Space Shuttle.

Liquid oxygen: LO2 is the main super cold oxidizer for liquid fuel rockets. LH2 fuel is even colder.

Nozzle cooled with cryogenic liquid fuel: Need pumps to keep the flow rate of fuel and oxidizer

Space Shuttle engines: Gimballing engines, with independent movement, allow tilting and rotation about the axis.
Directed thrust allows full maneuvering in the vacuum of space.

Handling Heat for Return Landing, materials are either insulating or sacrificial

Space Stations, Solar Power, and Astronauts

Layered ablative material: Material burns away instead of the metal underneath getting hot

Ceramic Tiles: Shuttle is coated in insulated ceramic tiles, so heat stays on the outer tile surface. The tiles are light.

Satellites and solar panels to keep the power: Each square meter of panels gives a few 100 watts, funded by NASA

Space suits and untethered flight in space: Compressed gas is the exhaust to move about. Suits also need to protect from extreme cold and solar radiation.

Fuels, nozzles, materials, space stations and electronics... all have been developed.
Now and in the future, rockets are in a Wild West new era of development, with commercial companies doing the innovating to reduce cost and improve access to space.

Recent Innovations in Space Technology

New technology is getting added to reduce cost to get to space, and maybe give non-astronauts access to space. Any candidate new technology, besides being new, needs to be reliable, less expensive, and useful. For example, SpaceX chose old stainless steel over new carbon fiber, because carbon fiber is too expensive and does not handle heat as well. Also, SpaceX and Blue Origin decided against liquid hydrogen in favor of methane, because methane doesn't leak as easily, isn't as cold, and it can be made on other planets.

"Innovations are less expensive rockets, automation for flight control, robotics, LEO small satellites ...Wow!"

Some of what exists already

Re-usable rockets, to not throw away money by dropping stages in the ocean.

Returning boosters with liquid fuel, from SpaceX
Legs extend and engines re-lite in last few seconds.

Vertical landing of first stage for re-use, from demonstration rocket from Blue Origin.

Spaceliner, version 2, from Virgin Galactic: Hybrid fuel sub-orbital plane returning after launch off mothership, in this case a glide landing

New large and less costly rockets, to practically bring people and survival equipment to Mars

SLS: Rockets to Mars, by NASA and Boeing
One launch has already brought a capsule around the Moon, using LH2 fuel

Launch of SpaceX Starship, first attempt, 2023.
This is a 2 stage rocket, using methane fuel. The upper stage requires re-fueling in orbit to go to the Moon. The rocket uses a 2 stage design to get to LEO and then needs a re-fuel station in orbit, supplied by other rockets.

Robotics, to explore outer space and planets without risking humans.

Sky crane to lower the rover, by NASA Jet Propulsion Lab
Many stages of decent help make a robust landing in low pressure atmosphere of Mars.

First helicopter flying on Mars, by NASA Jet Propulsion Lab.
Mars only has 1% the atmospheric pressure, so the helicopter blades need to spin very fast to get lift.

Small satellites, to get sensors and communication satellites up quickly

60 Starlink satellites stacked together before deployment on 2019, by SpaceX
Quick design and deployment

3D printing, to avoid many parts and hand labor

3D printing of rocket engine for advanced space manufacturing. 3D printing can print metal as well as plastic.

Robots, 3D Printing, supersonic flight helps space exploration and life here on Earth. Robotics can enable remove surgery if an astronaut gets injured. 3D printing can allow parts to be custom built on Mars.

Research Innovations in Space Technology

New technology is getting added to reduce cost to get to space, and maybe give non-astronauts access to space. Besides being new, the candidate new technology needs to be reliable, less expensive, and useful. For example, SpaceX chose old stainless steel over new carbon fiber, because carbon fiber is too expensive. Also, SpaceX and Blue Origin decided against liquid hydrogen in favor of methane, because methane doesn't leak as easily, isn't as cold, and it can be made on other planets.

"Innovations are less expensive rockets, automation for flight control, robotics, LEO small satellites ...Wow!"

Some of the current research

New rocket engine types, like ion rockets, to get rocket speed even faster over a long but steady time.

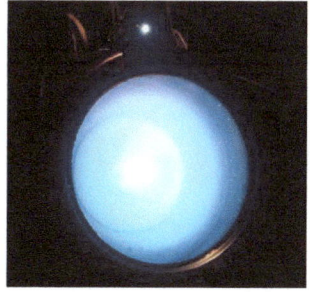

NASA Evolutionary Xenon Thruster (NEXT) ion thruster in operation

Deep space can use a gradual thrust from ion rockets. Ion rockets give steady low thrust, but gradually get the satellite to faster speeds than chemical rockets.

Clean up space junk in orbit, to avoid catastrophic accidents from collisions

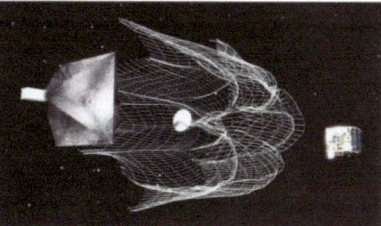

Net to capture space junk, built up over 50 years

There is a risk in orbit of getting hit with space junk, going faster than bullets.

Supersonic commercial flight, for convenience back on Earth, in development.

New 'Boom' supersonic design

Potential Concorde successor 'Boom Supersonic', using turbojet engines, with sonic boom directed upward, or broken up into smaller booms.

Nuclear thrust that does not exist yet

If we want to dart around our solar system in weeks instead of years, then we need the steady thrust from nuclear power. This has not been invented yet, but it is a necessary research direction.

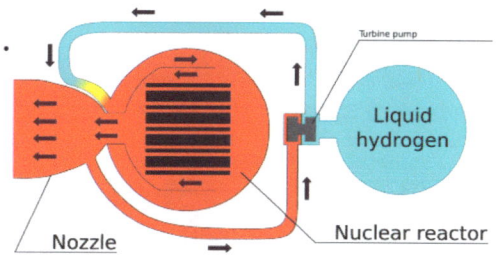

Fission heat: Concept of direct heating of exhaust gas passing through a hot fission source.

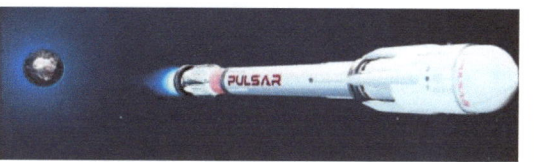

Potential fusion power enabling faster travel in the solar system.

Trip times can be reduced by more than half to Mars and to Jupiter.

Fusion: Magnetic coils to direct exhaust out the back

The hot exhaust will be so hot that we want to use magnetic walls, instead of melting metal.

Robots, 3D Printing, supersonic flight helps space exploration and life here on Earth. Robotics can enable remote surgery if an astronaut gets injured. 3D printing can allow parts to be custom built on Mars.

Practical Missions and Hardware

We had the Space Race, where we developed rocket technologies to survive in space and escape Earth. We currently launch science telescopes, and launch robotic rovers to explore Mars. We typically have 5 people in space conducting experiments in the Space Station.

If the planned Artemis program keeps going, we'll have people living on the Moon in a few years. The earliest would be 2026. Then, in a decade or two, we'll expand to Mars.

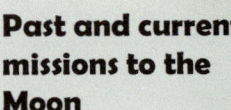

Past and current missions to the Moon

Lunar module on the Moon in the 1970s, in Apollo missions

New missions to the Moon

Lunar base for planned Artemis Moon missions, 2020s

Rockets will need to deliver all this equipment to the Moon according to the planned Artemis Moon missions.

There are still mission concepts and rocket hardware designs getting worked out to enable this delivery.

Probably many rocket companies will provide astronaut transportation, lunar buildings, and life support equipment. These rocket companies will include SLS, SpaceX, and Blue Origin.

Hubble telescope:
Pictures of the early universe.
(1990 -) The new Webb telescope is an improvement.

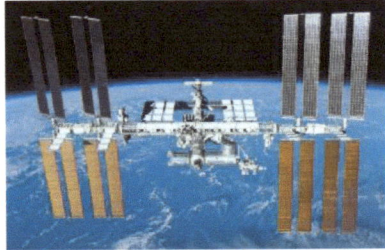

International Space Station
(1998 – took 10 years to assemble)

Perseverance Rover on Mars
(2021)

Sensor satellite:
1000s of satellites orbit Earth now, which provide communications and weather monitoring

These are technology and science missions. Technology can be many satellites orbiting Earth to provide communications. Technology can be making progress of a gradual goal of living off Earth.

Rocket Competitions, Amateur and Business

Here are some national rocket competitions in the USA, from middle school to business competitions. Many people enjoy the challenge and the combination of technologies that go into space flight. There is chemistry, there is mechanical engineering, and there are sensors and control systems.

Middle and High School

American Rocketry Challenge from the National Association of Rocketry (NAR)

NAR: Competition of various age groups

'The NAR is all about having fun and learning more with and about sport rockets. We are the oldest and largest sport rocketry organization in the world. Since 1957, over 100,000 serious sport rocket modelers have joined the NAR to take advantage of the fun and excitement of organized rocketry.'

National Association of Rocketry (nar.org)

College School

Experimental Sounding Rocket Association (ESRA)

College competition of multistage rockets and all chemical propulsion types (solid, liquid, and hybrid) are allowed

'ESRA hosts an Intercollegiate Rocket Engineering Competition (IREC) for student rocketry teams from across the USA and around the world. With a payload size of 8.8 pounds and target altitudes of either 10,000 or 30,000 ft above ground level, competing rockets are typically 4 to 8 inches in diameter and 8 to 20 ft. long.'

https://www.soundingrocket.org/

Businesses

Defense Advanced Research Projects Agency (DARPA), with a rocket challenge.

DARPA's competition to find a rapid rocket launch provider.

DARPA Launch Challenge:
To win the competition, eligible teams had to demonstrate that they could launch small national security satellites from practically any launch site in the US with very little heads-up. A company had to launch at least two rockets carrying DARPA payloads within two weeks of each other during very specific windows.

DARPA Launch Challenge

Middle Schoolers, High Schoolers, College Students, and Companies can all have different competitions.

Notable People in Rocket History

1880	1930	1940	1950	1970
Fuel development (liquid oxygen using cryogenic technology)	Liquid Fuel Rocket demonstrations and development	WW2	Space Race between USA and USSR	Commercial Satellites for weather, communications, Earth monitoring, and science

Louis Paul Cailletet in France and Raoul Pictet, 1877
In Switzerland, they succeeded in producing the first droplets of cold liquid air.
In 1883, Polish professors Zygmunt Wróblewski and Karol Olszewski produced the first measurable quantity of liquid oxygen.

They used cooling and expansion (the Joule-Thomson effect); oxygen was cooled while highly compressed, then allowed to rapidly expand, cooling it further, resulting in the production of small droplets of liquid oxygen

Dr. Goddard, 1926
Used new cryogenic liquid oxygen to make the first liquid fuel rocket, and used turbo pumps to feed the fuel.
USA

Konstantin Tsiolkovsky, 1903
Developed the Rocket Equation
Russian.
Instead of using a cannon with 1000s of g's, he figured out that gradual rocket thrust is more practical.
He also proposed multiple stage rockets, which is a natural result of the rocket equation.

Sergei Korolev, 1940-60
Developed the Russian multi-stage rocket, which launched the first satellite Sputnik and cosmonaut Gagarin to orbit the Earth. Korolev was brought out of a gulag as a political prisoner into the Red army, to work on rockets.
Ukrainian and Russian

Yuri Gagarin, 1961
First man in space to orbit Earth. During re-entry, he ejected from his capsule as planned and landed by parachute.
Russian.

Wernher von Braun, 1940-70
Developed the German V2 rocket and the USA Saturn V
German and USA

Neil Armstrong, 1969
First man on the Moon.
USA.

The invention and development of rockets has been a big combination of many developments from other fields, like fuels, electronics, light weight and strong materials. No one person did it all, but some remarkable people have done critical work.

Will the Movies Predict the Future?

Travel faster than light? Probably not.
We don't need to break physics and go faster than the speed of light to explore our own solar system, and maybe the closest star at 4 light years away. It may take a 100 years to get to the closest star, even using nuclear power, but we'd get there. Don't expect anything like visiting a new star every day or week, like Star Wars, Star Trek, or Marvel Universe, unless someone can break physics.

Star Trek: 'Warp 10, Scotty'

Star Wars: 'Don't want to fly through a star'

Marvel Universe, in the 'Thor' series and 'Guardians of the Galaxy'

Warp Drive: Travel faster than the speed of light. Due to Hollywood ambiguity, it is possible that Warp 2 is not twice the speed of light, but some undefined factor. It is also possible that the starships jump through worm holes in space, probably near black holes, that compress space.

Hyperspace: Travel in an alternate dimension that shortens distances between two stars. Why go directly the long distance between A and B, when you can jump into an alternate dimension.

Black hole travel: A ring star ship able to fly into a black hole, to jump to other parts of the universe. That requires super strong materials and some anti-stretch field that stops a gravitational gradient from stretching everything apart.

Populate colonies out in our solar system? Probably.
Solar system outposts can do science, tourism, and mining. For science, we want to investigate the other planets. For tourism, we want adventure. Tourism can also pay some of the bills. For mining, we don't want to transport all that building material from Earth. That would be prohibitively expensive. Some meteors might also have some very useful fuel, from methane or ice water, or useful minerals, like iron.

Single Stage to Orbit to a spinning space hotel?

Space hotels around Jupiter and Saturn? From '2001 A Space Odyssey' movie.

Modular habitat on Mars?

We can start moving across our solar system, like inhabiting Mars and the moons of Jupiter and Saturn. Out of our solar system is a bit tougher. The closest star to us is 4 light years away, and just our spiral galaxy is 100 thousand light years across.

Index

Air pressure, gauge	I-6-8, I-16-17
Arrow principle	I-69, I-73
Acceleration,	
• Newton's 2nd law	I-18
• Equations, definition	I-19, I-63, I-68
• Measurement	I-64-68
Acceleration, people's tolerance	I-74-79
Bottle rocket	
• Water	I-5-7
• Air	I-5
Bullet	I-10-11
Camera, video	I-61-68
Cannon	
• Chemical	II-72-75
• Rail gun	II-72-75, II-78-82
• Air drag	II-75-82
China	II-50, II-55
Drag, air	II-31, II-36, II-38, II-41-42, II-70, II-75-77, II-79-83
Drag, heat	II-8, II-41-42, II-70, II-75-77
Earth Spin	II-35-38
Elevator, Space	I-12-13, II-72-75, II-86-87
Engine, air breathing	II-61-70
Exhaust velocity	I-63-65, II-69-70, II-83-84, II-96-98, II-100, II-107-110
• Air bottle	II-108
• Water bottle	II-108
• Chemical	II-108
• Ion	II-98-100, II-108
Force (thrust)	
• Action/Reaction	I-14-19, II-107-110
• Measurement	I-61-68
Fuel rocket,	
• Solid toy Estes	I-81-84
• Solid space	II-24-26, II-28, II-30
• Liquid space	II-24-27, II-29-30
• Hybrid-fuel chemical rocket	II-30

Gravity	I-61-63, II-24-25
Gyroscope	I-21-24
Jet packs	I-56-57
Launch pads	I-69-73
Mars base	II-115-116, II-122
Moon base	II-116-121
Moon landing conspiracy	I-55
Movies	I-31, I-49-54, I-80, II-75-77
Newton's laws (see Force)	
Nozzle	I-7, I-17, I-20-21, I-23-26, I-61-67, I-82, II-26-28
Nuclear (see Rocket, nuclear powered)	
People, Engineers and Scientists	
• Goddard	I-21-22, II-130
• Korolev	II-51, II-130
• Von Braun	II-49, II-130
Pump, turbo	I-21, I-26, II-27
Recoil	I-14-18
Rocket velocity or speed	II-57-59, II-107-109, II-113
Rocket development	II-43-56
Rocket equation for speed	II-107-110, II-113
Rocket, fails	II-54
Rocket, ion	II-31-32, II-83, II-89, II-91-92, II-96-98, II-106
Rocket, laser	II-74-75, II-84
Rocket, military	II-52-55
Rocket, multiple stage	II-56-59
Rocket, nuclear powered	
• Nuclear powered electricity	II-91-92, II-93-94,
• Nuclear powered thrust	I-5, I-12, I-31, I-49-54, I-60, II-72-74, II-95-106
Russia	II-50-51, II-53-54
Shuttle, Space	I-6, I-8, I-24, I-27, I-44, II-28-29, II-41-42, II-124
Sling Shot, catapult	II-39-40
Thrust (see Force)	
Trajectory	II-35-41
Travel	I-12, I-32-37, I-45-48, I-74-80, II-61-69, II-95-98, II-116-122, II-125-127, II-131

Back Cover

Hope you had a 'blast'.

Court Rossman first saw and built water bottle rockets, as an adult, while helping with Cub Scouts. It seemed like a great introduction to hand's-on rocket building. He was impressed that there was a basic rocket to demonstrate the concept, and that the kids could build it themselves. Court certainly learned rocket concepts himself as a volunteer from doing the activity.

This book compares the water bottle rockets and toy chemical rocket experiments to real uses and applications, and then goes beyond standard rockets to possible future ways to launch payloads that are more efficient. Rockets have launched humans into the 21st century.

Court is participating in the emphasis on hands-on learning. Science kits are readily available these days, and that is great. He just wants to help that trend, so the next generation has practical knowledge and creativity.

Court has also published a similar book of 'Water Bottle Rockets', as well as 'Pinewood Derby Cars and Real Cars' and 'Magnets, Motors, and Generators'. Court has a life-long interest in physics and science, and has a Ph.D. in physics, and works on rocket sensors through his day job.

Thanks to the Cub Scout Pack that staged some Water Rocket activities. Thanks to Brian Stevens, who ran the activity. Thanks to Peach Rossman who helped with rocket launches and provided an abundance of criticism about layout. Thanks to Stephen McDowell for taking a launch video of the water bottle rocket. Thanks to people who posted pictures on the internet, many of which are used in this book. Thanks to Ross Wendell for helpful feedback. Thanks to family, Wayne Rossman and Richard Lafleur, also for helpful feedback. Thanks to Allan Rossman for drawing some sketches. Thanks to Paul Zemany for the Space Shuttle air drag comparison to the balloon acceleration, and a discussion of how to turn or change heading using fins in air.

Model of Dr. Goddard's first launch liquid fuel rocket

Astronaut jokes:
https://funkidsjokes.com/astronaut-jokes/
https://upjoke.com/astronaut-jokes

References:
Youtube channel: Kurzgesagt – in a Nutshell
https://upjoke.com/astronaut-jokes

www.ingramcontent.com/pod-product-compliance
Lightning Source LLC
LaVergne TN
LVHW071734060526
838201LV00039B/406